STO

YO-BUD-492

*1980s Project Studies/Council on Foreign Relations*

STUDIES AVAILABLE

REDUCING GLOBAL INEQUITIES

*Studies by W. Howard Wriggins and Gunnar Adler-Karlsson*

RICH AND POOR NATIONS IN THE WORLD ECONOMY

*Studies by Albert Fishlow, Carlos F. Díaz-Alejandro, Richard R. Fagen, and Roger D. Hansen*

CONTROLLING FUTURE ARMS TRADE

*Studies by Anne Hessing Cahn and Joseph J. Kruzel, Peter M. Dawkins, and Jacques Huntzinger*

DIVERSITY AND DEVELOPMENT IN SOUTHEAST ASIA:

The Coming Decade

*Studies by Guy J. Pauker, Frank H. Golay, and Cynthia H. Enloe*

NUCLEAR WEAPONS AND WORLD POLITICS:

Alternatives for the Future

*Studies by David C. Gompert, Michael Mandelbaum, Richard L. Garwin, and John H. Barton*

CHINA'S FUTURE:

Foreign Policy and Economic Development in the Post-Mao Era

*Studies by Allen S. Whiting and Robert F. Dernberger*

ALTERNATIVES TO MONETARY DISORDER

*Studies by Fred Hirsch and Michael W. Doyle and by Edward L. Morse*

NUCLEAR PROLIFERATION:

Motivations, Capabilities, and Strategies for Control

*Studies by Ted Greenwood and by Harold A. Feiveson and Theodore B. Taylor*

INTERNATIONAL DISASTER RELIEF:

Toward a Responsive System

*Stephen Green*

# Industrial Policy
# as an
# International
# Issue

# Industrial Policy as an International Issue

*WILLIAM DIEBOLD, JR.*

*1980s Project/Council on Foreign Relations*

McGRAW-HILL BOOK COMPANY

*New York   St. Louis   San Francisco*
*Auckland   Bogotá   Düsseldorf   Johannesburg   London   Madrid*
*Mexico   Montreal   New Delhi   Panama   Paris   São Paulo*
*Singapore   Sydney   Tokyo   Toronto*

The Council on Foreign Relations, Inc., is a nonprofit and nonpartisan organization devoted to promoting improved understanding of international affairs through the free exchange of ideas. Its membership of about 1,700 persons throughout the United States is made up of individuals with special interest and experience in international affairs. The Council has no affiliation with and receives no funding from the United States government.

The Council publishes the journal *Foreign Affairs* and, from time to time, books and monographs that in the judgment of the Council's Committee on Studies are responsible treatments of significant international topics worthy of presentation to the public. The 1980s Project is a research effort of the Council; as such, 1980s Project Studies have been similarly reviewed through procedures of the Committee on Studies. As in the case of all Council publications, statements of fact and expressions of opinion contained in 1980s Project Studies are the sole responsibility of their authors.

The editor of this book was Robert Valkenier for the Council on Foreign Relations. Thomas Quinn and Michael Hennelly were the editors for McGraw-Hill Book Company. Christopher Simon was the designer, and Teresa Leaden supervised the production. This book was set in Times Roman by Offset Composition Services, Inc.

Printed and bound by R. R. Donnelley and Sons.

**Library of Congress Cataloging in Publication Data**

Diebold, William.
Industrial policy as an international issue.

(1980s Project/Council on Foreign Relations)
Bibliography: p.
Includes index.
1. International economic relations.  2.  Industry and state.  I.  Title.  II.  Series: Council on Foreign Relations.  1980s Project/Council on Foreign Relations.
HF1411.D48    1980          338.9          79-9539
ISBN 0-07-016809-1
ISBN 0-07-016810-5 pbk.

1 2 3 4 5 6 7 8 9 R R D R R D 8 0 6 5 4 3 2 1 0

# Contents

# Foreword: The 1980s Project

In today's interdependent world, where governments have assumed broad responsibility for steering the course of their domestic economies, there is need to find ways to prevent the economic policy of one country from adversely affecting others. Furthermore, it is becoming increasingly clear that new sorts of collective efforts by governments are needed to facilitate and to smooth the process of structural change in the global economy. Yet, while the importance of international cooperation in managing change in an interdependent world is generally acknowledged, solutions do not seem close at hand.

All countries take a variety of measures to shape the structure of their domestic economies, to determine the long-run use of resources, and to affect the distribution of gains from economic growth—though many countries do not have comprehensive and consistent industrial policies. Sometimes the intent of the measures taken is to stimulate the development of new industry; sometimes it is to help workers and firms adapt to changes in the world economy. But often, as this book points out, the main effect of most countries' industrial policy measures has been to resist change, with damaging results to their national economies as well as to the economic well-being of others.

These and other problems of national and international industrial policies are the subject of this essay, which is part of a stream of studies produced by the 1980s Project of the Council on Foreign Relations. Each 1980s Project volume deals with an issue likely to be of international concern during the next 10 to 20 years.

The ambitious purpose of the 1980s Project is to examine important political and economic problems not only individually but in relationship to one another. Some studies or books produced by the Project will primarily emphasize the interrelationship of issues. In the case of other, more specifically focused studies, a considerable effort has been made to write, review, and criticize them in the context of more general Project work. Each Project study is thus capable of standing on its own; at the same time it has been shaped by a broader perspective.

The 1980s Project had its origin in the widely held recognition that many of the assumptions, policies, and institutions that have characterized international relations during the past 30 years are inadequate to the demands of today and the foreseeable demands of the period between now and 1990 or so. Over the course of the next decade, substantial adaptation of institutions and behavior will be needed to respond to the changed circumstances of the 1980s and beyond. The Project seeks to identify those future conditions and the kinds of adaptation they might require. It is not the Project's purpose to arrive at a single or exclusive set of goals. Nor does it focus upon the foreign policy or national interests of the United States alone. Instead, it seeks to identify goals that are compatible with the perceived interests of most states, despite differences in ideology and in level of economic development.

The published products of the Project are aimed at a broad readership, including policy makers and potential policy makers and those who would influence the policy-making process, but are confined to no single nation or region. The authors of Project studies were therefore asked to remain mindful of interests broader than those of any one society and to take fully into account the likely realities of domestic politics in the principal societies involved. All those who have worked on the Project, however, have tried not to be captives of the status quo; they have sought to question the inevitability of existing patterns of thought and behavior that restrain desirable change and to look for ways in which those patterns might in time be altered or their consequences mitigated.

The 1980s Project is at once a series of separate attacks upon a number of urgent and potentially urgent international problems and also a collective effort, involving a substantial number of persons in the United States and abroad, to bring those separate approaches to bear upon one another and to suggest the kinds of choices that might be made among them. The Project involves more than 300 participants. A small central staff and a steering Coordinating Group have worked to define the questions and to assess the compatibility of policy prescriptions. Nearly 100 authors, from more than a dozen countries, have been at work on separate studies. Ten working groups of specialists and generalists have been convened to subject the Project's studies to critical scrutiny and to help in the process of identifying interrelationships among them.

The 1980s Project is the largest single research and studies effort the Council on Foreign Relations has undertaken in its 55-year history, comparable in conception only to a major study of the postwar world, the War and Peace Studies, undertaken by the Council during the Second World War. At that time, the impetus of the effort was the discontinuity caused by worldwide conflict and the visible and inescapable need to rethink, replace, and supplement many of the features of the international system that had prevailed before the war. The discontinuities in today's world are less obvious and, even when occasionally quite visible—as in the abandonment of gold convertibility and fixed monetary parities—only briefly command the spotlight of public attention. That new institutions and patterns of behavior are needed in many areas is widely acknowledged, but the sense of need is less urgent—existing institutions have not for the most part dramatically failed and collapsed. The tendency, therefore, is to make do with outmoded arrangements and to improvise rather than to undertake a basic analysis of the problems that lie before us and of the demands that those problems will place upon all nations.

The 1980s Project is based upon the belief that serious effort and integrated forethought can contribute—indeed, are indispensable—to progress in the next decade toward a more humane, peaceful, productive, and just world. And it rests upon the hope that participants in its deliberations and readers of

Project publications—whether or not they agree with an author's point of view—may be helped to think more informedly about the opportunities and the dangers that lie ahead and the consequences of various possible courses of future action.

This study on industrial policy has been made possible by a generous grant from the Fritz Thyssen Stiftung of Cologne, Germany, which also supported a conference on industrial policy held at the Bellagio Conference and Study Center of the Rockefeller Foundation in March 1978. Additional support for the 1980s Project was provided by the Ford Foundation, the Lilly Endowment, the Andrew W. Mellon Foundation, the Rockefeller Foundation, and the German Marshall Fund of the United States. Neither the Council on Foreign Relations nor any of those foundations is responsible for statements of fact and expressions of opinion contained in publications of the 1980s Project; they are the sole responsibility of the individual authors under whose names they appear. But the Council on Foreign Relations and the staff of the 1980s Project take great pleasure in placing those publications before a wide readership both in the United States and abroad.

*The 1980s Project*

# Acknowledgments

In writing this book, I have had an exceptional amount of help. Some has been inadvertent; that is to say, governments, businesses, interest groups, and individuals connected with them have said and done things that illuminated my subject or caused me to see angles and problems—and occasionally possibilities—that might otherwise have escaped me. It would be invidious to single out anyone on this score. Very inadequate recognition of the writing of others can be found in the Critical Bibliography. The main help, however, has come from purposive talking—with me, to me, or among others in my presence. I can best indicate my debts by telling how this book came to be.

That industrial policy—as the term is used in this book—was a key factor in international economic relations that needed more attention became clear to me as I worked on a book that was published in 1972. I had other things to do that prevented my pursuing the matter, but some ideas took clearer form as I took part in the discussions guided by Miriam Camps that led up to her important essay, *The Management of Interdependence*. The chance to try out some of these ideas came when the Council on Foreign Relations followed up Mrs. Camps's work by organizing the 1980s Project. Its first director, Richard Ullman, and his successors, Edward Morse and Catherine Gwin, were sympathetic to the idea of using industrial policy as an organizing principle for a significant part of the economic work of the Project, but not to the exclusion of more conventional approaches to some issues. Sometimes the approach worked well, sometimes not. Without disentangling all the strands of the large and complex 1980s effort, it is impossible to acknowledge each debt, but the total contribution to this book has been substantial. Much but not all of the evidence lies to hand in the published products of the Project and the lists of people who participated in it, as authors or members of groups.

The direct approach to industrial policy that resulted in this book was largely financed by a generous grant from the Fritz Thyssen Stiftung of Cologne, Germany. I am most grateful for this support and also to that of other organizations which, by holding conferences and paying my expenses for traveling to them, permitted me to talk to many more people about the work I was doing.

Some exploratory work was needed to find a way of dealing with basic issues and still set manageable limits to what might otherwise become an inquiry into practically all economic policies of a large number of countries. A somewhat arbitrary but not overly strict focus on the international effects of national industrial policy measures seemed to provide the answer, and in the summer of 1976 I drafted a rather lengthy working paper which, with occasional amendments and supplements, became the basis for practically all the discussions that followed. Its baptism of fire was in three meetings of a group at the Council on Foreign Relations in the fall and early winter of 1976. Those who attended these sessions, presided over by Miriam Camps, were Solomon Barkin, Stephen Blank, Isaiah Frank, Joseph A. Greenwald, Catherine Gwin, Roger D. Hansen, Heinrich Machowski, Harald B. Malmgren, Edward L. Morse, Caroline Pestieau, Andrew Shonfield, Helena Stalson, Richard H. Ullman, Lawrence A. Veit, Raymond Vernon, Stephen J. Warnecke, Sidney Weintraub, Jerry Wurf, and John Zysman. Carol Richmond and Susan Sorrell wrote summaries of the discussions for me.

Other subjects occupied most of my time during the first eight months of 1977, but that fall I held intensive discussions of industrial policy with people in Japan and Western Europe. I then prepared further material for a conference which the 1980s

Project held at the Rockefeller Foundation's European Confer-
ence Center, the Villa Serbelloni at Bellagio, Italy, in March
1978. The carefully chosen specialists who took part engaged in
discussions that were of great benefit to me. Once again, Miriam
Camps presided with great skill. The others were Marc de
Brichambaut, François Duchene, Catherine Gwin, Takashi
Hosomi, Wolfgang Michalski, Edward L. Morse, Shinichi
Nakayama, Kazuo Nukazawa, John Pinder, Romano Prodi, Sir
Andrew Shonfield, Christian Stoffaes, Jan Tumlir, Louis Turner,
Frank Wolter, and John Zysman. Our deliberations were helped
by the hospitality and atmosphere provided by William and
Elizabeth Olson.

During the fall of 1976, Sir Andrew Shonfield, an old friend
and colleague and a pioneer in this field, was in residence at the
Woodrow Wilson International Center for Scholars of the
Smithsonian Institution in Washington. Whenever a Council
group met to discuss my paper, a second meeting was held to
discuss his work, and that was also of great help to me. These
meetings were financed by the Conference Board and organized
largely by Stephen Blank with some help from me. The participants in these sessions were Robert Black, Stephen Blank, Lee
Bloom, Miriam Camps, David Gordon, Peter Gourevitch,
Catherine Gwin, Walter A. Hamilton, Robert Heilbroner, Peter
Katzenstein, James Kurth, Leon Lindberg, Charles Maier, Andrew Martin, Edward L. Morse, Gordon Schwartz, Joan Spero,
Helena Stalson, and Steven J. Warnecke.

I am grateful to David MacEachron of the Japan Society for
inviting me to the American-Japanese conference at Shimoda in
September 1977, which threw light on some of the issues I was
studying and gave me the opportunity to discuss my working
paper with a number of people. James Abegglen was particularly
helpful in putting me in touch with Japanese officials, scholars,
and businessmen. The Keidanren was kind enough to bring
together an impressive group of businessmen and economists for
my benefit.

Steven J. Warnecke helped by organizing a conference on
subsidies as a tool of industrial policy, at which I clarified some
of my own ideas and learned a good bit about the thinking of

others. William Bundy and Ernst van der Beugel invited me to prepare a paper for the Bilderberg meeting in Princeton in April 1978, which permitted me to hear the views of a distinguished group of statesmen, academics, and businessmen and later stimulated reactions from a wider audience as well. In January 1979, when this book was all but done, a Ditchley Conference presided over by Miriam Camps provided a valuable last-minute assessment of the results of the multilateral trade negotiations as they bore on my subject.

Most important of all these parallel activities, however, was my work as North American rapporteur for a Trilateral Commission report on Industrial Strategies. I am very grateful to George Franklin and Charles Heck for inviting me to undertake this work, which began after the present study was well launched and was completed after the manuscript was out of my hands. The overlap in time and subject was sufficient for me to benefit considerably from exposure to the views of a large number of people at a series of meetings in Bonn, Paris, London, Tokyo, Washington, New York, and Edmonton. Their names appear in the Triangle paper published in September 1979, but I must give special thanks to my fellow rapporteurs John Pinder and Takashi Hosomi and to several people who worked with us, especially Eisuke Sakakibara, Ariyoshi Okumura, and Wolfgang Hager. Tadashi Yamamoto, Hans Maull, and Roger Hill, the secretaries of the Trilateral Commission in Japan, Europe, and Canada, have been most helpful. Fabio Basagni of the Atlantic Institute in Paris has contributed by organizing discussions leading to the preparation of a collective volume on industrial policy growing out of the Trilateral efforts.

Many of the people already mentioned have spent much time helping me to understand the issues dealt with in this book. The many others—businessmen, scholars, and officials of national governments and international organizations—who have talked with me are too numerous to be named. However, I owe a special debt to the following, who for one reason or another were not in the groups already listed: Masao Aihara, Michel Albert, Carlos F. Díaz-Alejandro, David Z. Beckler, Bernard Cazes, Robert W. Cox, Seamus O'Cleireacain, Etienne Davignon,

Theodore Geiger, Lincoln Gordon, Deane Hinton, Ghita G. Ionescu, John H. Jackson, Gunnar Adler-Karlsson, Abraham Katz, Mahn Je Kim, Kiyoshi Kojima, Hans Liesner, Roger Loutz, Robert Marjolin, Stephen Marris, Pierre Mathijsen, Roy A. Matthews, Judith Maxwell, Göran Ohlin, Saburo Okita, Gardner Patterson, Giuseppe Sacco, Mihaly Simai, Susan Strange, and S. Zottos.

Many of the people already mentioned have let me see unpublished papers which are too numerous to be listed. Honors for the number of pages go, I think, to Solomon Barkin and John Zysman. Through correspondence I have learned of the work of Dr. Colin Aislabie of the University of Newcastle, New South Wales, Australia, who has sent me a whole series of interesting analytical papers (which I hope will soon be a book).

David Steinberg of Washington, D.C., was one of the first people to argue that if the United States was to have a truly liberal trade policy it would have to have an industrial policy aimed at restructuring American industry. Though we have been out of touch in recent years, I remember his speeches and congressional testimony on the subject.

While working on this book, I was often asked to give talks about its subject matter. For providing occasions that required me to formulate my views and gave me useful reactions to them, I am grateful to The European University Institute, Florence; the University of Toronto and the Canadian Institute of International Affairs; the Ralph Bunche Institute of the City University of New York; the International Fellows program of Columbia University; the European Management Symposium at Davos; the Institute of World Economics and Politics in Moscow; and the Economic Council of Canada.

While raw materials issues have been somewhat slighted in this book, I should like to acknowledge the benefits I have gained from two sets of discussions. For several years, I have been a member of a kind of steering committee of a study of raw materials in Canadian-American relations sponsored by the World Peace Foundation of Boston and the C. D. Howe Institute of Montreal and guided by Alfred O. Hero and Carl Beigie. At the Council, during 1977 and 1978, I did the staff work for a series of discussions on the changing structure of the international raw materials industry presided over by Stephen Stamas. Publications expected to result from these activities will in some respects supplement this book.

My acknowledgments outside the Council on Foreign Relations have been many, but it is there that I owe my greatest debts. Two presidents, Bayless Manning and Winston Lord, have permitted me to follow the course I thought best in shaping this work and to take the time from other duties that it required. My colleagues on the studies staff and some of the others have had to do work that I might otherwise have done. As always, Janet Rigney and her library staff have diligently followed up my interests and provided me with the material I needed. Robert Valkenier edited the manuscript, put it in shape for the press, and provided much good advice. Patsy Gesell and Debra De Palma helped with further revisions. When this work started, Carol Richmond was my secretary and assistant. She was succeeded by Rashida Tewarson. Both have put up with a lot and have been essential to the completion of this work.

The support of the whole 1980s Project has already been acknowledged, but I should say a special word of appreciation for Catherine Gwin. While carrying a large load of responsibility and detailed work she has provided valuable criticism and all kinds of support and help. She has also been very patient.

Miriam Camps's key role in this project must be apparent from what has already been said. I am grateful for all the time, thought, and effort she has put into chairing meetings and conferences. My debt is even greater for her sustained interest in this study and the prods, challenges, and encouragement that have flowed from it. Her belief that it all made some kind of sense and should be set down sooner rather than later has been most helpful in keeping me going and, I suspect, has helped me indirectly as well through the influence of her views on others.

As in all the work I have done at the Council for years, I have been immensely helped by Helena Stalson. Her thorough knowledge of a wide range of subjects and her very independent lines of thought have supported my reasoning on some points and challenged it as to facts or logic on others. Either way she has contributed a great deal. She has caught me in errors and confusion that I am glad to have avoided and extended my knowledge and understanding by her own work.

As will be discovered by reading this book, some work that Eugene Staley did about 35 years ago is highly apposite to the problems of today. I am grateful for whatever caused me to remember these studies, though I suspect my debt is even larger for the impact they made on me at the time; they have probably been shaping parts of my thinking ever since, and all to the good. It was a pleasure to recall the time when he was a most active member of the group in the Council's War and Peace Studies that I worked for in the early 1940s, to reread some of his other work, and then to get in touch with him again. This is another debt I owe the Council.

My wife and children and, to a degree, even my grandchildren have had to put up with quite a lot during the long period I have been working on this book. I have been away from home a good deal more than I should have liked, pursuing the siren call of conferences and meetings when the words "industrial policy" or something similar were attached. And when I have been home I have spent rather longer at my desk or deep in a reading chair than is altogether compatible with paying adequate attention to others.

In spite of all this help, it is only with considerable trepidation that I have let this manuscript go to the printer. I could tell you how to improve every page; I have persuaded myself to take the risk of dealing simplistically with many complex issues. Sometimes this has been done against good advice but not, I hope, without good reason. But self-criticism is not the strongest suit of an author who may be temporarily obsessed with an idea, since, as Laurence Sterne said in *Tristram Shandy*, "there is no disputing against hobby-horses."

Naturally I have received more advice than can be taken, not just because of its volume but because so much of it was contradictory. I have tried not to take the easy way out and ignore arguments because they would cancel one another. But no matter what I have said, someone has thought me wrong. I have been charged with simply clinging to an out-of-date attachment to free trade ideas and of being a cartelist, of having a very American and United States–centered approach to the problems of the world, and of applying a double standard that excuses the behavior of foreigners while condemning that of the United States. As these accusations frequently came from old friends, it was tempting to say that they should know better, but instead I have taken each of these complaints seriously, at least to the extent of reexamining what I said, stylistically for clarity and substantively for cogency and validity. Often I have made changes on both grounds. If I am still vulnerable to the same objections, it is, in the case of cartelism versus free trade, because of the nature of the problem, while in the case of an unduly American view it is a defect of knowledge, understanding, and, I suppose, bias. However, anything I have wrong is less so for having been jumped on so firmly and frequently by so many people, and much that is right is all to their credit. I thank them. No one can hold them responsible for the result.

*William Diebold, Jr.*
August 1979

## 1980s PROJECT WORKING GROUPS

During 1975 and 1976, ten Working Groups met to explore major international issues and to subject initial drafts of 1980s Project studies to critical review. Those who chaired Project Working Groups were:

*Cyrus R. Vance*, Working Group on Nuclear Weapons and Other Weapons of Mass Destruction

*Leslie H. Gelb*, Working Group on Armed Conflict

*Roger Fisher*, Working Group on Transnational Violence and Subversion

*Rev. Theodore M. Hesburgh*, Working Group on Human Rights

*Joseph S. Nye, Jr.*, Working Group on the Political Economy of North-South Relations

*Harold Van B. Cleveland*, Working Group on Macroeconomic Policies and International Monetary Relations

*Lawrence C. McQuade*, Working Group on Principles of International Trade

*William Diebold, Jr.*, Working Group on Multinational Enterprises

*Eugene B. Skolnikoff*, Working Group on the Environment, the Global Commons, and Economic Growth

*Miriam Camps*, Working Group on Industrial Policy

## 1980s PROJECT STAFF

Persons who have held senior professional positions on the staff of the 1980s Project for all or part of its duration are:

| | |
|---|---|
| *Miriam Camps* | *Catherine Gwin* |
| *William Diebold, Jr.* | *Roger D. Hansen* |
| *Tom J. Farer* | *Edward L. Morse* |
| *David C. Gompert* | *Richard H. Ullman* |

Richard H. Ullman was Director of the 1980s Project from its inception in 1974 until July 1977, when he became Chairman of the Project Coordinating Group. Edward L. Morse was Executive Director from July 1977 until June 1978. At that time, Catherine Gwin, 1980s Project Fellow since 1976, took over as Executive Director.

## PROJECT COORDINATING GROUP

The Coordinating Group of the 1980s Project had a central advisory role in the work of the Project. Its members as of June 30, 1978, were:

Carlos F. Díaz-Alejandro
Richard A. Falk
Tom J. Farer
Edward K. Hamilton
Stanley Hoffmann
Gordon J. MacDonald
Bruce K. MacLaury

Bayless Manning
Theodore R. Marmor
Ali Mazrui
Michael O'Neill
Stephen Stamas
• Fritz Stern
Allen S. Whiting

Until they entered government service, other members included:

W. Michael Blumenthal
Richard N. Cooper
Samuel P. Huntington

Joseph S. Nye, Jr.
Marshall D. Shulman

## COMMITTEE ON STUDIES

The Committee on Studies of the Board of Directors of the Council on Foreign Relations is the governing body of the 1980s Project. The Committee's members as of June 1, 1979, were:

Barry E. Carter
Robert A. Charpie
Stanley Hoffmann
Henry A. Kissinger
Walter J. Levy

Robert E. Osgood
Stephen Stamas
Philip Geyelin
Marina v. N. Whitman

James A. Perkins (Chairman)

# Industrial Policy as an International Issue

# ONE

# The Nature of the Problem

The central thesis of this book is that a failure to improve the ways of dealing internationally with structural change and the problems arising from national industrial policies will seriously damage the world economy and international cooperation.

After this chapter briefly sets out the nature of the problem, the next shows why it is difficult—if not impossible—to see what the ideal solution would be. The bulk of the book then canvasses possible ways of improving matters. Existing measures for dealing with some problems are examined to find ways of reducing their inadequacies. The potential of some half-formed initiatives is explored, and imagination is allowed to play on some untried and rather ambitious innovations. Obstacles are looked at realistically, but the book ends with a fairly positive indication of what would be worth trying. Failure to move in the right direction, it is argued, will lead to economic damage, the deterioration of international cooperation, and increased friction.

The book's perspective is global and long-run. It deals with issues broadly and not in detail. Still, since the problems exist in the real world, something will have to be said about specific countries and industries; nor will it be forgotten that the long run is a succession of short runs.

## AWARENESS

Between the first draft of this book and its final version, interest in its subject grew immensely. A world struggling with obdurate economic problems for longer than it had supposed would be necessary came increasingly to think that it was dealing with structural difficulties and not only cyclical ones. Politicians and businessmen in several countries called for government to take the lead in shaping new industrial strategies. Past industrial policies were criticized for failing to deal with new problems or blamed for creating them. To cope with unemployment, inflation, and international imbalance, governments everywhere took measures that were not sufficiently thought through to be called industrial policies but that were intended to protect existing economic structures against foreign competition and the decline in demand or to stimulate new production and employment. There was talk of excess capacity in world industry and how to destroy or "sterilize" it. "Crisis cartels" made their appearance in several countries. One expected any day to hear the language of the Depression: "Business must no longer be allowed to produce tremendous surpluses without regard to consumption. . . . Major industries should be required by law to limit their production to an amount fixed by a government agency." "Rationalization" and other terms of the 1920s and 1930s were revived and used alongside the newer vocabulary about structure and industrial policy. Whatever the terminology—and the same words frequently meant different things to different people—there was no doubt that the prolonged recession of the mid-1970s and the unsatisfactory recovery from it accentuated the problems with which this book deals, and interest in them as well. The malaise and the concern were centered in the Western industrial world—the OECD countries—but there was a direct and significant involvement of everyone else: the oil exporters, the state trading countries, and both the more and the less advanced of the developing countries.

The advantages of heightened awareness are obvious, both in increasing appreciation of basic issues and in enhancing the willingness to do something about persistent problems. But there are disadvantages as well, stemming especially from the need to act quickly, the fairly narrow margin of maneuver that democratic governments have when they face both heavy unemployment and serious inflation, and the inevitable emphasis on the im-

2

mediate rather than the long run. Perhaps some of the actions of governments during this period will improve the long-run situation, but on the whole it is more likely that the net effects of measures taken to deal with the recession will reinforce resistance to structural change. How that result might be avoided is considered later, but there is one fact that warrants a certain amount of hope. Fear that each country might try to deal with its own difficulties by measures that would hurt other countries led the governments of the countries belonging to the Organization for Economic Cooperation and Development (OECD) to pledge that they would avoid such actions. The results were not perfect, but they were encouraging, even though they left countries outside the group with no assurance that their needs would be looked after.[1] How long the recognition of danger will inspire so sensible a reaction only time will tell.

The answer is of great importance to the themes of this book, as will soon become apparent. But it is of equal importance to think about these matters without giving primary attention to the events of the recession, however revealing and important they are for the study of industrial policy. The fundamental problems were discernible before the recession and before the energy crisis; they would have grown worse if neither had occurred; and they will persist in one form or another when the recession is long past and substantial adjustment has been made to energy changes. That is because structural change is inherent in the world economy and governments will continue to take measures (here called industrial policy) to help, hinder, or induce change or to adapt to it. There is, indeed, good reason to think that more use will be made of these measures in the future than in the past decades.

Although the world economy has undergone an enormous amount of structural change since the end of the Second World War and benefited greatly thereby, signs of trouble were clear by the late 1960s. Some reflected the inability of the extensive

[1] Though the pledge was originally given in 1974 when the prime threat was the upset to international payments resulting from the increase in the oil price, it was continued in force and in June 1978 was specifically related to problems of structural change (see chap. 3).

measures of international economic cooperation, which had accomplished so much in a quarter-century, to cope with changing conditions. Others came from the reduced ability of the world's economy, nationally and internationally, to absorb the costs of uneconomic practices as growth rates slowed down but not expectations. There was an increasing unwillingness to accept the political, physical, and moral consequences of giving priority to economic values. Still other problems arose from shifts in power in the world or the greater weight that had to be given to the needs and wishes of poorer but ambitious parts of the world's population. The impact of almost all these factors was magnified, at least for some countries, by the substantial degree of interdependence that had grown up in the world economy.

Neither the long-run nor the short-run perspective can be neglected but the emphasis of this book will be on the long run. It will also be on the international problems surrounding industrial policy, not on how each country can best cope with its individual problems. But we cannot ignore the fact that some kinds of national measures cause more disturbance to the international system than others. Nor can we confine ourselves to damage limitation. There is also the question whether by new kinds of international arrangements various combinations of countries can act together to bring about desirable structural changes in the world economy on terms that will both be widely acceptable and maximize benefits.

These delimitations do not so much narrow the subject as focus the attention. To narrow the issue any more would be to distort it. Proper analysis has to take into account a wide range of economic, political, and social issues that shape and are shaped by industrial policy, broadly conceived. Perhaps it is foolhardy to try to put all this in a short book, but there is need for an introduction to a subject that has not been fully recognized in the past. To see what the subject is we must somehow look at the whole, even if only in terms suitable for a primer. The problem is not that the issues themselves have been ignored in the past— many of them have been heavily studied and debated for centuries—but that their interrelation as parts of a complex has too often been ignored while the difficulties they create have increased.

4

From the foregoing enumeration of characteristics it follows that this book is written at an uncomfortably high level of generality. Unfortunately, a book twice as long would still suffer from that difficulty and permit only a slight exploration of some of the many paths that are pointed to but not entered on in this one. If the approach and analysis hold up, they will suggest further inquiries and provide a way to link up much of the excellent work being done on different parts of the subject. Some of that work is touched on here and there in the text, but not in any systematic or exhaustive fashion. Broader studies, dealing with some of the central themes of this book, are noted in the Critical Bibliography, where I acknowledge some of my debts.

This book provides an approach more than a set of conclusions. Still, all who write for the 1980s Project are under the injunction to be prescriptive. This book is, up to a point, but not on all issues. It suggests quite a few courses of action—says what to avoid and what to do more of, whether the prescriptions are old or new. But most of all, its basic prescriptions are to see the problems in the round and in the long run, to act on them with full consciousness of their international dimensions—which sometimes requires collective action—and to be aware that a combination of familiar issues may create a new set of difficulties and opportunities.

## WORDS ABOUT TERMS

*Industrial policy* is a term that has been used in various ways. Sometimes it refers to policy toward a particular industry, and only rarely does it denote comprehensive measures dealing with the whole distribution of economic activity throughout the country. Because of the familiarity of industrialization—the dominant industrial policy of developing countries—it seems natural to associate the term and its variants, such as *industrial strategy*, with manufacturing. It is preferable, however, to think of *industry* as covering all economic activities—a common enough usage, helped by the fact that for most industrialized countries in the postwar period agricultural policy has been the prime example of the special treatment of a segment of the economy.

Strict usage would suggest that the word *policy* be confined to deliberate, thought-out, systematic, and more or less consistent lines of action. But then one would ignore the largest part of what governments do in the field of industrial policy, where ad hoc, unsystematic, and sometimes inconsistent measures are far more common than their opposite. One should recognize that, as one of the pioneers in the field has said, "a collection of interventions by the state does not necessarily constitute an industrial policy."[2] Motives make a difference, and so does consistency; but we also have to be concerned with effects, intended or not, and actions that are piecemeal rather than comprehensive. Therefore, the term *industrial policy* is used in this book to refer to discrete governmental measures as well as to the sustained pursuit of certain ends or the persistent use of certain methods or devices.

The common characteristic of the industrial policies we are dealing with is that they concern the *structure* of an economy. That term itself is far from crystal clear and is sometimes used even more loosely than *industrial policy*. This is partly because it has become a rather popular way of emphasizing the importance of an issue or its difficulty. (Another source of confusion is that the term *structural* is used in various ways in such fields as linguistics, anthropology, and literary criticism.) Historically, structure has sometimes been distinguished from function, and sometimes the emphasis is on framework rather than on interactions within a system. In economics, the label is sometimes applied to factors that are assumed to be more or less constant, but that in fact sometimes change and then dislocate past reasoning. It is easy to understand what is meant by the structure of prices, of demand, of supply, and of many other phenomena; but these are only occasionally of central concern to us. In this book, *structural* refers primarily to relatively lasting arrangements affecting the use of resources and the patterns of world production and trade resulting from them. Occasionally, though, the term may be extended to cover the basic circumstances in which the allocation of resources is determined or the manner

---

[2]Lionel Stoleru, *L'Impératif Industriel*, Editions du Seuil, Paris, 1969, p. 157.

in which the international economy functions. Thus a significant shift in the government's place in an economy and the movement from largely fixed to largely floating exchange rates are structural changes.[3] The organization of industry also comes into the picture, but usually only as competition, monopoly, concentration, control, and the size of firms affect the use of resources and international relations.

The link between structural change and industrial policies is that the latter are primarily concerned with maintaining the structure or with changing it one way rather than another. Much of the time—probably most of the time—industrial policy measures are efforts to resist structural changes that would otherwise take place, as when a new and cheaper producer appears in the world to displace former suppliers. Sometimes the aim is to induce change, as when a country wishes to become more industrial and less agricultural or wants to produce technologically advanced products instead of those using lower skills. Sometimes the two are combined, as when a country seeks to develop new industries to replace those in which it is no longer competitive while protecting the latter against the full blasts of foreign competition until new jobs and alternative uses of other resources can be found.

Although the distinctions may not always be sharp and clear, it is helpful to think of industrial policies as divided into three categories.

Those that are *defensive* are mainly concerned with keeping in being some structural arrangement, such as domestic production of certain goods that would not survive international com-

[3]In a work that overlaps this one in certain respects but concentrates on growth, Lincoln Gordon cites "seven aspects of structural change which emerge most clearly from historical study of economic development": the shift away from agriculture to manufacturing and services; urbanization; the demographic transition most countries go through over time; increased savings in relation to national product; rapid technological change in methods and in what is produced and consumed; the increased share of the national product accounted for by the public sector; and changes in the international division of labor, including the terms of trade. Lincoln Gordon, *Growth Policies and the International Order*, McGraw-Hill for the Council on Foreign Relations/1980s Project, New York, 1979, pp. 7–9.

petition or a given pattern of employment. They often resist change by limiting imports or subsidizing domestic activities in one way or another. It is often not clear whether a defensive policy will be pursued for a long time because its purpose is a lasting one (such as national security) or is more likely to give way or erode when economic and political circumstances change (as happens in some cases of simple protectionism).

*Adaptive* policies facilitate structural change by helping to shift resources to new uses that do not require protection or subsidy or by increasing efficiency in existing lines of activity. Simply permitting market forces to work is an adaptive policy; so too is help to injured workers and communities if this makes the change politically and socially acceptable. Such a policy may have defensive elements, as when imports are slowed down during a transitional period, but its purpose is to dispense with these elements before too long.

The third type of industrial policy *initiates change* rather than simply responding to it. This is what governments do when they have programs of economic development for the country as a whole or certain parts of it and when they seek to become producers of goods or services not formerly made at home. The devices they may use are legion, as the chapters to come will show.

Whether the emphasis is defensive, adaptive, or initiative, and whether the aim is to preserve old activities or break into new ones, a wide range of motives may be at work. Employment, foreign trade, growth, wealth, and similar economic goals may dominate for the country as a whole or some part of it. But very often the economic aim is mixed with something else: security, diversification of economic activity for broadly social reasons, a belief in the values of specific kinds of activity (the family farm), a wish to retain some independence from the rest of the world, or simply the greater importance attached to some values other than those of efficiency and productivity. The reduction of pollution and the improvement of the environment often require changes in the structure of industry. Not least in the list of factors to be taken into account is the play of domestic politics that insists that certain interests be protected and others promoted.

8

In practice, the distinction between structural policies and other policies is unfortunately not as sharp as it can be made on paper. Macroeconomic policies that are concerned with full employment, inflation, stability, growth, and other general conditions of an economy are plainly not industrial policy. But the boundaries are blurred whenever a government is not indifferent to the kinds of production and employment that result from its efforts, or, even if indifferent, acts so as to aid one kind of activity and hamper another. Measures to counter a recession, for example, affect structure by either encouraging the existing pattern of employment or stimulating investment in new lines of activity. The strains on international economic relations created by national measures to increase employment, overcome balance-of-payments deficits, and meet other "temporary" needs are bound to create problems in industrial policy for other countries. After the event, one has no conceptual difficulty in distinguishing cyclical unemployment: It is what disappears when demand again reaches a proper level. But it is another matter to be sure in advance that one is not dealing with structural unemployment, which can be overcome only by a shift in resources or by protection against the changes called for by what has happened in the rest of the world. Opinions about this difference and how to deal with it are often basic issues of industrial policy.[4]

Other kinds of policies can also be distinguished from industrial policy in broad terms. Among these are policies aimed at the distribution of wealth and income in a society; the promotion of foreign trade; immigration and emigration; the allocation of resources to defense; public works of various sorts; social security; the provision of social services, education, and health care to the population; the protection of the environment; and the regulation of economic activity for a variety of purposes—from laws on pure food and drugs and the protection of consumers against fraud through the supervision of banks, insurance, and natural or man-made monopolies. Although their main aims differ, few of these measures are without impact on the economic structure of countries in something like the sense we are using

---

[4]The problems of the recession and of the place of industrial policy in the gamut of economic policies are reexamined in the final chapter.

9

it here; and often they will deal very directly with the same kinds of issues that motivate industrial policy. A certain coherence ought to result when a country's policies in these fields reflect the same sets of values and trade-offs among them that shape its industrial policies and its attitude toward structural change. That at least would seem logical; but no one should be very surprised to find that in pluralistic societies different values and trade-offs dominate different policies simply because of differences in the policy-making process, the interests and values of different groups, and the intensity with which they pursue one rather than another objective. Accordingly, there may be important questions of consistency between some measures of industrial policy and action in other fields.

Not only explicit policies in other fields have to be taken into account in delineating what we mean by industrial policy. Institutional factors such as the monetary and financial system within a country and internationally not only have an effect on structure but do much to shape the problems and possibilities of industrial policy. That is equally true of such things as government-business relations, the organization of labor, and prevalent attitudes toward reliance on market forces, among other factors. Similarly, we have to bear in mind that to have what is called "no policy" is a kind of policy if it means accepting whatever happens and permitting people to adjust to changing circumstances as they will or can.

Lest all this emphasis on industrial policy confuse an already complicated situation, two things should be made clear. First, many of the sources of structural change to which industrial policies respond exist quite independently of governments, lying in changes in technology, income, wants, needs, fashion, and productivity; they may result from entrepreneurial activity at home or abroad or the lack of it. Second, structural changes are not necessarily good or bad; and although many problems arise from resistance to them, other problems stem from the forces of change themselves and their impact on groups, nations, or the international system as a whole.

Instead of enlarging further on these generalities, it will be wise to get a rough idea of some of the concrete policies or

10

measures we shall be dealing with—and then to see precisely why they pose special problems in international relations.

## EXAMPLES OF ACTION

France and Japan provide the two clear-cut, sustained, comprehensive examples of industrial policy in leading OECD countries in the postwar period. In both cases the starting place was the need to build a new national economic structure to fit into a changed world. France began with the first Monnet Plan in 1947. Japan's effort dates from the end of the American occupation in 1952. As time passed, goals changed and to a degree methods as well—especially in France, where the government's power to direct activities waned somewhat as business became stronger and gained freer access to capital. Still, "indicative planning" was used to point out where the national economy needed expansion or strengthening, and government help often supported the indications. The Japanese, too, concentrated on identifying the activities that should be expanded and on pushing resources into them. Extraordinary rates of growth helped bring about major transformations that included not only the creation of whole new industries but much shrinkage in traditional activities. Skeptical scholars have raised serious questions whether *le Plan* in France and the system called "administrative guidance" in Japan are entitled to quite as much credit as has been claimed for them, but there is no doubt that what was done depended in each case on a rather special set of government-business relations. By the late 1970s, however, few people believed that the most promising road for the future lay along the same lines. In France, *le Plan*, as a concept and an organization, had lost its former power—at a time when, one might think, it was most needed. In Japan, there was extensive questioning and debate about what should be done if, as is widely believed, the problems of the future cannot be met by the methods and instrumentalities of the past.

Other countries have at various times had reasonably clear-cut industrial policies covering significant parts of their econ-

11

omies, though usually not the whole. The special treatment of agriculture is common to industrialized countries. Energy policy has been forced on almost all governments by the abrupt structural changes of 1973 and 1974; but it was an earlier field of activity for many of them, especially postwar Western Europe as it moved from a predominantly coal-based economy to the greater use of gas and oil. Transportation, too, has preoccupied governments, whether the emphasis was on the domestic network of rail, road, and waterway; the rate structure; or (for many countries) support of a national merchant marine and airline. Shipbuilding and the production of aircraft have frequently been the objects of government encouragement that was rooted in concern for both economics and defense. Policies aiding regions that are depressed or suffer handicaps in one form or another are very common in industrialized countries and have much to do with the national economic structure. Another partly disguised industrial policy is common to almost all the OECD countries: Export promotion by governmental credit, insurance, or other means gives a selective stimulus to certain parts of each national economy, usually the industries producing equipment and other capital goods. (In the United States, interestingly, cotton was once the main such beneficiary.) At the receiving end, in the developing countries, there is also industrial policy. It may be very specific, such as the grant of tax concessions and tariff protection to a steel plant, the requirement that automobile importers incorporate a certain amount of local supplies and labor in every vehicle they sell, or the use of export controls or taxes to force the local processing of raw materials. Measures may also be general, intended to encourage whatever manufacturing seems possible, with or without foreign investment, according to the local preference. Often the issues concern the production and processing of raw materials, a subject that cannot be explored as fully in this book as is justified by its place in the world economy.

A full account of industrial policies would have to deal with the movement of people. Even when shaped by quite other considerations, laws governing immigration affect the supply of labor and its composition. Sometimes a government aims to draw in people with particular skills and keeps out others. Willing immigrants shaped the growth of North America and Australia. Refugees from the East after the Second World War greatly increased West Germany's productive power. Workers from southern Europe and North Africa were essential to Western Europe's great economic growth in the 1950s and 1960s, and the forced return home of many of them eased the contractions of the 1970s. Affluence—perhaps abetted by other factors—has made some kinds of work unacceptable to many Americans and Europeans, making it likely that immigrant labor will have a lasting place in those economies. Japan's experience is different: There the great change was from prewar emigration to little or none in the period after World War II. For developing countries, too, emigration is a key factor, whether the stress is on gains through relief of population pressure or losses of scarce skills through the brain drain created by higher pay and wider opportunities in richer countries. But immigration can be important, too, whether of technical or administrative people and teachers in small numbers; whole teams of construction workers; or, in countries where money has grown faster than population or skills (as in Saudi Arabia), substantial numbers of Indian, Pakistani, and Korean workers who staff as well as build factories. The movement of people within a nation—from region to region, country to town, and town to city—can also be significant for industrial policy, whether such movements are to be induced, discouraged, or simply accepted as facts to be taken into account.

The experience of individual OECD countries with industrial policy varies greatly. Britain's is complex. It includes dealing with depressed areas in the 1930s; the nationalization of coal at the end of the war; the later, more controversial effort by the Labour Party to secure effective public control of the "commanding heights" of the economy; and in the late 1970s a considerable effort to stimulate investment that would raise productivity in key parts of the economy. This last was plainly labeled an "industrial strategy."

In the Federal Republic of Germany, in contrast, many people have been uncomfortable with such terms, which are taken to connote more *dirigisme* than is thought compatible with either the *Sozialemarktwirtschaft* stemming from Ludwig Erhard or the somewhat comparable reliance on macroeconomic management favored by the Social Democratic Party. Nevertheless, there are significant elements of what we are calling industrial policy in postwar Germany, going back to the arrangements for absorbing massive immigration from the East and the channeling of capital into key industries through the *Kreditanstalt für Wiederaufbau* in the 1950s. The difficult process of winding down the coal industry involved cooperation among business, labor, and government (at various levels) in a manner quite characteristic of the conduct of affairs in Germany. Banks have long been closely linked with industry, and competition blends with a good deal of consensus about the desirable structure of the economy. Keeping a lead in world markets is given great emphasis. A substantial range of subsidies and other governmental measures is intended to help achieve that result while leaving initiative to entrepreneurs and at the same time cushioning the processes of change as they affect small industry, workers, and regions that are not as well off as the rest of the country.

The history of industrial policy in Canada goes back to the National Policy of the nineteenth century, the tariff protection that was seen as the key to industrialization, the land policy that encouraged western settlement, and the building of the transcontinental railway to tie together the areas of economic activity stretched out in a narrow band just north of the American border. Special efforts have long been made to stimulate more processing of raw materials and in recent times to encourage the growth of secondary industries that will not only create employment but also bring more research, development, and high technology to the country. The pursuit of these goals has not been consistent, and debate rages about suitable methods. Provinces as well as the federal government are involved; hence different standards may be applied at different places and times, not only with regard to the proper use of raw materials but on such basic matters as the desirability of more or less foreign investment. One of the most fundamental questions that keeps coming up is whether (and if so, how) to restructure Canadian industry to produce a smaller range of goods, concentrating on larger-scale output of its best products for the domestic and world market.

Sweden can be said to have had something like the reverse of Canada's industrial policy. Foreign investment has long been controlled but there was far less protection of domestic manufacturing and as a result there has been specialization to meet competition at home and abroad (especially because of the small domestic market). There has also been acceptance of the fact that Swedish companies have to invest in productive facilities abroad if they are to remain competitive in some fields. But the most commonly cited Swedish industrial policy has been the deliberate reduction and even phasing out of labor-intensive industries while encouraging the shift of workers to other, higher-paid lines in which they could meet world competition without protection. To do this required a combination of trade measures, education, social security, subsidy, and a complex of steps usually summed up as "an active labor market policy."

The European Community during the 1960s devoted a good deal of attention to devising an "industrial policy," which meant at the time measures intended to make its enterprises more competitive with the large American companies that constituted *le défi américain*. The related efforts to formulate a science and technology policy for Europe also deserve the name of industrial policy, as do the efforts by various member states of the Community to undertake cooperative ventures in aviation, aerospace, nuclear research, and the like. Euratom and the Coal and Steel Community contained distinct elements of industrial policy, and the Common Agricultural Policy is a major complex of structural measures. In dealing with regional policy the Community has had a special and interesting role in trying to introduce some common standards for the different practices of its members, provide for a certain amount of common financing, and relate the various regional measures to other activities. It is especially in this last field that the Community and every individual member country finds itself pushed to something approximating industrial policy, however piecemeal or inconsistent, when it tries to deal on a sustained basis with what might be thought of as the geographically weak spots in its economy.

The OECD surveyed the industrial policies of its members— or, for the most part, what they said were their industrial policies—for which they usually professed such unexceptionable goals as growth, efficiency, and the easing of adjustment. The concluding report mentioned some of the measures governments took to this end: "financial and fiscal incentives; technical assistance, training, and a wide range of consultative and advisory activities; policies within the framework of government procurement and contracts for technological development (R & D contracts); and direct State participation in industry."[5] But the list goes on almost indefinitely: the regulation of foreign or domestic investment; taxation and depreciation; direct government financing and other measures affecting access to capital; aid to small business; policies to promote (or inhibit) competition and to encourage or discourage mergers; the building of infrastructure, the regulation of transport, and the setting of freight rates; environmental measures and relief from them. Planning measures, whether indicative or compulsory, sectoral or comprehensive, come into the picture. Regional measures, whether they are intended to revive depressed areas, open up new territories, or ease the transfer of people from one to the other, are all likely to contain strong elements of industrial policy, even when they have other purposes as well.

The long list bears out the point made earlier that to survey the situation accurately one must take into account individual measures and not just full-blown policies. Showing that these measures are inconsistent may be very important but does not permit us to dismiss them. However, the length of the list is a warning that if every appearance of such widespread practices were taken to pose a problem of "industrial policy as an international issue," the subject would be blown up to an unmanageable size. Up to a point one can use fairly simple reasoning. It is one thing to see how six or eight of these practices converge in, say, a French effort to create a computer industry, and quite another to study the tax structure of every country to see if it favors one kind of investment more than another. Nevertheless, the question of where to draw the line will reappear (in a somewhat different form) when we come to consider how one can best try to work out rules and procedures for dealing internationally with national measures of industrial policy. That is not

[5]Organization for Economic Cooperation and Development (OECD), *The Aims and Instruments of Industrial Policy: A Comparative Study*, Paris, 1975, p. 132. (For other reports in this series, see the Critical Bibliography.)

simply because some kinds of measures lend themselves to codification reasonably well and others hardly at all, but also because some kinds of industrial policies reduce international friction and others are almost bound to increase it. It also makes a difference what countries resort to what practices; in that respect the description of the industrial policy of the United States is of some importance.

It also presents some difficulty. The term *industrial policy* is hardly known in the United States except as it applies to what some other countries do. The American response to the OECD inquiry pointed out that there were no federal administrative arrangements to carry out industrial policy, "since the American philosophy of economic progress has never called for a 'co-ordinated' Government attempt to intervene in the operations of various industries. Intervention has normally been ad hoc, to deal with particular situations. . . ."[6] There is no question about the lack of machinery; but more is being said here than just that the United States has not had a coherent and comprehensive structural policy. The language reflects a widely held American view that industrial policy is practiced only by countries that rely on governmental direction of the economy instead of on market forces and private enterprise. The attitude is understandable enough but is not entirely justified. One can hardly ignore the kinds of industrial policy measures the United States has taken. Moreover, the situation may be changing.

The United States has its share of fairly durable measures affecting the structure of the national economy. Farm policies, subsidies for shipping and shipbuilding, depletion allowances for extractive industries, and regulation of the structure of freight rates are neither new nor temporary. In the Kennedy Round the U.S. government was able to make large reductions on some tariffs (automobiles) and not on others (chemicals). Textiles were protected by quotas legitimized by international agreements created on American initiative. Later, shoes, color television, and

---

[6]Organization for Economic Cooperation and Development (OECD), *United States Industrial Policies*, Paris, 1970, p. 35. The document "summarizes a presentation made by the United States Delegation to the OECD Industry Committee. . . ." (p. 5).

steel were shielded from foreign competition by agreements limiting the exports of other countries. "Buy American" laws not only affect the treatment of domestic and foreign products but distinguish among products as well; exemptions are provided for certain goods produced in certain allied countries and for a wider range of products from Canada. Government purchases at all levels equal about one-quarter of the GNP, and some sections of industry depend almost entirely on the government. The Lockheed Company was kept alive by financial measures judged to be in the public interest. The Joint Economic Committee of Congress publishes studies of the extent and form of subsidies paid throughout the economy. Tax laws are altered according to what is thought of their effect on business investment. Domestic oil production was protected on grounds of national security before the events of the 1970s made energy policy a central subject of debate.

More comprehensive industrial policies have not been unknown in the American past. Alexander Hamilton's *Report on Manufactures* of 1792 was an explicit and well-thought-out proposal to encourage the growth of industry, attract foreign investment, and bargain for access to European markets for American exports. State and federal aid in the building of canals, roads, and other "internal improvements" from the 1820s to the 1850s may not have been very well coordinated, but it certainly reflected a concept of national economic development. So did government help to railroads, the banking laws, the Homestead Act, and the subsequent administration of forests and minerals on public lands. High tariffs for many industrial products after the Civil War were linked with free entry of some supplies that farmers wanted in a great political compromise that also reflected a concept of national economic structure. Trust-busting followed, another kind of industrial policy that is still with us. In the Depression some people called for "comprehensive planning," and for a while the National Recovery Administration (NRA) was thought to be providing it, though before the Act creating it was declared unconstitutional, the NRA had plainly turned into a form of self-government for business.

It is certainly true that in the period after the Second World War the emphasis of major American policies at home and abroad was to broaden the area in which market forces and private enterprise could play. But it is not preordained that this emphasis will always characterize American policy (even with allowance for exceptions to the principles). The energy measures of the 1970s will for some time to come affect not only energy but the rest of the national industrial structure as well. There are many proposals for enlarging the government's role in science, technology, and R & D, at least partly to foster the growth of new industries. In 1977 the steel industry for the second time in a decade required government help to deal with difficulties caused in part by imports, but this time the approach went beyond temporary protection to what was unmistakably a set of industrial policies (see Chapter 4). Environmental measures are debated in terms of their differential effect on industries. The concern felt in the 1970s about future supplies of a number of products and the conundrums of stagflation moved some people, including some businessmen, to propose at least a limited kind of planning. The aim was to work out the requirements of meeting major national needs or simply to indicate to businessmen the economic setting in which they would have to operate over a period of time. Nothing serious has come of this interest, and it may dissipate; but even if that happens, there will continue to be a major element of American life that has to be thought of in terms of industrial policy: the supervision of markets and the governmental actions necessary to make them work well.

In other words, to choose to rely on market forces and on less rather than more government interference with private business is to choose a particular kind of industrial policy, not to dismiss the need for one. Moreover, such a choice is rarely absolute; we have tariff protection and many other familiar measures of industrial policy because people are unwilling to accept the results of unfettered competition. To increase their willingness to do so is often a good objective of government action, and one can make a strong case for an industrial policy that mostly confines itself to helping instead of hindering adjustment while at the

19

same time easing the position of people who are hurt in the process. To increase the flexibility of the national economy could be an admirable objective of industrial policy, but it would not consist of doing nothing. In a world of partial interventionism, "free" markets can produce distorted results. How to define and produce fair competition presents another set of problems. And private businessmen are as likely to try to suppress competition as to promote it if they are free to do so. That is one of the reasons that antitrust policy is industrial policy.

Indeed, it may be the most distinctive American contribution to the subject. Not that the United States is as alone in the world as it once was in these matters; but it remains the exponent of a more highly developed, perhaps more radical, enforcement of competition on reluctant businessmen than other countries have undertaken. The question of market forces and competition in the service of industrial policy will arise at a number of points in this book. Here only two points need underlining. First, "the market" is not some homogeneous behavior pattern that exists whenever governments are not intervening. Markets differ greatly from one another in performance and results. Products, processes, and the structure of firms all contribute to the outcome. Among the factors determining the nature of a market is the set of laws and governmental policies that apply to it and the way the private entrepreneurs (and anyone else involved in the market) act in the light of how they expect these laws and policies to be invoked. Second, there is nothing automatic about antitrust policy, American or any other. The law is the law, but how it is applied depends on a variety of circumstances and these have much to do with the shape of American industry—and could have more.

The choice of when to prosecute and how to interpret the applicability of the United States law to various activities rests with officials of the Department of Justice. Their judgment and standards are different at different times. They are not independent of the law but it is in part shaped by them, as it is by judges. The remedies sought, the consent decrees negotiated, and the arrangements imposed by the courts entail judgments not only about the law but also about the structure of the national economy. Although Americans have not thought in these terms, such considerations are similar to those that shape industrial policies in other countries—even if they sometimes promote opposite ends. The Department of Justice is not wholly in charge; the courts are independent, and those who feel damaged can sue (including foreigners) even if the Antitrust Division takes no initiative. Not all the results are intended; companies have said they invested abroad for fear that expansion at home would attract prosecution. Uncertainty about how the antitrust laws apply and when they will be invoked undoubtedly affects business behavior.

It would take changes in law, concept, and atmosphere to see American antitrust policy being used primarily as an instrument to pursue the kinds of goals generally associated with industrial policy. But the possibility would not be too farfetched if the United States were to develop a more conscious industrial policy. The oil companies were permitted to work together to bargain with foreign suppliers. Do not the sharp differences of opinion about the wisdom of prosecuting IBM depend to an important degree on differences about the effect that that action is expected to have on competition within the American economy and the ability of American industry to compete abroad? And if one's industrial policy is to use market forces to make adjustment whenever possible, something will have to be done to make sure that market forces work.

Our survey of examples is far from complete. It has produced illustrations, not an exhaustive catalogue or typology. Little or nothing has been said about the times when a government's concern with the fate of a particular enterprise—Lockheed, British Leyland, the Boussac group—results in actions that have a significant effect on the structure of the economy and its foreign economic relations as well. Often an industrial policy rests on what can be done to make a single company successful as the "national champion" in some new field or simply as a profitable competitor in world markets. And when firms are not allowed to fail because of the repercussions that are feared, new resistances to structural adaptation are likely to be created. Another subject only touched is the provision of public credit to a firm

21

or a whole class of firms to help expand an economy's capacities in certain fields—or simply to become more competitive. Still further illustrations will appear in the chapters that follow.

What will not appear, for lack of space, is what might be called private industrial policy. Business firms, especially large firms that either account for a substantial share of a country's output of certain things or operate in a number of countries (or both) have an influence on the operation and structure of the world economy that touches the very stuff of industrial policy. Sometimes they create problems for one or more governments; sometimes they bring about adaptation and change in ways that avoid or even eliminate problems that governments would have trouble dealing with. That is not why the business firms do these things; nor do they do them simply in response to the immediate demand for their products. They look ahead; they plan; they undertake activities that cannot be profitable for some years to come, and then only if they have calculated correctly. Businessmen take some risks and avoid others; they concern themselves with growth, survival, change, and other factors that are not altogether easy to assess or predict. Banks and other sources of funds make the same calculations about business. Naturally consideration of these activities plays some part in the pages that follow, but the activities are not dealt with systematically or in the detail they deserve.

Perhaps the illustrations in this section have been sufficient to make clear what kinds of things we are dealing with when, at some risk of abusing the language, we use broad terms like *industrial policy* and *structural change* to cover so many things. Enough has surely been said to show that part of our problem is that we have to be concerned with an extreme variety of measures, including the comprehensive and the particular, the routine and the exceptional, the immediate and the long run, the intended and the unintended (so far as the structural results are concerned), the defensive and the aggressive, and so on. What remains for this chapter to do is to explain why all these measures taken together—or at least a very large number of them—pose a set of problems the world has not faced before and why, if the challenge is not recognized, the world will slip blindly into great difficulties.

## THE INTERNATIONAL PROBLEM

If the world has lived this long with such a blooming, buzzing confusion of industrial policies, why should they now pose a major international problem? The answer can be given briefly, but its full purport can be seen only through the later chapters.

Structural change in the world economy is essential to progress. If industrial policies are devoted mainly to resisting change, the loss of efficiency, productivity, and flexibility will mean that the world will have fewer goods and services to meet its needs than it would otherwise have. Although industrial policies are shaped primarily in response to the play of national political forces, they often impose serious and very inequitable burdens on foreigners. If improved ways are not found for dealing with these problems through international agreement, there will be increased friction among countries and a deterioration of international economic relations. This does not just mean that the period ahead will be more difficult than the last few decades have been, but that much that has been accomplished since the end of World War II will be eroded and eventually lost.

Take the situation in international trade. Its great expansion in the 1950s and 1960s was a major factor contributing to the prosperity of the period. Unprecedented removal of trade barriers stimulated the exchange of goods and encouraged increased specialization and productivity through investment and technological innovation. There were fewer dislocations and disturbances than might have been expected from this process, partly because the general expansion made adjustment easier and partly because a number of the changes were spread over a period of time. Nevertheless, there was a good deal of resistance to shifts in trade in many parts of the world economy. Japan's great export expansion met barriers of many sorts. There was much less removal of trade barriers in some fields—textiles, clothing, certain chemicals—than in others. Agriculture largely escaped the whole process. Almost every major country had some sectors it insisted on protecting. Although the OECD countries extended especially favorable treatment to the exports of developing countries in some respects, they were on the whole more restrictive in dealing with the products of those countries than in trade among themselves. The cotton textile agreements of the early 1960s, which were extended to man-made fibers and woolens in the 1970s, were efforts to slow the rate of change. As tariffs were substantially reduced or removed, it became clear that much of world trade was restricted or distorted by nontariff barriers of various sorts and a whole series of measures favoring domestic industry, such as subsidies and tax concessions. Thus, on the one hand, resistance to structural change was checking trade liberalization in some key areas while, on the other hand, where the tariffs and quotas were removed, national industrial policies were increasingly revealed as directly affecting other countries. By the early 1970s it seemed apparent that existing trade arrangements were inadequate to cope with these difficulties and might themselves be undermined.

The international flow of capital and the expansion of direct foreign investment has played a major part in the structural changes of the past few decades. There were no multilateral agreements on the scale of the General Agreement on Tariffs and Trade (GATT), but many national measures taken or agreements made between governments and investors influenced the structure of world trade and production. Some of these involved tax concessions, subsidies, and the grant of privileged positions in the domestic market. In other cases business gained access to a market by promising to export a certain amount from the new facilities. Thus the industrial policies of some countries produced problems of adjustment for others. Development financing tended to focus on national needs, but it often had important international impacts as new facilities substituted for imports or created new export capacities. Artificial exchange rates, subsidies, variations in taxation, the incubation period for new industries, and intracompany trade often made it hard to know whether shifts in production and trade responded to true differences in competitive advantage. In the interests of assuring themselves of supplies of energy and other raw materials, protecting investments, and holding export markets for capital goods, industrial countries made special arrangements with developing nations that had a distinct bearing on the patterns of production of still other countries. Often the result seemed to challenge the future viability of long-established industries in older producing centers. Thus, in this field as in trade, structural concerns plus industrial policies began putting a strain on the willingness of governments to tolerate the relatively free movement of capital.

The accumulation of resistances to change and of possible distortions in the world economy began before the energy crisis and the recession of the mid-1970s. But these events have made them worse. If, in the future, growth in the industrial countries is slower than it was in the 1950s and 1960s, matters will become still more difficult. On the one hand, it will be harder to find ways to absorb workers displaced from declining industries; on the other hand, the burden on the more productive parts of the economy of carrying the less productive parts will increase. The need for the efficiency that comes with adaptation to structural change will increase, but the ability of countries to adapt will be reduced. Countries that resist change will find it harder to earn their way in the world as their costs become higher than those of new producers abroad.

If the gloomy forecasts prove wrong and growth rates are high, adaptation will be easier and failures to adapt somewhat less costly. But even a much-improved situation will not eliminate the need to find better ways of dealing internationally with industrial policy issues. The rough sketch already given shows that national measures of industrial policy are so numerous and various that it is implausible to suppose that they will be given up on any large scale. On the contrary, there are good reasons for supposing that even in prosperous times governments are likely to make increased use of industrial policy measures in the future and to be more concerned than in the past with the structure of their economies.

In part, this is a matter of what is needed to help bring about change. Conventional macroeconomic policies no longer seem altogether adequate, at least in the mixed economies of the industrialized countries. Exports of manufactures from the developing countries—which have not been as great a pressure for change as shifts in competitive strength and technological change within the industrial countries—will increase and require structural shifts in the older producing centers unless new trade barriers are erected. It may very well be that in the modern world international shifts in comparative advantage—the factor that makes international specialization so valuable—take place more rapidly than they used to. The speed with which capital, management, and technology can move from one country to another suggests this; the margins by which low labor costs were offset by low productivity seem to have narrowed. The increased speed and reduced costs of transportation and communication and the spread of the habit of comparing every place within a global horizon also play their parts.

Industrial policies are called for both to keep ahead of this process and to slow it to a politically and socially tolerable level. Closely related are the trade-offs in rich industrial societies that give environmental considerations, stability, job security, and leisure higher value than they had before. The wish to put a floor under poverty, to raise the minimum social services the state provides for all, and to achieve more equitable distribution in general creates a demand for an arsenal of industrial policies of one sort or another. It is a rare country that is so little involved in the economy of the rest of the world that its structural measures will not affect others or be affected by what they do.

Even if there is more reaction against these domestic tendencies, or at least an effort to rely heavily on market mechanisms instead of government intervention or nationalization, the international issues will not go away. The measures will not be uniform throughout the world. As was argued earlier, the reliance on market forces requires policies to make the markets function well. Not all countries will pursue the same course in these matters or even agree on what they want from the markets, how they should function, and how much competition there should be (and among whom). National actions will clash, and even a good deal of similarity in actions will not assure the same results in international markets that countries try to obtain at home.

If major countries used their industrial policies to facilitate adjustment, even if it were spread out over a period so as to make the pace of change politically acceptable, there would be fewer international problems than if they all resisted change or tried to pass off its costs onto others. Still, this would be no cure-all. Adjustment implies a shift of resources toward new uses of greater value to the national economy. The steps taken to attain that structure may affect other countries. If each country ignores what the others do, it may not be able to achieve its own aims. Resistance to the new changes by one or more countries will simply create a new set of distortions. To the basic problem of improving methods of accommodating divergences in national industrial policies should be added questions about the possibility of devising measures of *international* industrial policy through common action by several countries.

It may seem strange to hold up such a prospect when there is already so much confusion about what can and cannot be done by national measures; but, as is explained in Chapter 5, we are not totally without some relevant experience. More important is the underlying rationale. The realities of the postwar world have borne in on people an older truth, that individual national states cannot fully satisfy the needs and aspirations of their citizens by themselves or in isolation. In different ways and with different degrees of success they have joined together to accomplish a variety of common purposes. Some of these already involve aspects of industrial policy and structural change. Difficult as the task may be, might they not consider doing more? If so, what? Should the emphasis be on pushing further the already highly developed cooperation among the OECD countries, or on dealing with the extraordinary shifts in world manufacturing that can be foreseen in relations between the developing countries and the old industrial areas? Or should the emphasis be on a few especially troublesome industries?

Any particular forecast may be wildly wrong, but we can be quite sure that there will be substantial economic change during the next few decades. Some countries will become more industrialized than they are; new geographical patterns of production and trade will take shape; individual industries will rise and decline in relative importance, globally and regionally; new industries will come into existence; technological change will alter the character of existing industries. Governments will foster some of these changes and resist others; industrial policy in one form or another will frequently be their major instrument. In each country groups will be differently affected by these developments and will favor some and oppose others. Given the range of issues involved, the complexity of the trade-offs, and the differences in circumstances, it seems likely that when a national consensus is achieved on matters of industrial policy, it will more often than not clash with the consensus within another nation. And when there is a willingness to act in industrial policy, it may require the coordination of positive measures taken in different countries, which is often harder than carrying out agreed measures to remove obstacles to trade and payments. It follows that the problems with which this book is concerned are inescapable.

They may take different forms from those we expect. The complexity of the economic issues alone could have that result, but more than economics is involved. The aim of industrial policy is often to impose social criteria on the values of the marketplace or to shape the life of a society according to a scale of values that covers more than material satisfaction. Looking outward, a country may also pursue economic policies for highly uneconomic aims. Some may be bound to bring it into a conflict with other countries or at least to emphasize relative power. The aims of these policies may be basically defensive, as in the pursuit of some minimum level of security that is believed to go with a certain kind of economy and to be worth paying for even if it reduces the gross national product. There may be a sense that certain economic conditions are necessary to national sovereignty and independence. And even if the aims are never achieved, societies may go on pursuing them.

A convergence of all these interests or international agreement on the economic and noneconomic values that would permit common action in industrial policy by more than a few countries is not something to be taken for granted. Whether it can be created or encouraged is a question better left for the end of this book than speculated on at the outset. There can hardly be a consensus if the issues are not clearly understood. To achieve some measure of that understanding is a major purpose of this book. But even if the issues are clear it may not be possible to achieve broad agreement on ends, much less means, as the next chapter demonstrates.

# TWO

# Why the Solutions
# Are So Difficult

To map a route, it helps to know where you are going. Unfortunately, those concerned with the international problems created by national industrial policies lack the guidance of any generally accepted idea of what an ideal solution would be. They are not even as well off as their predecessors who in the 1940s worked out the postwar trading system. Many people then regarded free trade as an ideal, but even theoretically its main virtues were postulated on conditions unlikely to be met in real life. Its classical formulators allowed an important exception for infant industries, of which there were likely to be many in the postwar world. Adam Smith himself recognized the priority of defense over opulence, and security was the main thing the United Nations was created for. As the theory said nothing about how the benefits of the optimum allocation of resources would be shared around the world, it would have been irresponsible for any government to accept global free trade as the ideal without some assurance of what other policies would prevail in the world.

What did exist, in spite of all the qualifications, was a significant consensus among people in key positions that it was highly desirable to reduce the great accumulation of barriers to international trade that had been built up since the early 1930s. The practical task was to find ways of persuading governments to move in that direction when they had so many other pressures on them. For that purpose no one needed to subscribe to an ultimate goal. It is no accident that neither GATT nor the more ambitious Charter for an International Trade Organization (which never took effect) said anything about free trade or about the ultimate condition they aspired to achieve. The signatory governments simply undertook to move toward the reduction of tariffs and the elimination of discrimination, quotas, and some other trade barriers. Nevertheless, it is doubtful whether there could have been even that much agreement on the direction in which to move without the intellectual foundations laid by a century and more of theory and considerable experience of what it means to make extensive use of trade controls.[1] There is no such basis for a consensus on industrial policy.

Matters would be different if the opening sentence of the OECD survey already quoted could be taken as gospel: "Industrial policies are concerned with promoting industrial growth and efficiency."[2] So they are, much of the time; but as often as not the concern is to protect some existing activity at home against the

---

[1]The consensus was not complete. The biggest differences concerned the pace of liberalization, how it should be applied to countries with balance-of-payments difficulties, etc., and not the basic idea. Here and there one found people who favored the fairly free use of trade barriers for the kinds of nation-building reasons identified with Hamilton and List. But few of these would go so far as to favor autarky, so there was room for compromise. The priority some people attached to full employment over removal of trade barriers could be met (not altogether satisfactorily) by various devices and the knowledge that no amount of paper commitment to trade liberalization could be expected to win out over serious prolonged unemployment. A more fundamental difficulty was posed by those who believed that freeing trade would upset national planning or socialism. Here the task, again dealt with in only a partially satisfactory way, was to work for links between planning and the market in the first case and to develop rules concerning state trading in the latter. Again the real compromise was practical rather than theoretical, since all-out planning and 100 percent state ownership and control as the definition of socialism did not win out in any of the key countries. In short, the question became one of linking mixed systems in which the mix varied from country to country—a problem also faced in dealing with industrial policy.

[2]OECD, *The Aims and Instruments of Industrial Policy: A Comparative Study*, op. cit., p. 7. In fairness to the authors of the report it should be said that they immediately recognize that these words do not mean too much and quite quickly move into a discussion of issues hardly suggested by the rather anodyne opening.

results of a new efficiency that has arisen abroad (so to speak). General acceptance of growth and efficiency as goals would not eliminate conflicts between national policies, but it would provide a basis of compromise and potential reconciliation that does not now exist. To be sure, per capita growth of income remains a target of the macroeconomic policies of most countries. Their industrial policies, however, are more likely to be concerned with the growth of particular parts of the economy (or sometimes their contraction). Even if several different countries were trying to stimulate the growth of the same industry, it is not impossible to imagine ways in which the advantages they seek can be shared on some equitable basis if they also adhere to the standard of efficiency. But if there is a conflict between efficiency and full employment, the latter is likely to be given priority. Again, the goal is one best pursued by macroeconomic policy, and in periods of growth governments may be satisfied with that course. But when the results are not good, industrial policy too will have an employment-creating function, as it may also for certain areas even in normal times.

Highly as one may value efficiency, it is obviously not unreasonable for a society to prefer not to accept as inevitable the loss of output from unemployment. Alternatively, the definition of maximum efficiency might have to be rethought to include the full use of resources. One could then say that "the aim of industrial policies should be to make the greatest possible progress towards an objective that is formulated as some weighted sum of income and employment."[3] That formulation is an improvement, but to accept it as the ideal would be to leave out the more complex goals involving environmental, social, and various other aims that countries often pursue in their industrial policies. One can say that they should not be taken into account, or that whenever noneconomic values are taken into account they should

---

[3] Bohuslav Herman, *The Optimal International Division of Labor*, International Labour Office, Geneva, 1975, p. 103. This interesting study is one of the few attempts to define an international optimum for industrial policies. It is a thoughtful piece of work and touches on a number of points considered later but does not deal with the whole range of national aims taken into account in this chapter.

be treated as trade-offs involving a departure from an economic ideal. That is how economic analysis usually approaches public policy, and it permits a degree of rigor that has its merits. This book, however, sacrifices that possibility in the hope of coming a little closer to the real issues of industrial policy.

A second set of difficulties stands in the way of accepting the income-plus-employment formula as an ideal industrial policy. Suppose it is applied in one country in a way that interferes with the optimum solution in another country. Does one country give way to the other because it can better afford the sacrifice on grounds of wealth or level of development? Do they split the difference, suboptimizing and leaving each with still another problem? Lack of an agreement satisfactory to both is clearly likely to stimulate one or the other to take steps that may leave both worse off. This set of questions and the beggar-my-neighbor process it conjures up arise when other standards are applied to industrial policy as well. They will need further attention. But first we need to explore a little more fully the difficulties of defining an ideal industrial policy judged in terms of global welfare.

## THE GLOBAL VIEW: CONFLICTING CRITERIA

Imagine, then, an authority empowered to set the goals for industrial policy for the world. It need not persuade national governments of the merits of its solutions but must think of global welfare in the broadest sense, which includes satisfying the wishes of people as much as possible. For the time being the difficulties of putting policies into effect can be left aside except to the extent that they are inherent in the pursuit of several ends at once. Policies do not need to be uniform all over the world and can take account of differences in conditions or in the preferences of people. Time is not a problem, since the authority is defining an ideal toward which the world will work.

Somewhat greater difficulties arise from the fact that industrial policy does not exist in isolation. To be rigorous, one ought to make assumptions about the effects of macroeconomic policies on full employment, stability, growth, and other conditions influencing global welfare. In the process one would probably define away many of the difficulties that most require attention. Consequently our discussion is blurred around the edges.

It may also be blurred in the middle: The nine sections of this chapter that follow sometimes overlap. They are also not strictly uniform regarding the kinds of problems they present for the formation of industrial policy. Further, they are not all equally important; and part of the problem is that different people give them different weights in each case and that the same person will rank them differently in different circumstances. What they have in common is that each embodies a set of values that someone will favor as the best basis of an ideal global industrial policy. A person who gives primacy to one or more of these considerations will see others as constraints on the ideal policy. At this stage of the inquiry, however, this book is still neutral; each section that follows sets forth criteria that have to be given some weight in trying to construct a global ideal. To discuss them properly would require a treatise on social philosophy; therefore these paragraphs are best thought of as notes about points that will bear on later chapters as well as this one.

### Growth

This is a macroeconomic objective that cannot be achieved by industrial policy alone, but it enters into the shaping of a global ideal for several reasons: (a) Without growth one cannot satisfy the aspirations of large parts of the world's people for improved conditions. To move in that direction will require structural changes that an ideal industrial policy ought to foster. (b) Some of the aspirations themselves concern the growth of certain kinds of activities in parts of the world where they do not now exist; in addition to favoring this kind of expansion, the ideal industrial policy has to take account of the impact of these structural changes on the rest of the world. (c) Controls or limits on growth will be wanted by some groups to conserve resources, limit pollution, and provide space, leisure, and other benefits. Others will value such benefits less highly than the economic gains from growth. While overall growth itself need not be an objective of global industrial policy, it is probably a necessary condition for achieving some of the ends of that policy. It will also entail structural changes, which industrial policy must at least adapt to and sometimes foster.

## Stability

Like growth, stability is generally thought of as a primary aim of macroeconomic policy and the possible contributions to it by industrial policy at first seem fairly small. But the structure of an economy surely has something to do with its stability. Diversification is generally supposed to be more stable than monoculture; it is widely believed that an economy with a number of small firms can adjust more easily than one dominated by a few large ones, though the possibilities the latter have for internalizing adaptation (expanding one activity while contracting another) point in the other direction. Just as most people wish to combine growth with stability, so they would like changes to come about in an orderly way whenever possible. Thus one test that will be applied to an ideal global industrial policy is whether it contributes to stability.

It must be remembered, though, that the concept of stability is a rather slippery one. An economy in a stable state might have no growth; but without some economic growth, social and political stability may be threatened. Is a stable society one that keeps everything the same or one that changes continually in fairly small ways to avoid the accumulations of dissatisfaction that may break out in revolution? Assurance that a known set of laws will determine the outcome of an issue is surely an element of stability, but some discretionary power may improve the ability of authorities to adapt to changing circumstances. An effort to maintain the stability of a national economy by shutting out imports or other external disturbances may promote stability in one place at the expense of stability elsewhere. The efforts that people make to keep their own position in society stable helps explain why so much of industrial policy is defensive instead of

34

adaptive. They often mislead themselves in these efforts and the policies become self-defeating. Jan Tumlir put it well in a most thoughtful lecture:

The rapid economic progress which liberal international policy makes possible generates growing expectations of further progress which, fomented and exploited by the politicians, eventually outgrow the system's capacity to deliver. The popular expectations focus on stability in particular; stability not only of one's income but of one's position in the social group, and thus of the rate of growth of one's income and of its relation to the incomes of others. Eventually, a degree of stability comes to be desired which makes stable progress impossible. Economic progress implies novelty and social adaptation to it. But before this insight dawns upon the society, the state has been called upon, and has promised, to make possible progress without change.[4]

## Efficiency

A key criterion for industrial policy, efficiency depends on many things that go far beyond it. Much discussion is misleading when it deprecates efficiency as part of the threat to human values that some people think comes from technology and the dominance of the marketplace. In the fundamental sense of getting the greatest output for a given input, efficiency is hard to dismiss as a major means of achieving almost all goals, including leisure, more equitable distribution, environmental protection, and adapting economies to slower growth.[5] It is true that in certain circum-

[4]Jan Tumlir, *National Interest and International Order*, Trade Policy Research Center, International Issues No. 4, London, 1978, pp. 6–7.

[5]Emphasis on distribution often blinds people to the importance of production, but one of the greatest egalitarians saw the connection. As he sat in the British Museum in the 1830s thinking through what was essential "to organize a great community according to the fundamental rules of equality," Etienne Cabet soon saw "that above all what was needed was increased production in agriculture and then in industry." "Comment Je Suis Communiste," quoted in H. Lux, *Etienne Cabet und der ikarische Kommunismus*, Dietz, Stuttgart, 1899, p. 84.

stances an insistence on efficiency would be incompatible with the preservation of certain values and ways of life for some people—which poses the recurrent problem of who makes what choices and who carries the burden of the results. The particular importance of the efficiency criterion is that so much industrial policy is defensive, guarding established producers against new competition. This can be done in ways that permit efficiency to win out, but only if that purpose is given major emphasis.

It could be argued that the efficiency criterion for industrial policy comes close to being the same as the ideal of world trade liberalization. That would be true if efficiency were taken as the sole aim; but that cannot be, as this chapter is demonstrating. Moreover, to take this as the ideal would fly in the face of the fact that one of the main reasons industrial policies are widely used is that people have been unwilling to accept the consequences of free trade, any more than they accepted it as the objective of the trade liberalization to which they subscribed (no matter how loosely statesmen and journalists speak of "the end of free trade"). Sometimes, though, a defensive industrial policy may be justified as leading to efficiency. In terms of the categories sketched in Chapter 1 that result would turn it into an adaptive policy, but one cannot always tell in advance. It would be hard to argue that the efficiency of the Japanese economy of the 1970s was not in part the product of the protection and governmental help of the 1950s and 1960s, or that the high productivity per man in American agriculture was not brought about in part by the support prices and subsidies of past farm policy that certainly did not seem to be rewarding efficiency at the time. The classical exception to free trade—infant industry protection—has its modern application not only in developing countries but whenever some new activity (sometimes in an old industry) is shielded from the competition of more efficient producers on the ground that it will take time for the new producer to become as efficient as they. Unfortunately, the methods of determining the chances of success are not very good; the result is not always the one hoped for, and to continue the protection if the activity does not become competitive—as often happens—is to increase inefficiency in the world.

Thus efficiency and free trade are not identical except under certain conditions. But at some point competition must be the test of efficiency, and often it may be the best means of bringing it about. If, however, competition is allowed to lead to monopoly, efficiency may suffer once again. Generally speaking, though, trade barriers have to be regarded as likely to interfere with efficiency except when they are used temporarily to promote it. If the goal of an industrial policy is something other than efficiency, then, of course, trade barriers or any other instruments have to be judged by different criteria. Perhaps a rough initial approximation might be to say that if industrial policies do not promote efficiency (on a global scale), the reason why should be made clear along with the cost. How that cost should be shared then touches another key element in an ideal global industrial policy: equity.

Efficiency is a more complex concept than is suggested by the picture of one person at a machine producing what 10 people produce by hand. Technical efficiency is not the same as economic efficiency, which takes account of costs. Time is a factor (in the tortoise-and-hare sense as well as for continuity), and so is some degree of stability. It is not efficient to have no security of supply or to try to put either machines or workers in and out of employment according to fluctuations in costs between 99 cents and a dollar. But this is no place for a discourse on the full meaning of efficiency. For most of our purposes, a rough test of efficiency is international competitiveness over a sustained period under conditions of fair competition (which also needs defining). As the efficiency criterion is so often referred to in this book, the reader should keep in mind that it is a kind of shorthand for a concept that is not as simple as it sometimes seems and that the existence of it is not always easy to determine.

### Full Employment and Use of Other Resources

Again, macroeconomic considerations take first place but may need to be supplemented by structural measures to assure full employment. When industrial policies promote full employment in one place, one must determine whether they interfere with full employment elsewhere and then who makes that loss good, who decides, and who pays. The definition of full employment of resources other than labor raises questions about conservation, the environment, rates of growth, etc. There is a connection with efficiency. If automation throws people out of work, is not the increased efficiency of that process offset in some sense by a decrease in efficiency in the national economy, at least so long as their labor is left unused? That transitional unemployment is essential to efficiency and adaptability is easily demonstrated, but prolonged unemployment that does not yield to anticyclical measures is properly taken to be structural. Like so many of the other criteria, this one also raises the questions of who makes the trade-offs and who pays for them.

## Choice

Ideally, everyone ought to be able to earn a living by the activity he prefers. If a person chose idleness, or activities not valued by others, or at which he was inept, his return would be only that minimum that society decided it was right and proper to pay to anyone to keep body and soul together—plus satisfaction. Otherwise, the return for labor would depend on demand and skill, and that would, of course, influence choice. All this is utopian; and so would be the industrial policy necessary to make it a reality, for it would have to provide an immense range of choices in every place or something like complete global mobility, which would require not only free migration but some sort of common standard of education and an extraordinary degree of cosmopolitanism in social relations, language, and much else. Moreover, production on the scale and with the productivity needed to provide with any decency for the world's population entails a degree of social and economic organization that may well be incompatible with truly free choice for all. But such speculation about the human condition carries us beyond where we are entitled to go in our quest for the ideal industrial policy.

Though our global formulator of industrial policy—let us give him the Benthamite title of Legislator—may have to dismiss the extreme, he can hardly ignore the need to include in his ideal some movement toward widening the range of choices open to people. Most nations try to increase opportunies (if not for the whole people then for the privileged), and our Legislator is simply performing the basic societal functions on a global basis. Although there is no conflict between choice and the full use of resources, there may well be between choice and efficiency, growth, and perhaps stability.

## Participation

This is a label covering some interconnected activities that have to be taken into account in thinking about an ideal industrial policy. Even if we judge it utopian for every individual to be able to choose his work, it is not too farfetched to argue that he should have some voice in the matter. That voice might influence the kinds of economic activity that take place in one's country, or province, or neighborhood, and thus the choices that are open. But as it takes more than wishes to make jobs, such a voice might be effective only if clear alternatives were posed or as opposition to certain kinds of economic activity or in trying to establish the conditions in which economic decisions made by others had to be carried out. How much the voice is heard will depend in part on the political system and in part on whose voice it is. An entrepreneur has the best chance to exercise choice, if the government permits. A worker has a different and more limited opportunity, and consumers and taxpayers still others.

Consideration of participation by individuals leads into other questions of industrial policy. There is the role of groups, whether unions, business organizations, cooperatives, or something else. There is the question of what level of government makes key decisions, and of who determines the efficiency–full employment mix or the trade-offs between production and pollution. We have eliminated nation-states for the moment, but even a global policy might be improved by devolution of decisions to regions or localities. Then there is the question, Who decides who is entitled to decide which issues? But that is one of the really basic political problems, lying beyond even the broadest bounds we can give to industrial policy. There is, however, one further set of issues that cannot be ignored: those concerning participation in decisions affecting the conduct of enterprises and perhaps whole industries. Here the questions include worker participation in management, public representation on company boards, self-government by industry, government-business relations, and still other matters. (These relations are viewed in another perspective in Chapter 6.)

The participation criterion is plainly not one that will command unanimous support. It is likely to be judged in part by the results it produces in terms of efficiency, equity, and other values. Even among those who regard participation as a value in itself, how it is to be achieved and how far carried in industrial policy will be matters for dispute. The emphasis is likely to be very different in different parts of the world. Nevertheless, in the late twentieth century and when discussing ideals, it would be difficult to imagine a satisfactory industrial policy—broadly conceived as it is here—that did not take into account the matter of participation, in at least some of its numerous meanings.

## Compensation

If it is not a contradiction in terms—and I do not think it is—an ideal solution must include ways of coping with its failure to meet its own ideals. To the extent that people have to do things they would rather not do because it is to society's interest that they do them, they should be compensated for this loss of freedom. This might simply mean higher pay for what is to an individual a less attractive job (not easy to implement if there is also a principle of equal pay for equal work and others are willing). One could be led far afield thinking what else it might be—priority in upward mobility when the time comes? (or isolation so that discontent does not spread?)—but we are concerned here only with principles. Whether people who are somehow required to work at less than their highest ability, or productivity, are also to be compensated may be an even trickier question; if not compensated, may they not sooner initiate changes that will improve the lot of others as well as their own?

One can also not stop with society in the abstract. Supposing

40

one locality makes a choice about its own industrial policy—say, to limit smelting to the hours when the wind blows away from the town—and thereby damages someone else, in this case those who need the metal. The first group pays for its own choice by selling less metal, but does it also owe some compensation to those who are deprived of the supply and have to look farther and pay more for a substitute? Perhaps the answer should depend in part on how powerful or rich either group is or what reasonable expectations have been created by past relations. Or the key difference may depend on the nature of the choice; public health and safety carry weight that comfort and esthetics may not. Like some of the other issues raised here in terms of groups, this is one that will reappear when we return to the world of nations.

## Equity

In fashioning the aims of global industrial policy and then in supervising the pursuit of it—with whatever degree of intervention or nonintervention the concept calls for—the Legislator will have to satisfy the world's standards of equity. Perhaps this is only to paraphrase what has already been said under other headings, especially about compensation; but it is just as well to emphasize that an ideal industrial policy must respond to people's ideas of how its burdens and benefits ought to be shared. Since these ideas are likely to change over time, we need not concern ourselves with any particular set of views. Sometimes it may be possible to meet the standard of equity through taxes and measures affecting the distribution of wealth and income in society rather than by altering industrial policy. Much of the time, however, the structure of industry itself will be at issue. Where shall high-value-added industries be put? Whose market position shall be preserved for how long when new competitors appear? An ideal industrial policy will seek to minimize the conflicts between equity and efficiency and other criteria, but it will not completely remove them; therefore the questions of who chooses the trade-offs and how their costs and benefits are allocated reappear in a very fundamental form.

41

## Change and Adaptation

Whatever industrial policy for the world the Legislator might devise, it would not set the global division of labor for long. An ideal industrial policy should encourage innovation and improvement; whether it did or not, change would come from a variety of sources. To deal with change is a prime requirement for every industrial policy, and it seems reasonably clear that an ideal policy must aim at several results: (a) It should encourage changes that will promote the ends of the industrial policy (efficiency, full employment, or other aims) and not permit the maintenance of the status quo to interfere with such changes. (b) It should minimize the disturbances and possible waste that go with shifts in the use of resources. (c) People who are put out of work or otherwise hurt by these shifts should be helped to shift their activities (through education, help in finding new jobs, and other means) and shielded from the full burden of this change (by supplementary unemployment insurance, severance pay, etc.). (d) People permanently left in a less good position than before should be compensated in some way (possibly by early retirement with increased pension). Thus the costs of social gain should not fall more heavily than is inevitable on a particular group of people.

To meet these standards it may be necessary to slow the pace at which new sources of production are allowed to take over markets and drive out established producers. This reduction in flexibility does not seem to be a serious disadvantage so long as there is no doubt that the change will take place. However, too much slowing down can be costly to the economy and start a cumulative process that becomes a vicious circle.

*　　*　　*　　*

These nine criteria do not exhaust the subject, but they show the range of issues that have to be taken into account in fashioning industrial policy, ideal or real. There is nothing surprising in the fact that the criteria conflict with one another—a normal state of affairs in dealing with complex issues. By itself this would not mean that there could not be a global industrial policy that would provide the optimum combination of aims (if there were a global Legislator). It could not, however, be a static policy. The weight given to different criteria would change over time as people's preferences and status changed (wealth, education, skills). Even if choice and participation were dropped as criteria, the continuing structural change in the world economy would require adaptation with a shifting mix of efficiency, employment, security, equity, and other factors. Thus flexibility over time would itself become part of the definition of an ideal global industrial policy. Another need would be the capacity to effect change and not just adapt to it.

As we shall not soon have a global Legislator, we need not pursue these possibilities further. Enough has surely been said to demonstrate that while there may be an ideal global industrial policy in the sense just described, it is hardly identifiable in any concrete way in advance; and it certainly is not as clearly and simply characterized as the ideal of global free trade, even with all its qualifications. This does not mean that the criteria give no real guidance or that they are all equally important. My discussion has already reflected some judgment about the greater significance of some than of others. By the end of the book it should be possible to say more about those features that are indispensable to desirable industrial policy, global or national. It should become possible to point a direction, if not to describe an ultimate destination. Whether the result will command a consensus is another matter. But no prescription can be written without taking more account than we have done so far of the national industrial policies shaped by governments whose criteria are rarely global.

## WHEN GOVERNMENTS DECIDE

We turn away from our global make-believe and introduce reality in the form of nation-states as the primary determiners of industrial policy. What changes have to be made in the list of criteria? All nine still seem relevant. The most important difference from the situation of the global Legislator is that whereas his constitutional and decision-making activities were vague because wholly hypothetical, those of nation-states are real. They are not, however, immutable. The role of government varies from country to country and time to time. The private economy is of decisive importance over much of the world—within nations and between them. The powers that governments have in principle cannot always be translated into effective practice. Nevertheless it is largely national governments that make industrial policy. It follows immediately that two more criteria have to be added to our list.

The tenth criterion results from the fact that when the first nine are applied nationally it stands to reason that different nations will make different trade-offs among them. Therefore the ideal global industrial policy must be able to accommodate differences in national industrial policies. The eleventh criterion is that the international economic system must be able to deal with or remove difficulties between countries arising from their national industrial policies.

The difficulties may come from different trade-offs between criteria in national industrial policies, the pursuit of conflicting objectives, or simply the impact of one country's actions on another. Even an identical set of values in all countries would create such conflicts, since the definition of goals on a national basis will produce different results from their definition on a global basis. It is unnecessary to spell out the matter; the balance of payments and national security can be taken to stand for all those things that a nation has to think of simply because there are other nations in the world. Going beyond the minimum requirements of survival, a nation may want respect, power, influence, domination, friends, and other things. Some can only be had to the extent that other nations do not have them (first place in anything, more power than someone else), while some are best pursued in common with other countries (collective security, peaceful settlement of disputes, stable money). National policies are likely to involve both kinds of activities. Certainly, most national industrial policies are intended in part to serve the aims of national security, political strength, the ability to influence others, or the balance of payments.

This last criterion becomes something of a basket category into which much of the rest of the book could be fitted. What remains to be done in this chapter is to comment on the kinds of interests that industrial policies are intended to serve and the questions that are thereby posed for the international economic system. The matter is a good deal more complicated than would be suggested by the common custom of saying that governments will pursue their national interests. So they do; but what are the national interests of a given country at a given time?[6] It is with the answers to this question, repeated over and over in many places at many times, that a large number of international economic problems are concerned. People often speak as if the answers were clear and more or less the same for all countries all the time. This is not correct, nor do governments act as if it were; moreover, except in extreme circumstances, the people of a country are only rarely in general agreement—among themselves or with their government—about the true interests of the nation. In industrial policy, these differences are often rooted in the domestic economy.

Perhaps for that reason, the foreign side of industrial policy is frequently discussed as if the neomercantilist view of national interest could be taken for granted. Exports are good; imports are what you take because you have to; foreign competition in the domestic market is generally undesirable but sometimes a necessary price for exporting; a balance-of-payments surplus is intrinsically more desirable than a deficit; and so on. It is, in short, a fairly conventional view; and, needless to say, there is a case for most of its points, but not always and not when carried to extremes. They are mostly half-truths, and the introduction of the other half complicates matters.

Some of the obvious limits—to the concept, let alone the practice—have become familiar through long years of discussion of trade policy. People are consumers as well as producers and gain from foreign goods in cost, quality, and choice. Domestic producers perform better if they are exposed to foreign competition.

[6] There is a sense, of course, in which the national interest is whatever the government wants at any given moment; but this approach is intellectually empty.

45

Protected industries are likely to charge higher prices and pay lower wages than others. As taxpayers, people do not want to see their government paying unnecessarily high prices for supplies because they are domestically produced—especially if they are also poorer goods. Taxpayers also have an interest in economizing on subsidies and knowing what value is received for the cost. Exporters have an interest in imports both because they give foreigners the wherewithal to pay for what the exporter wants to sell them and because they affect the exporter's own costs. If all your inputs cost more because of protection than those of your foreign competitors, your future is limited. If your workers have to pay higher prices than the rest of the world for food and clothing, your wage bill will increase.

Limits to simplistic neomercantilism are also set by a country's relations with the rest of the world. Rarely can one country damage another with impunity; retaliation is the other side of cooperation and sometimes calls it into being. Two neomercantilistic policies facing one another can produce reasonable compromise, but not always easily. For lasting arrangements, reciprocity is an essential, but the kind of rather fraudulent statistical reciprocity that long characterized tariff negotiations is neither feasible nor desirable in working out the kinds of compromises industrial policy conflicts make necessary, except possibly in the quite short run. But, in the short run, power may also be decisive and is not necessarily enhanced by mercantilist measures. The national interest in the economic welfare of other countries is widely recognized in words but not always in practice. For many countries, however, foreign policy considerations provide a broad and realistic approach to concepts of national economic interest.

Another limitation on neomercantilism is the development of the international economic system and the associated rise in living standards around the world. Autarky—which once had a literature written by advocates—has few attractions these days except for dreamers; Tibet and Burma are not models for many. Trade barriers at the levels of the 1930s would be regarded with horror by people who do not always realize that the achievements of the 1950s and 1960s are not immune to abuse. This does not mean that every aspect of interdependence is highly valuable or that some countries may not sensibly cut some interconnecting strands from time to time. Nor can there be a guarantee that some countries—not necessarily the most powerful—may not be able to exploit the system by clever policies and get a free ride with more or less damage to others.

Nevertheless, it is true that the industrial policies of the future will have to take account of the fact that, for better or for worse, the world largely accepts the need to fit each national economy into the global economy. In one of the pioneer works in this field, Lionel Stoleru, a French economist, said that because it had joined in the creation of the Common Market, France would have to learn how to make industrial policy with open frontiers. A disjointed series of government interventions would not suffice; nor would it be sufficient to bolster the weak spots in the national economy and nurse sick industries. France had given up protectionism, at least as far as Europe was concerned. Thereafter, the aim of industrial policy had to be to promote the ability of French firms to compete in the international market. That did not mean giving up indicative planning or government aid to industry. Employment, security, and technological advance would be given weight in shaping industrial policy; but unless an industry offered the promise of becoming competitive, there was little to be said for supporting it. The next step was to join forces with the other Community countries in shaping a European industrial policy.[7]

In the years that followed, France made some progress along these lines, but no one could call the results a complete success. Nearly a decade later another young French official, Christian Stoffaes, looked back to the earlier book and said that France needed "a new industrial imperative . . . but this time we have to face the world, not just Europe."[8] He, too, took international competitiveness as the necessary standard and argued that France had lost ground to the high-technology producers in the

[7] Stoleru, op. cit.
[8] Christian Stoffaes, *La Grande Menace Industrielle*, Calmann-Levy, Paris, 1978, p. 20.

industrial world on the one hand and the low-labor-cost producers in the developing world on the other. A new concept of planning, sharpened and highly selective instruments of government aid, and a substantial restructuring of French industry were necessary to create the kind of flexible entrepreneurship France would need to thrive in a changing world economy. All this would require considerable changes in the attitudes of the French toward their economy.

It is not the first time that French intellectuals, facing hard problems at home, have articulated a need which if not universal is nearly so. How to meet this need is a matter that will receive attention throughout this book. What these last few pages have tried to establish as a starting point is that it will not suffice to think in terms of conventional neomercantilism, especially if one's aim is to create a strong national economy with a healthy balance of payments and an industry that can export successfully around the world.

Although the domestic content of industrial policy is often very large, the interplay of domestic and external economic interests is a characteristic of all foreign economic policy. The usual sequence of events is as follows: A conflict of domestic interests is compromised in a way that requires taking certain action that affects the rest of the world (say, raising a certain tariff and giving a producing group a subsidy to offset the resulting higher costs). When challenged from abroad, this arrangement is then declared to represent "the national interest," something one has to struggle for. Getting no satisfaction, foreign countries retaliate. Who is hurt in the first country? It may be anyone, depending on what the foreign country can do and thinks best. It may be someone who has nothing to do with the whole issue or the weaker party to the original domestic compromise. Occasionally the foreign country is in a position to take measures that it thinks may help to bring about the kind of change it wants—or perhaps even prevent the step from being taken in the first place.[9] Usually,

[9] When in 1969 the European Community was threatening to move against American soybean exports, the U.S. let it be known that its retaliation would hit automobiles, other manufactured goods, and brandy, a combination thought likely to bring pressure sufficient to prevent the step—as it did.

though, it is only when the foreign aspect is brought sharply into focus by foreign reactions that this dimension of the national interest is fully taken into account in shaping industrial policy.

Is it not possible, however, that the growing prominence of industrial policy will itself help to bring about a change? In domestic disputes conflicts of group interest within the society are often clearly recognized—they are the natural order of things— and policy is shaped by a political struggle or settlements that provide compromises or compensation. If domestic groups become acutely conscious of their own stake in the international economy, they will do more than in the past to inspect the impact of industrial policy measures on the rest of the world and the reactions that may follow. The result would be to bring more sharply into focus the real meaning and effect of various measures of national economic policy instead of obscuring the costs that fall on the rest of the world, as often happens now. This process is likely to be enhanced by the international affiliations of various groups, labor and business. One can speculate about the growth of international coalitions among interest groups, each working for changes in the policies of its government. Effective or not, this sort of trend would help clarify the issues.

That is the optimistic view. A more pessimistic one is that precisely because industrial policy issues involve so many domestic arrangements, governments will be less willing to deal with them internationally. Cooperation abroad will spell contention at home. Complex political compromises involved in industrial policy measures that are possible within a national political system may be untenable (or unreachable) if they are subjected to the play of forces from abroad. Reactions during the recession point in this direction, as is hardly surprising; but one should not forget that earlier there was already a considerable growth of opinion to the effect that increasing interdependence was undesirable if it put too many constraints on freedom of action at home. *Freedom of action* in this proposition often means simply the substitution of domestic for international pressures on the government. Somewhere between the pessimistic and the optimistic views, and easier to forecast than either, is the complication of domestic and international processes by which industrial policy decisions are made. The intellectual task of analyzing their impact will not be simplified.

In addition to the long-familiar play of pressure groups, another newer domestic factor shaping industrial policy in some countries has international implications. This is the emphasis that has been given in the latter part of the twentieth century to the exercise of power by units smaller than nation-states and the related tendency to emphasize the participation of affected groups in decisions bearing on their interests and, to a degree, in the management of economic units. At one end of this list are the questions of devolution: What powers should be given to Scotland and Wales? What will regional economic administration come to mean in France and Italy? Are the powers of Canadian provinces over raw materials and investment compatible with the formulation of homogeneous national policies? How differently will New York City act if its access to credit comes under federal control? At the other end are such matters as how co-determination in Germany and other countries affects the way both labor and management see their interests, whether self-management on the Yugoslav model is a pattern useful for other developing countries, and the whole set of questions about the proper relation of government to business which are given different answers in various parts of the world. These matters affect other aspects of international economic relations as well but have a special bearing on industrial policy. They sharpen its domestic political edge. Much industrial policy concerns regional differences. Trade-offs are almost certain to be made differently at different levels.

The international effects are likely to be felt in four ways. First, having to take account of regional differences and the distribution of power, national governments will make different industrial policy choices than they would otherwise. If a smaller share of the textile, clothing, and furniture industries were in Quebec, Canada might not be so solicitous of their need for tariff and other protection. Second, to the extent that the real power rests in less than national units, behavior is likely to be different. "Buy British" and "Buy Scottish" come out differently, though whether the latter will encourage production in Scotland or Scottish purchases from cheaper suppliers than those in England is not foreordained. Third, the dispersal of power can reduce the ability of the national government to pursue an effective or a consistent policy of its own in a variety of fields. Government procurement is normally a major tool of industrial policy but the impossibility of Ottawa's dictating to the provinces in the matter led a committee of the Canadian Senate to conclude "that government procurement in Canada as a policy instrument for restructuring, reorganizing and strengthening the Canadian secondary manufacturing industry, cannot be relied upon to play a major role."[10] Not everyone agrees with this view. The fourth effect of the dispersal of power is that international commitments become difficult to make when states or provinces can deal independently not only with procurement but taxes, subsidies, and production. Whether the result is more international friction, less intervention and more reliance on market forces, more frustration of sovereigns who cannot govern, or new coalitions and alliances creating a surge of multilateral cooperation is a matter for speculation, but later rather than now.

No one knows how far devolution will go, but even if it stops, industrial policies will be influenced by the participation of entities whose perspective affects the balance that becomes the national interest. A large multinational corporation sees the problems of its industry differently from a small national one (and may help shape more than one "national interest"). The world's industrial policy problems in textiles, with thousands of producers, are different from those in aluminum, with a high concentration of production in large international companies. American oil policy in the 1960s balanced the interests of big internationals and the more numerous domestic producers, a distinction that was somewhat blurred by the links between some companies in both groups. It will be argued in Chapter 6 that how national labor movements are organized influences the way workers see their interests, a matter of very considerable importance to the

---

[10]*Canada-United States Relations*: vol. II, *Canada's Trade Relations with the United States*, Report of the Standing Senate Committee on Foreign Affairs, published under the authority of the Senate by the Queen's Printer for Canada, June 1978, p. 61.

shaping of industrial policies. Co-determination in Germany and the relation between employer and employee in Japan obviously influence the way both management and labor approach questions of industrial policy. More examples could be added, but enough has been said to show that conventional lines of thought about the nature of national interest are inadequate either for the shaping of industrial policies intended to maximize welfare or for the analysis of their effects.

In discussing "the right level of management," Miriam Camps thought it "probable that some problems should now be pushed down from the national level to the local level; others, pushed up to regional or global levels."[11] Like devolution, the movement in the opposite direction has major implications for industrial policies in their national and international dimensions. That was Stoleru's argument, but other countries have not gone as far as those in the European Economic Community. Nevertheless, different combinations of regional groupings in other parts of the world have their effect, along with nonregional efforts to deal with economic issues intergovernmentally. Sometimes the effects, like those of devolution, weaken the ability of a national government to pursue certain kinds of industrial policy. France could not control American investment the way it once wished to because the Common Market treaty prevented it from keeping out goods from American-owned plants in other Community countries. Sometimes, however, the main effect—and sometimes motive—of the broader-than-national arrangements is to make possible measures of industrial policy that would have been difficult if not impossible for a country acting alone. The members of the International Energy Agency think they can provide greater mutual security together than they could separately. Scientific and technical cooperation is another obvious case. This kind of development changes perceptions of interest so that the range of possibilities for industrial policy is also altered.

One of the most important issues raised by the reaching out beyond the nation-state is what combination of countries is best

[11]Miriam Camps, *The Management of Interdependence*, Council on Foreign Relations, New York, 1974, p. 99.

for what purposes. The six countries that formed the European Community seemed the right combination at that moment; then more were added. Even so, a number of structural issues go beyond what the enlarged group can handle, and in addition, many measures of individual policy have been kept in national hands from the beginning. The OECD, which brings together the main industrial countries of the noncommunist world, seems well suited to certain kinds of problems but not others. The key trade issues are handled in the much larger GATT, but not always in ways that involve its full membership or affect them uniformly. Although one would think that global arrangements were necessary in many fields, they are actually few in number, largely because of the very practical difficulties of reaching meaningful agreement among so many. Many so-called North-South issues are dealt with in UNCTAD, but often at the price of generalizing issues that need more nuanced treatment.

International action affecting industrial policy also takes place outside formal organizations. Sometimes only two countries are involved, as in the Canadian-American automobile agreement, and sometimes more, as in the five-country Andean Pact with its common policies toward foreign investment. Governmental arrangements may provide the framework for private activities, as happens in most arrangements between Western governments and the Soviet Union. Relations between industrial countries and their suppliers of energy and raw materials bear on the industrial structures of both countries in a variety of ways. There is little point in arguing the merits or demerits of different combinations in general terms. After digging more deeply into some of the problems of industrial policy, we return to this question in Chapter 7. But as the groupings mentioned and others turn up in the pages that follow, it is well to keep in mind two of the standards by which each has to be judged: what it makes possible for the participants and how it affects other countries. The exchange of mutual benefits by a few countries often means that others are kept from gaining a comparable advantage or even have new burdens thrown on them. Yet it may also be that the benefits such arrangements provide for a few key economies may create considerable advantages for others who deal with them. Another aspect of the limited and exclusive arrangements that needs watching is their tendency to pull apart countries that might otherwise work together. They may also add to the rigidities that bilateral arrangements introduce into the world economy.

There is a related set of questions about what might be called the proper international division of labor in industrial policy. If some key countries follow certain principles of industrial policy, might that suffice to create a reasonable amount of order in the international economy while other, probably economically less important, countries are left free to pursue other practices, provided they do not go beyond some reasonable boundaries? Another way of putting the matter would be to ask how many of the world's problems would be solved if, say, the OECD countries all adhered to a certain set of industrial policy arrangements. If the developing countries were left out of these arrangements and committed only to somewhat looser obligations, would that do much damage to the world economy? Would special arrangements to deal with particularly difficult problems be preferable to more comprehensive understandings? Or do we have to try to bring substantially all countries into the same network of agreements?

The answers to another set of questions will also be basic to the conclusions of this book: When is it necessary to deal internationally with industrial problems? Should one try to provide ways of handling a very wide range of issues or focus on a few that seem most crucial and dangerous? Can one act in advance to prevent difficulties from developing, or will it be necessary to wait until someone's interest is seriously enough threatened to create a willingness to act that was lacking when the evidence was only analytical and intellectual? Answers to these questions have a bearing on one's judgment about still another difficult issue. When should a country, in its own best interests, unilaterally adapt itself to circumstances, including the mercantilist industrial policies of others; and when should it hold to its old course until others are also ready to change?

A third set of questions concerns the best way of attacking industrial policy issues. Does the new emphasis on these questions provide a good basis for governments to negotiate about industrial policy as such? Or would it be better to build on existing arrangements for trade, investment, and other matters that deal with industrial policy in fact but not necessarily in name? Is some mixed approach preferable?

These questions—what issues, under what heading, by whom— may sound procedural, but they are vital to the substance of what can and cannot be done to treat national industrial policies as international issues. They are also issues that cannot usefully be discussed without a good deal more material before us. Some of this is provided by the next three chapters, which deal, respectively, with the possibilities of pressing further some established lines of international economic cooperation, the strengths and weaknesses of attacking the problems of specific industries or sectors, and the positive measures of new international cooperation that might be desirable for coping with foreseeable (or existing) problems of structural change in the world economy. Chapter 6 surveys some basic factors that shape national industrial policies. The conclusions to be drawn regarding what combinations of countries might achieve what results are considered in Chapter 7. The concluding chapter is less a summary than a limited synthesis based on a second look at some basic issues.

## TRIAL BALANCE

This chapter has carried us from an effort to find an ideal type of global industrial policy to the posing of some pragmatic-sounding questions. Although no formula was found and the questions simply introduce later discussions, the chapter has shown that simple formulations will mislead us, whether they are supposed to state a novel global aspiration or apply rather familiar ideas about national interests. It is not enough to take a stand for or against planning or the market, to suppose that all government intervention has bad economic effects or surely serves the public interest. The pursuit of national interests has been seen to be an inadequate description of or prescription for foreign policy, economic or otherwise. "Industrial policy" itself is not something one can be for or against, since the term covers so many different kinds of activity. We have gained some sense of the complexities to be explored in the discussion to come. Finally, in spite of all the negatives, there has been some positive fore-shadowing of what we should be looking for as we suggest how the world can improve its handling of the international issues arising from conflicts of national industrial policies.

We know that national industrial policies should attach major importance to efficiency, broadly defined. This is true whether the main aim of the industrial policy is economic welfare or something else. A good part of the time the measure of efficiency will be the ability to meet fair competition in the world economy. It does not follow, however, that simply letting market forces play is an adequate prescription; for a variety of reasons it may often make sense to seek laissez-faire's ends but not by laissez-faire's means.

Structural change is an inescapable fact of the world economy, and adaptation to it is vital not only to the improvement of the economic condition of most people but also to the maintenance of the levels of production and consumption already attained. A great deal of past and present industrial policy has been used to resist such changes and has thereby damaged not only other countries but frequently the nation making use of it. A major need is to find policies that facilitate structural change, which sometimes means initiating it or anticipating problems before they become acute. It is also necessary to protect people who suffer in the process, help them make changes, and make ad-aptation politically more acceptable. A slowing of change may be essential for these purposes, but people should recognize the risks of simply trying to preserve the status quo.

It would be a mistake, however, to draw from this chapter only the conclusions summarized in the last two paragraphs. Much has been passed over quickly in the earlier pages; and perhaps too little emphasis has been put on how large a change in people's habits, ways of life, expectations, and ideas of what is proper may be demanded by the prescription to adapt to shifts in the world economy, especially if the process is accelerating. There is nothing surprising or reprehensible in resistance, and it may well be that in the interests of some of their people societies will sometimes reject some changes altogether. Naturally there are consequences of such choices, and societies must be prepared to accept the cost to the rest of the economy of whatever combination of protection or aid is necessary. Time is a factor, since costs that are acceptable for a temporary period can become unbearable in the long run. All that can be asked is that the choices be made knowingly and the costs borne by those responsible for the choice rather than thrust in some fashion on the rest of the world.

Roughly the same can be said about the use of industrial policy to promote ends other than efficiency, however broadly conceived. Goals may be of direct value to individuals—the environment, leisure, security, ways of life—or they may concern national strength and prestige or arise from the pursuit of foreign policy aims or specific national interests. They may be imposed by an undemocratic government. Whatever one may think of the merits of any given case or any class of objectives, it would make no sense to try to study these issues on the assumption that only "economic" issues are, or ought to be, pursued by industrial policy.

No doubt it is idealistic to rate highly the goal that people—individuals, groups, nations—ought to be able to make basic choices about their economic and political milieus but should not be able to thrust the cost of those choices on others. Still, something like this conclusion seems hard to escape if one thinks at all in terms of democracy and global welfare. The prescriptions with which this book ends certainly fall far short of that ideal. They deal primarily with one aspect of the problem, the international issues arising from the pursuit of national industrial policies. These problems arise whether the aims of the industrial policies are called "economic" or something else, but the nature of the possible remedies may vary. All that this chapter has provided is a starting place.

Another, and perhaps more limited starting place, can be found in the statement of the heads of government and state of the leading Western countries in the communiqué of their summit meeting at Bonn in July 1978:

We welcome the statement on positive adjustment policy made by the OECD Ministers. There must be a readiness over time to accept

and facilitate structural change. Measures to prevent such change perpetuate economic inefficiency, place the burden of structural change
on trading partners and inhibit the integration of developing countries
into the world economy. We are determined in our industrial, social,
structural and regional policy initiatives to help sectors in difficulties,
without interfering with international competition and trade flows.[12]

As far as it goes, this declaration squares with what has been
said in this chapter. Even if the aim is less sweeping than what
has been suggested here, the stated determination is an ambitious
one. A year later, the communiqué from the Tokyo summit said
much the same thing in different words. What we need are some
reasonably concrete ideas about how to put these ideas into
practice.

[12]*Department of State Bulletin*, Government Printing Office, Washington,
D.C., September 1978, p. 4.

# THREE

# Following Old Roads into New Territory

The way national industrial policies threaten international economic cooperation became clear first in trade. Interestingly, it was both the successes of trade liberalization and its failures that showed the need to find new ways of dealing with industrial policy. Since the process is not over—though in places it has come to what looks like a dead stop—trade liberalization provides an avenue into the possibilities worth exploring and then points to a second area in which governments have been very active but international cooperation more limited: the treatment of foreign investment.

Agriculture was effectively dropped from the trade liberalization process in the early 1950s. The Americans took the first formal action, and by the time they were ready for a change, Europe was not. Few serious students of the subject have thought that there was much chance of applying trade liberalization practices to farming (except here and there for a few products or when the value added by processing and packaging becomes so great that the products can be treated as manufactured goods). The reasons lay partly in the domestic politics of key countries, partly in the methods by which farm policies were carried out, and partly in the objectives of those policies. If domestic prices were being held well above world levels, it made no sense to admit cheaper foreign products. And if farmers were being paid to restrict production or the government was buying their surpluses, a ban on imports seemed in order. Suggestions were made for international agreements intended to reconcile these aims, instead of concentrating on the trade barriers that were largely symptoms of the underlying problem. The chances provided by the Kennedy Round for doing this, at least between Europe and the United States, were passed up; and a decade later American negotiators in the Tokyo Round were using the original futile rhetoric about liberalization. Though the analogy with problems of industrial policy is interesting, the agricultural question will not be pursued here. The experience is a warning of how failure to deal with underlying problems can all but nullify efforts at trade liberalization—or even cooperation.

A second exclusion came later and took a different form: textiles. Cotton cloth, yarn, and garments in the 1960s and those of woolen and synthetic fibers in the 1970s were in effect excluded from the normal rules and processes of trade negotiation and subjected to more restrictive arrangements in which importing countries had a strong position. There was, however, recognition of the fact that a shift was taking place in the location of textile production, to which world trade would have to adapt. Resistance to those structural changes produced a not very encouraging kind of international industrial policy that will be examined in the next chapter.

No other industrial products were given such extensive, formal exemption from normal trade rules. In most fields the removal of trade barriers was carried much further than most people thought likely when the process was started in the late 1940s. Inevitably there was a great deal of adjustment in the economies of most countries engaged in international trade (not all of it stemming from trade liberalization, of course). But there was also much resistance to adjustment. It showed up in a number of different ways. European countries were slow to reduce barriers to imports from Japan, which was seen as a dangerous competitor, first in the field of relatively cheap, labor-intensive goods and soon after in the provision of high-quality consumer goods produced by very modern means. The United States, which had reduced barriers to Japanese goods quite early, dealt with similar problems by insisting on the limitation of Japanese exports of various products as they became particularly troublesome. The same techniques were used toward Hong Kong, Taiwan, and then a series of developing countries as they shipped increasing quantities of manufactured goods to the older industrial countries. Shoes, consumer electronic goods, and some other products met with fairly general resistance; in addition, almost every country had a certain number of what are best thought of as "hard cases" in which either the threat to domestic producers was thought to be great or their political strength kept the government from acting.

The result was that a number of tariffs were reduced less than the average and sometimes reductions were withdrawn and new import barriers imposed. All these cases had elements of old-fashioned protectionism—the simple political strength of protected interests and the unthinking acceptance of the status quo as the proper order of things—but sometimes the basic issue was the pace of change or adaptation. It is hard to say how often explicit judgments about the desirable structure of the domestic economy determined what was done, but the resistance to imports often rested on tacit attitudes on that subject. Japan's success as an exporter did much to push industrial policy issues to the forefront. Europeans and North Americans who felt threatened often attributed Japanese competitiveness to that country's industrial policy, especially its unique government-business relations. The same explanation was given for the difficulty Western sellers had in penetrating Japanese markets.

Whether the developing countries should regard the preferential tariff treatment they receive from richer countries on many products as one of the successes of trade liberalization is debatable. The general principle is in practice shot through with selectivity, limitation, and frequently arrangements that withdraw the preference once imports pass a certain level. All these plus a number of other restrictions which industrial countries put on imports from the developing countries reflect resistance to change. It is worth noting, though, that the special treatment of developing countries in GATT had its origin in some rudimentary ideas about industrial policy. That is to say, from the beginning GATT accepted the need to industrialize with some protection against imports. Later steps exempting less developed countries

(LDCs) from most GATT obligations, including that of providing reciprocity for tariff concessions, were in a sense the infant industry exception writ large. There was, however, no selectivity in the process except as each individual country chose to apply it. This probably hurt many developing countries, and the lack of reciprocal bargaining certainly accounts for some of the present unsatisfactory restrictions. Whether progress in thinking through the proper matching of industrial and trade policies in developing countries can be combined with improvement in the adaptation arrangements in the older industrial countries so as to create some new kinds of international industrial policy measures, at least in a few fields, is something we shall consider in Chapter 5.

However, the question of adaptation in the industrial countries cannot be left until then. Though one of the most pervasive of all industrial policy issues, it has a special focus in trade policy matters, since there are some international rules about restrictions imposed when imports create "market disruption" or are said to injure domestic producers. Because these rules have not been satisfactory, their revision became one of the key issues in the Tokyo Round of trade negotiations that concluded in 1979. It marks a point at which industrial policy comes sharply into focus within the accepted framework of trade cooperation. What this opportunity could lead to is a question to be taken up after seeing how the successes of the past trade negotiations have transformed the Multilateral Trade Negotiations (MTN) concluded in 1979 into the first major round of multilateral negotiations about national industrial policies.

## NONTARIFF BARRIERS AND INDUSTRIAL POLICY

By the time the Kennedy Round was over it was clear that the postwar effort to liberalize trade had achieved great results but would soon confront unprecedented problems. After the pledges made at Geneva in 1967 were carried out, tariffs in the great industrial centers of the world would be at historically low levels. Though the effective protection was greater than some of the low nominal duty rates suggested, tariffs were no longer the determinants of production they had once been and were of little importance for many segments of world trade. Many developing countries had highly protective tariffs; but in the OECD countries the duties that were high enough to be troublesome involved the hard cases referred to above—that is, industries believed to present particularly difficult problems of adjustment. But even though tariffs were of secondary importance, trade was not free in the classical sense. Many different national policies or specific measures not always part of a general policy continued to limit the importation of foreign goods or put domestic producers at an advantage compared with their competitors abroad. Nontariff barriers (NTBs) was the label generally given to this whole variegated collection, though some actually made use of tariffs and others were better described as trade-distorting practices.

Whether there was an actual increase in the use of these measures for protectionist purposes as tariffs fell is a matter we need not debate.[1] It is enough that the stripping away of other barriers made the NTBs more prominent, with two very direct consequences. First, anyone who believed that the trade liberalization process was desirable now had to think in terms of the removal of nontariff barriers, which was going to be a more complex affair than the familiar reduction of tariffs and quotas. Second, a failure to make visible progress in that direction ran a serious risk of losing the ground already gained by tariff reduction. For one thing, governments would be tempted to meet difficulties by resorting to nontariff barriers to do what they had promised not to do by tariffs. For another, the differences in the kinds of NTBs made it easy for people in one country to believe that their foreign competitors were being given unfair advantages. This was a key element in the growth of American economic nationalism after the end of the Kennedy Round.

It was inevitable, therefore, that negotiations about NTBs should be a major item on the agenda of the Tokyo Round. And it was especially unfortunate that those delayed negotiations should finally have taken place at a time when the recession had

[1] There is no doubt about the increased use of subsidies and other aids later on to cope with the recession, but that is a somewhat different matter.

increased the amount of government intervention in economies and made optimism about an expansive future scarce. At the best of times, strong measures to deal with NTBs would have been difficult to work out largely because of the close connection between NTBs, domestic economic policies in general, and industrial policy in particular. No special difficulty arises when NTBs are primarily substitutes for or supplements to tariffs and quotas. At least in principle one can treat these NTBs as plain trade barriers, though the formulas for reducing them may have to be novel. Many NTBs, however, result from applying domestic regulations concerning health, safety, the environment, industrial standards, etc. Though not always easy to deal with, these are the least objectionable as long as they are not subterfuges for protection and apply equally to domestic and foreign goods. It is probable, however, that the majority of NTBs or trade-distorting practices are connected with efforts to produce certain results in the domestic economy. Sometimes the achievement of these aims—economic, social, environmental, or whatever— may require the checking of imports or the fostering of exports. When such effects are incidental to the main purpose of the domestic measures, they may be inescapable or it may be possible to eliminate or mitigate them. Often, however, it is a matter of dispute what effect these measures have on foreign trade and the interests of other countries.

One can hardly be hopeful about how far governments are likely to go, for some time to come, in subjecting these practices to international regulation. That is, however, the key question raised by the Tokyo Round, which has provided new means of dealing with some NTBs but relatively few firm assurances about what practices will be banned or permitted in different circumstances. Among the many arrangements resulting from the Tokyo Round, this chapter concentrates on two major instruments of industrial policy: subsidies, by far the largest category of NTBs, and government procurement.

Two basic facts about subsidies are their variety and ubiquity. Subsidies are not limited to direct payments from government to businessmen or farmers. They can take the form of tax concessions, losses by state enterprises, payments to workers that might hold down a firm's wage bill, low transport rates, cheap leasing of public property, the provision of some kinds of public services, and a host of other devices. If the government lends money to enterprises at low interest rates or preferential terms, the subsidy is clear; but it is also present in guarantees and many other common financial practices, including sometimes the provision of funds itself. Some forms of help are available to almost anyone; more are limited to certain kinds of producers or those who produce certain things. Some aid is intended to offset the burden created by other governmental policies: for example, the setting of environmental standards. It is not always easy to tell how a subsidy affects foreign trade; the distinction between subsidies paid on all production or consumption and those directly linked to exports and imports is not sufficient. Governments use subsidies for a very wide range of purposes, only some of which are primarily concerned with foreign trade.

The GATT rules, as of the beginning of the Tokyo Round, were fairly loose and not well enforced. They concentrated on export subsidies of certain types but recognized that more general subsidies could also affect trade. When a country was damaged by another's subsidies, it could levy countervailing import duties equal to the amount of the subsidy.[2] There was a large element of unilateral determination in these provisions. Consultation was provided for, and governments had an obligation to provide information about their subsidies, but there were gaps in what was in fact done. There has been much dissatisfaction with these provisions for some time but little agreement as to how they could be improved.

Some of the problems of improving the GATT rules are illustrated by regional development policies, which exist in most countries and use many kinds of subsidy. It is held by some that if the payments only equal the added cost of doing business in

[2] A key issue in the MTN was to make the United States conform to this provision, since the American countervailing duty law, which did not require a demonstration of damage, predated GATT and remained in force. However, the particulars of this dispute can be ignored here to concentrate on the larger issues. Obviously such a discrepancy is incompatible with the strengthening of international methods for dealing with subsidies.

a disfavored area there is no distortion, only rectification. This seems dubious, but what criteria are to be used? Even the definition of the kinds of locales that "deserve" help becomes unclear if one thinks of the kinds of handicaps that have held back development in remote regions, difficult terrain, or places with infertile land, as well as the kinds of decline that have taken place in once-thriving cities. As imagination plays over the possibilities, one draws back from the prospect of trying to lay down usable international criteria in any detail. But is it a satisfactory alternative to say that whatever a government may do under the heading of "regional policy" is exempted from its obligations to other countries? Or that when others are affected by such measures they are free to protect themselves, compensate for the damage, or try to force a change? Should it make any difference whether the regional policy primarily supports weak producers or tries to put them in a more competitive position? If the aim is adjustment, how is the alternative industry to be chosen to replace the weak one? If in a short time it too becomes a declining industry, what responsibility does the government have; and is it to be assumed that the rest of the international community has tacitly given its approval to whatever measures of support seem necessary?

The dilemma in dealing with subsidies is clear. To try to deal adequately with all of them would require an immensely complicated international agreement regulating the domestic behavior of governments far more thoroughly than would be acceptable. To confine the focus so as to rule out certain practices because they damage others or distort the results being sought by trade liberalization is to invite bureaucrats to find alternative legal ways of attaining the same results. The methods of subsidy are about as fungible as money.

Practical ideas must drive between the horns of the dilemma. Some subsidies would be banned: those most closely substituting for import barriers or given only to exports. Other practices would be more or less sanctioned: aid for regional development, for example, provided it took certain forms and was given in specified circumstance. A government might, however, be required to consult with others if they felt it was using this privilege illegitimately or in ways that damaged them. In between, the greatest part of the terrain would be covered by an agreement going as far as proved possible. This would include some principles suggesting what kinds of objectives governments could pursue with subsidies without there being any prima facie objections and what sorts of results were to be avoided. Methods as well as objectives might come into the recital of these principles. Publicity and information should be insisted on. Consultation about the application of the principles to cases would be essential. This might operate on the basis of complaints from any country that another's practices were injuring it, or might involve some more systematic review. Standards for judging injury could be set and their application put in the hands of some kind of impartial body. If an injured party got no satisfaction, it would have the right to react or countervail in some prescribed fashion.[3] A country persisting in the use of subsidies that violated the code—again as judged by some kind of international body— would be subject to some form of collective sanction or pressure.

The line of argument sketched so far emerged from some years of study of the problem. The subsidies code negotiated in the MTN takes more or less the same approach. It is weaker than one might hope in some respects and, inevitably, there are a number of gray areas where the language will speak differently to different readers. It would be out of keeping with the character of this book to analyze the MTN codes in any detail. So far as subsidies are concerned, there are two essential points. First, the code goes further than anything before in recognizing that subsidies of all sorts may have an impact on other countries. Second, the meaning to be given to this statement will be determined by the negotiations and consultations among governments resulting from the rules laid down in the code (and the related procedure for settling disputes). What the code provides is a procedure for applying principles to cases, not a detailed body of substantive rules about the forms and purposes of subsidies.

[3]The new subsidy code also tries to deal with the problem of damage by the effect of subsidies on a third market that one country loses to a subsidized seller.

Out of the procedures and consultation there may grow up a body of custom or common law that will strengthen the principles, give more concrete meaning to some of the language, and narrow the areas in which governments refuse to tie their hands. But this can only happen if governments want to build up the area of agreement, not if their main objective is to preserve their freedom to subsidize. The new code had its roots in conventional trade negotiations but can lead quite far into measures that deal with the international consequences of national industrial policies. Whether the potentiality will be made real depends partly on the intentions of governments; they may choose to confine the procedure as much as possible to established trade policy issues. But what happens will also depend partly on whether there is an emphasis on continued cooperation, in which case the logic of interdependence will put more industrial policy issues on the table. If cooperation is not valued highly, the failure to look at these questions will reduce the value of the trade cooperation so that one country after another will feel justified in making an exception of its activities.

This is equally true of the rest of the MTN results. Some degree of preferential treatment of domestic producers in government procurement is almost universal. The pre-MTN rules were even weaker than for subsidies so it was natural to think of discriminatory government procurement primarily as a trade barrier. Past proposals have been for a code that would permit increased competition and provide more "transparency" by ruling out practices that conceal the extent to which governments discriminate against foreign suppliers. The code that emerged from the Tokyo Round has such features. How far will this go in limiting the ability of governments to favor producers simply because they are domestic? Will the provisions to assure transparency work? It is not going to be easy or quickly done to build up a substantial area of international agreement on what constitutes proper market behavior for large public purchasers. The questions involve competitive bidding, specifications set out according to international standards, advertising in the newspapers of remote cities, long-run contracts, renewal orders, premiums for customer loyalty, allowances for experience and quality, and many other factors. There is also the question of when to take account of the difference in the bargaining power of those who buy paper for the U.S. government and for San Marino.

Another set of questions concerns the exceptions to the code, starting with security. Most governments will continue to buy at least some arms at home to maintain a defense capacity. Allies can share the burden (or benefits) by buying from one another. Will the term *security* be interpreted to permit maintaining (or building up) a domestic capacity for production of much more than arms? There may also have to be exceptions for procurement by public authorities at different levels, since various kinds of local preferences may be part of the politics and economics of a region. Moreover, in some countries constitutional provisions make it impossible for the central government to dictate the purchasing policies of states, provinces, or even cities. As countries vary greatly in the degree of government ownership (railroads, utilities, tobacco and match monopolies, steel plants, etc.), a general rule about public procurement would have extremely uneven effects. In the MTN the time-honored process of reciprocal trade bargaining was given a new cast when governments swapped entities in an effort to arrive at an equitable settlement. Good enough for a start, the result can hardly be defended as the most rational solution of the problem. It is, therefore, worth thinking how far one might carry a procurement code in the future.

Should special treatment be provided for sectors of economies heavily dependent on government purchasing patterns? Shifts in buying (this year domestic, next year foreign) could be very disturbing and, politics apart, it would not always be clear that the gain of buying cheap would outweigh other losses, especially if the government had to respond to the problems of the disturbance in one way or another. Clearly, there are some difficult questions about how an international code should apply to the use governments make of procurement as an instrument of industrial policy.

If certain common practices are thought unlikely to cause serious international difficulties (say, the support of small business), it can hardly make sense to rule out the use of discriminatory government procurement for those purposes. Even when there are international repercussions, government procurement may have advantages over other devices that one would not want to lose by making the international rules too limiting. Whereas a tariff raises prices across the board and encourages a diversion of resources from other uses, government buying can be more narrowly targeted. One could buy at a premium from the high-cost producer in the remote area without giving unnecessary protection to efficient producers in the rest of the country. It may even be the case that if the government purchased a certain number of high-cost, special-purpose computers, for example, a local firm could sell its other equipment at competitive prices. Businessmen can be left free to buy from abroad if they wish (at zero tariff) and so not suffer a disadvantage compared to their foreign competitors. The technique is not limited to promoting advanced industries. If the United States Army and federal prisoners were supplied with high-cost shoes and clothing from Appalachia, the urban dweller might well lose less as a taxpayer or consumer than if all imports of these products were taxed.

Selectivity would also increase the government's ability to press for the kind of performance it thought reasonable instead of providing the promiscuous assistance of a tariff or quota. In an effort to conserve resources, the government could have a differential buying policy that, for instance, assured exhaustion of mines in which costs rise as the veins thin out without giving other producers an incentive to produce faster than is thought desirable. If the objective were to help a domestic industry adapt itself to foreign competition by eliminating some activities and concentrating on others, government procurement could be a fairly flexible instrument for both sustaining the weak sections and encouraging the strong.

Certain kinds of subsidies can be limited to parts of an industry or individual firms in much the same way as selective government procurement. There may, of course, be immense difficulties within a country in following this kind of policy. It is based on plain discrimination among companies, affects competitive relations, underlines the fact that money is being taken from one part of the country and given to another (and not necessarily for accepted regional reasons), runs obvious risks of corruption and political manipulation, and can be highly objectionable in principle to those who believe that discretionary power in the hands of officials is always less desirable than laws that apply uniformly to all. No doubt these difficulties explain why the targeting techniques are not more common. They are, however, more widely used than may be realized, as when important firms are in danger of failing or a single national champion is being built up to fend off foreign competitors or provide new capacities of production. Selectivity is only slightly disguised by establishing classes of companies eligible for aid in countries where there are few producers. Some of the ideas being discussed in Canada about the need to provide a larger home base for a smaller number of companies that can become internationally competitive suggests that there may be an increased interest in company-directed measures of industrial policy in the future. In any case, the main point relevant here is that when compromises have to be made between limiting what governments may do and minimizing trade distortion or the impact on other countries, selective measures may have advantages over more sweeping ones that have sometimes been overlooked.

Another aspect of government procurement that is often overlooked is discrimination among foreign suppliers. This would be eliminated by a code that emphasized competitive bidding, but such a rule is not likely to be without exceptions. Some will be overt, as in procurement arrangements within the European Community or the Defense Production Sharing Agreement between the United States and Canada. Discrimination will be less easy to detect when a government uses its discretion to buy from a country it wishes to favor for political or commercial reasons. Since governments and government-owned enterprises are major importers in many developing countries, industrial countries competing for export markets may value their individual bargaining positions more highly than a code that deals strictly with discrimination. There is a merging here of thought about government procurement with the larger subject of state trading, another field in which the GATT rules are inadequate but which does not seem to have been the subject of major negotiation in the Tokyo Round.

The topic is a complicated one but has a good deal of importance for industrial policy. Government-owned corporations are often major instruments for shaping the economic structure of developing countries and may very well take into account more than the "commercial considerations" enshrined in the GATT formula.[4] In the industrialized world, government decisions on the purchase of supplies from abroad are often made conditional on the supplier's commitment to buy or manufacture components or other supplies in the purchasing country and sometimes to establish whole new lines of production there and research and development centers as well. This practice is particularly common in the procurement of civilian or military aircraft but is used more widely. It can be carried on in reverse if a government-owned raw material company, for example, will sell only to buyers who will provide it with processing facilities or technological help or something else—or perhaps to those who buy other products as well. It is a reasonably safe bet that the Tokyo Round's code on government procurement will not go far toward regulating such practices, and that they will consequently stay on the list of unsolved international problems stemming from national industrial policies.

If international codes are successful in introducing more transparency into subsidies and government procurement, they may not only influence the way these devices are used but also put some limits on them. Taxpayers tend to look at government expenditures rather critically, whereas consumers are notoriously lax in complaining about prices that are raised by tariffs. With more information citizens may raise more questions about subsidies and the costs of preferential government purchases. It will not always be easy to tell whether the government is getting its money's worth or whether a subsidy is serving its professed purpose, but transparency will probably stimulate scrutiny. The result ought to be a clarification of some industrial policy issues, but it may also intensify the tendency groups already show to

[4]The definition of commercial considerations is one of the problems with state trading rules. Another is how much state ownership—and at what level of government—is necessary for an enterprise to come under the rules. Control over trade, particularly through the licensing of individual transactions, sometimes amounts to almost the same thing but is not generally thought of as state trading.

seek less vulnerable forms of protection. The issue is part of a larger one: How far will international arrangements alter the way governments carry out industrial policies or, perhaps, their ability to do so? A further question, which would surely lead to very different answers, is what the effects would be if private people were permitted to appeal to international agencies when they felt that foreign governments (or their own) were violating the international rules—even if their own governments were not prepared to make the same objection.

Assuming that the MTN codes come into force (no government had acted on them when this book went to press), it is not possible to judge what their effects will be from their texts. While advancing somewhat beyond past GATT rules about particular practices, their essence lies in the procedures they set up to permit countries that feel damaged by the practices of others to bring complaints and then to insure that something happens: a change in the practice, a dismissal of the complaint, a compromise solution, or permission for the complainer to retaliate (when his case is valid and the offender will not budge). If these arrangements work, they will deal with a significant number of problems arising from national industrial policies. But if they do not work as expected, if governments prove unwilling to use them, or if countries in violation never mend their ways, industrial policies will continue to undermine and eventually nullify trading arrangements. Although the objectives of trade cooperation and of reducing the international difficulties stemming from industrial policy are not identical, they do converge over a considerable range. NTBs are part of this, but a much greater degree of convergence appears when we consider the relation of adjustment policies to the use of the safeguard clauses provided in international trade agreements.

## ESCAPE CLAUSES AND INDUSTRIAL ADAPTATION: GATT PRACTICE AND OECD PRINCIPLES

Even the countries most committed to trade liberalization are not prepared to give up completely their right to impose import controls in difficult circumstances. Defined in various ways, the escape clauses found in almost all agreements center on the inflow of foreign goods at a pace, price, or volume that threatens to drive domestic competitors out of business faster than their workers and other resources can be shifted to other uses or than the government is prepared to see them go. Of course, such escape clauses can be abused, but they are endorsed by the stoutest advocates of freer trade; without them, governments will either not agree to trade liberalization or will break their commitments under pressure. However, if the escape clauses are too easy to use, the system may also break down, since some governments will be unable to resist domestic pressures to invoke them and others will see no means of restoring equal advantage except to retaliate or withdraw concessions.

A combination of these factors led to dissatisfaction with the safeguard clauses of GATT (primarily Article XIX) and made repairs to them a major aim of the MTN negotiations. Failure to find an improved solution would be a constant hazard to whatever degree of trade liberalization might otherwise result from the agreements on tariffs and NTBs. It was therefore ominous that the major countries could not agree on a safeguards formula when other matters were largely settled in the spring of 1979. Whatever arrangements are finally worked out will have to be judged by how far they improve on existing arrangements with regard to the degree of international sanction required for the use of safeguards, how long they could be kept, and how the time gained was to be used.

If the problem giving rise to the use of import controls is temporary, the issue is of no particular interest to us. Nor need we concern ourselves here with what forms import control should take. Though the definition of the conditions that justify invoking the escape clause is a serious and complex matter, we can safely leave it aside to concentrate on how the time gained is used. It makes no difference whether the competition that is creating "market disruption"—however defined—results primarily from a past trade barrier reduction or from some other change that has put the domestic industry at a disadvantage. The principle should be that temporary protection is granted on condition that the time gained be used to make adjustments. The goal should be to make lasting protection unnecessary without making the burden of adjustment heavier than necessary. Most countries have some kind of mechanism for aiding adjustment and relieving the pressure, but these arrangements often leave much to be desired. Though it may be best to leave the importing country fairly free to decide how it brings about change, the other members of the international community who are affected should have some way of satisfying themselves that this process is taking place and of helping to push it to completion.

The simplest arrangement is a time limit and that has been used in the past; but if nothing is done about adjustment, the limit is likely to be extended and protection prolonged. Matters would be improved if outside countries were put in a position to examine what was being done by way of adjustment, whether through annual reports, frequent meetings of a surveillance committee, or consultation on particular measures affecting them. Built-in objective pressure would also be desirable, such as a declining level of protection. Prolongation of protection beyond an initial period might be penalized by some such method as requiring payments to the countries that are being deprived of a market or giving them permission to retaliate by trade measures of their own.[5] More important, however, is pushing the process of adjustment forward by one means or another. For that some

---

[5] Monetary compensation is perhaps best limited to cases in which there are large differences in wealth (see chap. 5). The reverse, international financing of a national adjustment program, also belongs in a broader category than the present one, though it could have a part in increasing the international influence on the adjusting country. A delinquent country's payments might go into this fund as fines rather than to other countries as compensation. Foreign trade retaliation ought to be confined to violations or extensions of the adjustment period; one of the weaknesses of past GATT practices is that when a country invoked the escape clause, others were entitled to withdraw comparable concessions; so it was, in effect, punished. This was one of a number of reasons that countries avoided the formal procedure. See the case for a two-track approach made by Anthony M. Solomon, "Safeguard Mechanisms," in C. Fred Bergsten (ed.), *Toward a New World Trade Policy: The Maidenhead Papers*, Lexington Books, Lexington, Mass., 1975, pp. 277–281. Another complaint was that GATT rules required the import controls to be applied equally to goods from all countries even though only one or two were causing the trouble. Efforts to permit the selective use of controls became one of the most contentious issues of the Tokyo Round, with major implications for trade policy that cannot be explored here.

standards are required, and it is here that honest men may differ and parties at interest are bound to. That is one reason why the adjusting country needs leeway to decide what it is to do, but it is equally a reason why other countries have an interest in what the new situation is going to be, as well as whether the old one is really ending.

Even if it is agreed that the result should be a situation not requiring protection (or in which the government is willing to take the consequences of not providing protection) and that this is something like the international competitiveness referred to earlier, it is not always clear from the outset how to arrive at that point. We tend to speak of an industry being threatened by foreign competition (and unless a substantial part of the industry is in difficulty, the general protection provided under an escape clause is hardly justified). In fact, though, the range between the most and the least efficient producers in an industry can be great and the consequences of the pressure will vary accordingly. Companies and workers also differ in their ability to change their activities. Better management may be enough to cut costs, but not always. Sometimes what is needed is only investment in new equipment or support for expansion. Location is often crucial for alternative jobs and sometimes for costs. A certain segment of the industry may already be competitive and the problem may be that of high-cost producers. Percy Bidwell said long ago that tariff changes usually "determine only the dimensions of the industry," rarely its life or death.[6] Even in the textile industry, thought of as the classical case of the inability of high-wage countries to compete in labor-intensive activities, there are all sorts of highly competitive firms in rich countries and there are very capital-intensive processes as well. Still, it is true that over time very large shifts in industrial structures occur, and there are lines of activity once strong in Europe or North America that are now vestigial there but thriving in other parts of the world. Quite often, therefore, the aim of adjustment will be to shift people, management, and capital out of past lines of activities into new ones.

[6]Percy Bidwell, *What the Tariff Means to American Industries*, Harper for the Council on Foreign Relations, New York, 1956, p. 289.

When there are major shifts, the heaviest cost of adjustment is likely to fall on workers. They may have to change jobs, industries, location, and the kind of work they do. Those who are older may never gain the skills in new occupations that they had in their old ones. At any age a person may justifiably resent having hard choices and limited alternatives forced on him. Better income support and assurances of job security are needed than governments can usually provide. Japan's exceptional arrangements worry Western entrepreneurs, but they need careful study, not writing-off as exotic peculiarities. The sympathetic treatment of labor is not, however, to be equated with the idea that changes in jobs are unacceptable. To be assured of a future in a declining industry is not the best kind of security for an individual. To employ a large part of the labor force in inefficient industries is not something many economies can afford. As people become better off, incentives to change lose their attraction and the ability to resist pressure increases. But without flexibility, economies lose their ability to make it possible for their people to live well. Somehow security and change must be brought together, not treated as opposites.

While the origin of escape clauses lay in the fear that tariff reductions might lead to greater imports than were expected, market disruption can have many causes. A change in technology or the productive ability of a new center abroad may be far more important than a tariff reduction made years ago in creating the situation that requires adjustment. It is best to deal with such cases in the same way and not try to be too strict in establishing cause and effect. Should the same be said about an industrial decline occasioned largely by domestic developments? Such elements are rarely altogether absent when industries prove especially vulnerable to import competition. Still, one might doubt whether import restrictions were justified in such cases. But as long as the adjustment measures took account of the domestic difficulties and did not throw the whole burden on imports, it might be best to accept some import restrictions as a way of assuring both international surveillance and accompanying measures that would create pressure to carry out adjustments. These measures, only hypothesized here, would mark a considerable advance in the international management of international issues.

A similar argument would apply to the idea that a country should sometimes be allowed to limit imports temporarily to permit some otherwise healthy domestic industry to become competitive in a new product. This is a more dubious proposition, and there might be considerable dangers of abuse unless it were strictly supervised. It should also be limited to cases in which it was clearly in the interest of the government to have the activity become viable as quickly as possible. There might even be a contractual obligation on the part of the protected industry to produce specified results by a certain time, after which the import limits would be dropped. If a country could not get prior international approval for measures of this sort, other countries could be expected to retaliate. To avoid an unraveling of trade cooperation, it would be worth considering if a formula could be found permitting a country to limit imports temporarily up to a certain share of trade (or domestic production) if it could claim to be meeting identifiable criteria of purpose and promise.[7]

All these possibilities represent things that might be done. What cannot be evaded, however, is the need to have some means of determining what postadjustment situation would be satisfactory. The same question arises as in regional policy. Is it sensible to say that country A should go out of the production of X without asking what it should get *into* the production of? Suppose it switches workers and capital to the production of Y just as everyone else is doing the same thing, and the same problem reappears in a few years' time, perhaps as demand for Y falls. Should the calculation and risk be entirely that of the importing government, or might there be international consultation and advice about its best choice? Might there even be an approved list and a disapproved list of activities put forth by some international body? A country that shifted to something on the approved list (or gained some other form of international endorsement) might reasonably be given some assurance by the

[7]This is one possible formalization of the idea that every country can go in for a bit of protectionism without inciting much foreign reaction—what Stoffaes calls *le crédit de protectionnisme* (*La Grande Menace Industrielle*, p. 329). He is also an advocate of contractual arrangements with industry, which have had a place in French industrial policy for a long time.

international community that for a stated period of years it would not be exposed to damaging competition in its home market. But how could this be done? The prescription may be too rigid, denying consumers in the importing country the benefits of reductions in the cost of production that may take place during the stated period or depriving efficient producers in other parts of the world of fair access to a market. Could one have criteria that would avoid these risks? Would such an arrangement give new producers not parties to the original agreement an unfair advantage, or would it expose them to discriminatory protective actions?

In the minds of many people there are no good answers to these questions. Nor could the international system offer much promise of carrying out such complex arrangements. Therefore, it is widely argued, the shift should be left to the market. No doubt that will often be the best way, but is it an altogether satisfactory answer? An entrepreneur who has made a mistake should take the loss and, if necessary, go bankrupt. But the problems we are discussing arise because governments are not prepared to see that happen until an alternative activity has been provided for workers, communities, and perhaps whole regions. Without some assurance that "the market" is good at forecasting in this particular field, or some safeguard if mistakes are made, another round of protection and another infusion of public help become necessary. All the problems of the purpose and direction of national industrial policy are posed again.

Even if a country fully accepts the target of competitiveness for an adjustment program and works hard at it, there may be situations in which that result cannot be attained except on unacceptably harsh terms. Public support may be inevitable. Even when productivity is low, employment is often greatly preferable to idleness for economic or humanitarian reasons. If alternative employment is not easy to find, the problem is likely to be chronic for a long time. Such cases hardly seem suitable to the kind of international surveillance that would help speed short-term adjustment. But international repercussions ought to be given the same emphasis as domestic ones in determining what help will cost least, create least inefficiency overall, and do least damage to those whose return or livelihood is reduced by the subsidy of others. Subsidies and the use of some kind of government procurement seem more likely to meet these criteria than would trade barriers if the industry is small enough; if it is extensive, the opposite may be true.

Even if competitiveness is accepted as a vital need for the economy as a whole, and therefore most parts of it, some economic activities will be supported or protected for a variety of reasons. These cases should not be treated as if they simply presented especially difficult problems in adjustment. Until the societies find the cost too high they will maintain these activities. The broad issue is one touched on before: Who pays for whose choice? Where is the balance to be struck between national autonomy and the cooperative "management of interdependence" (to use Miriam Camps's expression)? These questions clearly cross the border from trade policy into the kinds of industrial policy issues that the world does not yet handle in a satisfactory way.

We are, in a way, brought back to the not very encouraging example of agriculture. So far as I know, no one has yet invoked industrial policy as a reason to excuse a country from its trade policy obligations, as has long been done with regard to agriculture.[8] In fact, though, this is what the special arrangements for textiles and steel amount to, and the reference to exceptional circumstances that justify inaction in hard cases has overtones of this argument. A further accumulation of cases, owing in part to the recession of the mid-1970s and the unsatisfactory recovery from it, would begin to look like a partly rationalized set of exceptions on industrial policy grounds. Another way in which this tendency might express itself is the exceptions to rules limiting the use of subsidies and government procurement. The best chance of keeping these tendencies within bounds may lie in improving safeguard arrangements along the lines suggested

[8]Security has generally been recognized as justifying exceptions to trade obligations but has not presented problems on the scale of agriculture. This is probably because of a more or less tacit recognition that unless everyone interprets security in fairly narrow terms, much of trade liberalization will be undermined.

above. While formal changes and alterations of commitments can only come through changes in GATT, key countries could give assurances as to how they would use the time gained or set standards by which national adjustment programs could be judged. Just that seemed to have been done in an OECD document announcing principles agreed on by the OECD Council when it met at the ministerial level in the middle of June 1978.[9]

These principles, referred to as "general orientations," concern adjustment policies as a whole, not the GATT safeguard rules. Indeed, there is no specific connection with the MTN. The keynote of the document is that in dealing with unemployment and other results of the recession, governments are in danger of taking supposedly short-run measures that will turn into lasting resistance to structural change. The same session of the Council renewed the pledge referred to in Chapter 1 to avoid beggar-my-neighbor measures, and the "orientations" can be read as spelling out some of the meaning of the pledge's general language. The statement also followed a good deal of activity by senior members of the OECD Secretariat who were worried about the special arrangements for steel, shipbuilding, and some other industries being worked out in the European Community. (See Chapter 4.)

The emphasis in the OECD statement is similar to that of the earlier part of this chapter: The need to cushion the impact of structural changes in the short term should not lead to protective measures that prevent the adjustment from taking place. The difficulty of making these changes in bad times is recognized; but unless the structural shifts take place, the chances of resuming satisfactory growth and achieving full employment are reduced. There should be as much reliance "as possible on market forces to encourage mobility of labour and capital to their most productive uses."[10] The pursuit of other social and political "goals

[9]OECD Press Release, "Policies for Adjustment: Some General Orientations," Presse/A(78) 23, Paris, June 15, 1978, Annex II, pp. 12–17. (Mimeographed.) With negligible changes the text appears in *The OECD Observer*, July 1978, no. 93, pp. 10–12.

[10]Ibid. Quotes on pages 81–84 are from this document.

should be sought through policies which minimise any resulting costs in terms of reduced economic efficiency." When general policies do not suffice and measures are taken to deal with industries, sectors, or individual companies, they should be limited in time and include plans "to phase out obsolete capacity and re-establish financially viable entities." Costs should be clear, private risk capital should be involved, and competition should help insure efficiency and good management. Regional policies ought to help the strong as well as the weak, and national security should not become a cloak for protectionism.

In policies aimed at "picking the winners" it is reasonable to "supplement market forces" by government help with research and development, urban and environmental programs, and the provision of access to capital for small and medium firms. Desirable features are suggested for an active labor market policy and the reconciliation of the need for job and income security with mobility. Regional and agricultural policies, regulation, and various other matters are also touched on, and the statement concludes with a paragraph on international cooperation. This emphasizes that defensive policies in one country make adjustment policies in others harder to carry out, so cooperation on the adjustment policies themselves is in order.

It would be easy enough to dismiss the statement as largely a collection of pious platitudes. No great subtlety is required to find loopholes and qualifications that any government could say applied to its special circumstances. Other passages balance one statement against another in a manner quite familiar to readers of documents produced by international organizations. It would be a mistake, though, to dismiss the document on those grounds. Its emphasis is clear; much of it is reasonably detailed and concrete; the problems it addresses are real. The document embodies a definite point of view and responds to serious fears. It is stronger than most statements coming from the OECD or other intergovernmental bodies. It appeals throughout primarily to the national self-interest of countries rather than to the possible effects of their actions on others or on international trade generally. The validity of this line of argument is well borne out by studies showing the damaging effects of protecting employment by letting people work in uncompetitive industries. Not only does the productivity of the economy suffer and its flexibility as well (if labor does not move to more efficient sectors), but there is also an inflationary effect.[11]

I believe the OECD statement on "orientations" to be the first multilateral agreement on adjustment policy. It is therefore also an agreement on industrial policy, though it does not take account of all aspects of that large subject. For example, it gives no guidance in the fields where the main aim of policy is not to adjust to external competitive pressures but to initiate change or preserve noneconomic values. Where skepticism is in order is on how much weight governments will give to their mutual good advice. "Orientations" must be less strong than "principles," but the communiqué says the ministers "agreed on" them. It does not appear as if the groundwork for the statement included the building of any very broad consensus among national bureaucracies and business or labor groups. Therefore the influence of the orientations may depend on how effectively they can be put forward as a high-level agreement that now has to be implemented. The endorsement at the Bonn summit referred to at the end of Chapter 2 might be seen as a step in that process. However, much will have to be done at what is somewhat invidiously called "the working level." A possibility would be to set up a review procedure in which national adjustment policies would be examined as, in other parts of the OECD, aid policies are looked at in the Development Assistance Committee and macroeconomic measures in Working Party 3. If such consultation included the exchange of information about policies being considered or problems that might require action should they not improve, another step would have been taken toward international cooperation in new fields. Further movement toward hearing complaints about the impact of what others did might seem a natural evolution, but it would require some common acceptance of standards or the taking on of specific international obligations,

---

[11] The case is well made in Richard Blackhurst, Nicolas Marian, and Jan Tumlir, *Trade Liberalization, Protectionism and Interdependence*, GATT Studies in International Trade, no. 5, Geneva, November 1977; and United Nations Economic Commission for Europe, *Structure and Change in European Industry*, New York, 1977.

which would then have to be linked with the Article XIX arrangements of GATT.

The member countries of OECD not only account for a very high percentage of the world's production but also comprise the established centers of industry, where the largest changes have to take place to meet shifting competitive conditions around the world. Much of the adjustment will be to trade among themselves. Even if they lived up to the principles only in that respect, it would be progress. The last paragraph of the statement says, however, that "collective agreement on the need to shift from defensive to more positive adjustment policies . . . is also an affirmation of Member countries' willingness to adjust to changes in their trade in manufactures and other products with developing countries." This answer, at a verbal level, to an unasked question stimulates some others which we shall have to take up in due course: Is the commitment unilateral, or is some reasonable reciprocity expected from the LDCs? Is the determination as firm with regard to North-South trade as in trade among the members where the conditions to which one is supposed to adjust presumably vary within narrower margins? Does the fact that this is a "collective agreement" mean that individual OECD countries will be offering the LDCs better treatment than if each had acted alone?

## GOVERNMENTS AND FOREIGN INVESTMENT

There is no GATT for international investment; nor is it very likely that any large number of governments will soon agree on a set of reasonably firm rules that could be applied to a significant fraction of the international direct investment that has been a key factor in the growth and integration of the world economy, or on the kinds of financial measures that would greatly shape portfolio investment.[12] There are, however, many partial inter-

---

[12]Financial structures have a part in this whole story but are omitted here, along with such related matters as the bearing of the international movement of funds on national industrial policies, access to the Eurocurrency market, cooperation to regulate that market, etc. There are comments on some but not all of these points in chaps. 5 and 6.

national arrangements that have an effect on investment, production, and trade and either reflect fairly clear-cut industrial policies or are among the measures shaping national economic structures. Some of these are bilateral treaties between governments providing for mutually satisfactory treatment of their investors in the other's territory. Here the standard may be equal treatment with other foreigners or national treatment (i.e., the foreigner is treated the same as domestic corporations), or the emphasis may be on certain specified conditions and rights. This last sometimes looks like better-than-national treatment if the foreigner is given guarantees not extended to domestic companies, but the reality is usually some blend of all these, since even the promise of national treatment is usually somewhat shaded in practice. The host government's right to control foreign investment is never entirely lost, but among the countries of the European Community the basis has been laid for greater freedom of industrial establishment by foreigners. The Andean Pact established common policies dealing with foreign investors, though national differences remained strong. Of major importance are the understandings between large foreign investors and the governments of the countries where they either wish to establish themselves, seek concessions for extractive work, or already have a certain presence. A quite different kind of measure is to be found in the codes concerning the behavior of multinational enterprises that have been worked out in the OECD, explored in the United Nations, and, within limits, set up by some groups of recipient countries. There is, finally, some regulation of investment abroad by governments of the countries from which most of the investment comes.

International investment is often thought of in terms of the movement of capital and the effects of investment on national balances of payments, and such considerations often shape national policies. However, measures of the sort that we have been calling industrial policy can also play a dominant role, whether the emphasis is on the structure of the economy in the sense of the allocation of resources or of control over its operation. Even when national policies amounted to little more than encouraging direct investment, the results played a large part in bringing about structural change in the world economy.

Among the industrial countries the main emphasis has been on the fairly free movement of enterprise. There are numerous exceptions, but Japan was the only major industrial country that consistently combined restrictions on foreign investment with great growth. The result was a Japanese-owned industry using foreign technology but only gradually opened up to foreign investment. This restriction may well have had much to do with Japan's ability to carry out an industrial policy that relied heavily on business cooperation with government. Other countries took less stringent measures to assure themselves that the presence of foreign companies would redound to the national benefit. Often the interest in having investment in certain activities or in a certain place has led governments, national and local, to provide a variety of incentives to foreigners, including tax concessions, provision of infrastructure, and sometimes direct subsidies. Investors sometimes have to make commitments about employment, the use of domestic supplies, and the volume of goods they will export.

Developing countries, too, have made such agreements and solicited foreign investment by a variety of measures, including sometimes the guarantee of a near monopoly of the domestic market. However, uneasiness about foreign domination and surges of nationalism have often led LDC governments to take measures that discouraged foreign investment, at least for a time. The governments of raw-material-producing countries have been particularly dependent on large foreign companies to explore, dig mines, bring technology for mining and refining metals, and provide overseas markets as well. But as time passes and the terms of old contracts often come to seem onerous, governments move to improve the terms and enlarge their share of the income while the foreigners find themselves the victims of an "obsolescing bargain," as Raymond Vernon has called it.[13] Such shifts, including sometimes nationalization and the emergence of national producing corporations, as in oil, bring further changes in the shape of the international industry. Production, finance, and

[13]Raymond Vernon, *Sovereignty at Bay: The Multinational Spread of U.S. Enterprises*, Basic Books, New York, 1971, p. 46.

marketing are all affected and so are ideas about secure access to supplies. A specific shift is toward satisfying the old aspirations of producing countries to see a higher degree of processing of their raw material at home. Even when this is done without export taxes or controls, it is likely to entail a substantial problem of industrial adjustment in the older processing centers (which are frequently in the main consuming countries in Europe and North America).

The principal reason there are no comprehensive international investment agreements is that the investors and the invested-upon have always seen themselves as on opposite sides of a wide division. Another is the ambivalence of most countries about wanting (or feeling they needed) foreign investment and accepting it on terms that assuaged their uneasiness about the foreign investor, especially if it was a large multinational enterprise. One of the reasons the Charter for an International Trade Organization (ITO) never came into effect was that a belated effort to include in it an investment code was made in response to American business groups, who then disliked the results. Efforts to negotiate investment codes in the 1950s and 1960s produced meager results, because the moving force was always Europeans or Americans interested in more liberal treatment for their business abroad. Even among themselves the industrial countries had limited success with OECD agreements, but the problem was not a very serious one. Developing countries' efforts to get United Nations agreements controlling the activities of multinational corporations were based on the view that these were extremely powerful organizations that could move freely around the world and tell governments on what terms they would do business in their territories. The modest results of the international action have been far less effective than the measures individual governments have taken to deal with the companies, whose power was clearly a good deal less than was widely believed.

Once it is realized that comprehensive one-sided arrangements are impossible, the focus of interest should shift to the possibility of an international agreement on investment that establishes rights and duties for both governments and private firms and for both host and home governments. This has been the kind of thinking behind suggestions for a GATT for investment (in which behavior would be codified by practice, not all prescribed at the outset) or the financing of resource development in ways that involve the World Bank or other international financial institutions as partners plus guarantors of the legitimate interests of both sides. Various combinations of agreements among groups of countries can be imagined that could be interlocked in one way or another. It is also plausible that agreements on taxation or other particular aspects of investment and corporate behavior should be worked out. It does not seem likely, however, that the time is ripe for any comprehensive investment agreements involving a large number of countries.

This does not mean that there will be no international agreements affecting direct investment, even though the situation is completely different from that in trade, where the MTN provides an immediate test of how far governments may prove willing to go. In fact, the MTN itself has a direct bearing on the matter. Codes on subsidies and government procurement will affect investment as well as trade both directly and indirectly. The indirect effect comes from the fact that much investment is still stimulated by the wish to get behind foreign trade barriers, whether they take the form of tariffs or something else. The direct effect comes from the fact that the tax concessions and other subsidies of many different sorts that are widely used to attract foreign investors may be subjected to rules established in the new codes. No doubt governments will be chary of tying their hands in these matters, but it is often not easy to draw a line between a subsidy to promote domestic development and its effect on foreign trade. The classic example in recent times is the Michelin tire case. The Canadian government, as part of its regional development policy, provided aid to the French company to establish a plant in Nova Scotia; its products were then subjected to countervailing duties by the United States because they had to be regarded as subsidized competition for domestic producers.

There are undoubtedly many more cases of this sort in both developed and developing countries that have so far escaped countervailing measures. If the MTN subsidy code fails to deal with them in some reasonably satisfactory way, it seems probable that governments will more and more frequently act on their own. That seems especially likely because plants are often established on terms that require that a certain share of their output be exported. Unilateral action by countries that feel themselves damaged may well give rise to bilateral understandings and possibly to something broader. Suggestions have been made for new kinds of multilateral agreements to cover these practices, combining some of the features of a subsidy code with arrangements about the conditions of investment and the definition of fair trade.[14] While the prospects of something so ambitious may be dim—it might come after much more trouble rather than before—there is little doubt that a dynamic process is at work which will either produce new agreements or multiply international disputes about trade and investment. In the process, existing agreements about trade may be undermined and new restrictions put on investment.

There may also be an effect on the policies of capital-exporting countries toward the activities of their companies abroad. If the national interest of host countries leads to bargains with foreign companies, people in the countries where these companies are based will ask if they are being put at a disadvantage. Although the case against "exporting jobs" is not as clear as American unions (and others) have believed, there can be problems of adjustment that may call for measures comparable to those aimed at easing changes in trade patterns. In any case, international direct investment is one of the main forces for structural change in the world and operates by changing national economic patterns. It therefore cannot escape national industrial policies and whatever international measures they give rise to.

There is also a reverse influence to be taken into account. To the extent that governments, for whatever reason, increase their concern with foreign investment, incoming or outgoing, they will have to think increasingly about the structures of their own

[14]A number of possibilities are considered in C. Fred Bergsten, Thomas Horst, and Theodore Moran, *American Multinationals and American Interests*, The Brookings Institution, Washington, D.C., 1978.

economies. In the past the dominant movement of national policies, with or without international agreements, was toward increasing or preserving the relatively free flow of investment capital and the right of companies to establish themselves more or less where they liked. A focus on national industrial policies could reverse that direction. But if new agreements keep the channels open, governments may find themselves dealing with the results—or the expected results, since they will often act in advance—by measures of industrial policy other than controls over investment. As the investment policy followed by each or the bargains it strikes with companies or other governments will be one of the main means by which one country's industrial policy creates problems for others, that, too, may become a goad toward international action.

## ANSWERS

We began with the question whether the pursuit of the fairly familiar processes of international negotiation about trade and investment could do much to deal with the international problems raised by national industrial policies. We have arrived at fairly clear answers.

In the case of trade, major progress in dealing with subsidies, other nontariff barriers, and safeguards along the lines suggested in this chapter would do much to reduce some of the problems of industrial policy. This is not to say that many problems would be eliminated; the full meaning of the agreement would still depend on what use governments made of the kinds of consultative and disputes-settlement arrangements that are bound to be an important part of any major advance in this field. If, however, little use is made of the procedures provided by the MTN, or if they prove weak, national industrial policy measures will continue to undermine trade principles.

The OECD statement on adjustment policies is a major new development, affecting both trade policy and some central issues of industrial policy. If governments take it seriously, it can substantially strengthen any good results from the MTN and may offset some of its weaknesses.

In the case of investment, there are neither clear lines nor a central set of negotiations that might produce major developments. However, fragmented negotiations are likely to increase in number. Their potential for producing useful understandings in any given case is real enough, but it is hard to judge what their cumulative effect might be or what the chances are of their developing into broader arrangements.

Different as the situations in trade and investment are, the two cases have some significant similarities. It is hard to be optimistic about how much is likely to be accomplished by existing patterns of negotiation focusing primarily on standard targets of trade and investment policy. Modest results will do little to meet the difficulties arising from national industrial policies and may sooner or later weaken the existing arrangements and lower the level of cooperation.

The difficulties in trade and investment negotiations frequently stem from national industrial policy measures and the unwillingness of governments to alter them. This will become increasingly clear to more people as time passes. Heightened awareness may increase the willingness to reach wider areas of agreement on trade and investment problems and, in turn, can increase the effects of those negotiations on international industrial policy issues. It is quite clear, however, that these approaches are not adequate for dealing with industrial policy issues as a whole unless they develop into something quite different from what negotiations about trade and investments have been in the past. Whether any other method—a direct attack on industrial policy issues, more numerous negotiations about limited parts of the problem, or something else—could make greater progress is something we are not yet in a position to say.

# FOUR

# Answers by the Piece: The Sectoral Approach

Industrial policy is usually about individual industries. Even if governments are concerned with several different industries at the same time—defending shoes and trying to encourage the production of computers—each program is likely to stand on its own feet. Protectionism may, like Tolstoy's happy families, be all alike, but in different industries it may produce different results, and if governments are to encourage adjustment, they have to do so differently from case to case. Perhaps it is inevitable that much discussion of international action to deal with structural change—and probably even a greater share of the action—should be cast in terms of what can be done about a given industry.

None of this is very surprising or, for that matter, very enlightening. But questions arise that our survey must consider. Is the industry-by-industry approach to structural change the best? Are the solutions to be found in arrangements that treat each sector differently?[1] Affirmative answers seem implicit in most of what governments have done in recent years to deal with sick or declining industries.

The recession of the mid-1970s increased the number of industries in trouble; but in speaking of three of these—textiles, steel, and shipbuilding—the Commission of the European Community was surely right to see a "worldwide structural crisis"

---

[1]There can be difficulties in defining industries that affect both diagnosis and possible solutions, but these are left aside for the present.

and not just a temporary state.[2] Perhaps energy should not be thought of as a single industry, and its troubles are of a different sort, but it has called for an unprecedented national and international sectoral approach. What happens in energy has an exceptional and perhaps unique set of repercussions throughout the rest of the world economy, but changes in any major sector will affect others. Agriculture, that ever-recurring example, also illustrates aspects of the sectoral approach, but none that are very helpful to our present inquiry (except for some might-have-beens discussed later in connection with steel). The aircraft industry has been the subject of many national and some international measures based on its special characteristics. There has also been much discussion of whether future trouble could be avoided by international preventive measures in the chemical, automobile, and electronics industries.

Case studies in any depth of these industries are beyond the scope of this book. It is not even feasible to provide a detailed history of the industrial policy measures that have been taken in such key sectors as textiles and steel. We must, however, look briefly at the experience in those two basic industries if we are to make a realistic assessment of how the sectoral approach has been used and what it has accomplished. After that we may take a longer and more speculative look at what might be done in the future, given the difficulties of the sectoral approach.

One of its very practical advantages is focus. We have seen how difficult it is to deal with all the different kinds of subsidies and other trade-restricting practices or to provide for all contingencies before they arise. The sectoral approach is itself selective and becomes even more so if action is not taken until need arises. The ability to contribute to foreseeable results narrows the range of countries to be considered. Though not every key country may be ready to move at the same time, what one or two do will itself create a situation likely to require the others to act. Thus the sectoral approach tends to confine action to real needs felt by people who can do something about it.

[2] *Bulletin of the European Communities*, Office for Official Publications of the European Community, Luxembourg, No. 11, 1977, p. 9.

It is not hard, though, to assess these sectoral characteristics more negatively. A selective mechanism that picks only industries in trouble may not be the most constructive instrument for dealing with structural change. How often will it really be possible to secure a balance of advantages and concessions among a number of countries within the confines of a single industry? Is it realistic, since every input is someone else's output and vice versa, to suppose that the "solutions" arrived at in one sector will not create new problems for other sectors? The industry-by-industry approach has been used before to organize cartels, and it is obvious that the sectoral approach is often likely to take on some of their restrictive characteristics.

The balancing of these factors, and others, has to be postponed until after our rather selective review of the sectoral experience of the recent past. There is, however, still another question that must be kept in mind. In textiles and steel the international measures on which we shall be concentrating were taken in response to trade problems. The methods, for the most part, have been trade methods. But the real issues are issues of structural change, in the terminology of this book. It is important, therefore, to observe to what extent the textile and steel measures have, or might become, industrial policy methods and what relevance the answer has to the assessment of the sectoral approach.

## TEXTILES

John F. Kennedy carried into the office of President of the United States at the beginning of 1961 an electoral pledge to do something about the impact of foreign imports on the American textile and clothing industry. On top of the time-honored reflexes of a New England politician in defense of the waning of the activities that had made his section of the country an early industrial center, there had been a demand for action endorsed by enough Representatives and Senators of both parties from many parts of the country to make it likely that Congress would act if the President did not. Import restrictions unilaterally imposed would violate American commitments and encourage other countries to retal-

95

iate. To avoid that and keep open the possibility of another major American initiative in trade policy, it was necessary to find a new international device and also to keep the textile industry and its supporters from blocking new trade legislation.[3]

Public and private investigation by the executive branch set out the dimensions of the problems of the industry and possible remedies. The State Department took soundings abroad. Most continental European countries had tighter restrictions on imports than the United States had, so there was little room for "burden sharing." But Britain, which had treated India, Hong Kong, and other Commonwealth countries rather well, had larger imports of cotton goods compared to domestic production than the United States. Japan was the biggest exporter, but Hong Kong's shipments were rising fast. After a fairly long period of strenuous negotiations, a multilateral agreement covering cotton goods and clothing was worked out among the principal supplying and consuming countries and put under the aegis of GATT.[4]

The essence of the agreement lay in the stipulation that a country that felt damaged by imports of cotton goods could call on each of its suppliers to hold back shipments and, if they did not agree, could impose import quotas. The unilateral actions or bilateral agreements could not cut imports below the level of a recent base year and were to permit an annual increase of 5 percent. Existing quotas (mostly those of the continental countries) were to be enlarged. A limited amount of multilateral surveillance of the bilateral arrangement was provided.

Thus the United States became largely responsible for a major sectoral innovation in trade policy. Bilateral agreements to re-

[3]As the Trade Agreements Act was about to expire, some action was necessary unless the President was to lose his ability to reduce tariffs by negotiating with other governments. While postponement of renewal was seriously considered, concern about how the Common Market would affect American exports and the consequences of Western Europe's division into two trading areas (the Six and the Seven) gave rise to what became the Trade Expansion Act of 1962, which gave the President more power in this field than any predecessor had had and led to the Kennedy Round of GATT.

[4]There were in fact two agreements, a short-run one of 1961 and a long-run one that replaced it a year later. There were later amendments and extensions. The text gives only a rough picture.

strain the export of products were not new. Here, too, the United States had pioneered in pressing Japan to impose "voluntary" restraints on its shipments of cotton textiles and some other products during the 1950s, and the practice had spread to other countries. The significance of the Long-Term Cotton Textile Arrangement was that it formalized the practice, virtually insured that it would become general, and established some multilateral standards. Naturally, Japan, Hong Kong, and other suppliers were not very happy with the result but probably believed that the alternatives would be worse. Until the agreement was signed, President Kennedy kept alive an internal procedure that could have led to the imposition of import controls on grounds of national security. If he did not act, his negotiators told the others, Congress undoubtedly would. The Europeans were in a secondary position. Some worried about their own markets in the United States but knew they were not the main targets; others had no special reason to be upset by a procedure that would limit the liberalization expected of them. Americans who favored trade liberalization disliked the whole thing but reasoned, with varying degrees of conviction, that 5 percent a year was better than the cutbacks that might come through unilateral measures that would also violate international obligations. Moreover, by giving ground in the difficult textile sector it might be possible to move ahead in other fields with new trade legislation. The industry and its supporters could always find room for complaint but had no real assurance that the alternatives would have provided more protection. There were advantages in being recognized as a special case, since there was no great public sentiment favoring protectionism at that period.

Like the process by which it was reached, the agreement has major elements of ambiguity. On the face of it, there is nothing despicable in the idea that a major industrial shift should be orderly and managed so as to minimize disruption in old centers while permitting new suppliers with low labor costs to increase their share of world trade. One could applaud such an agreement as a sound innovation in international affairs, especially if it kept individual importing countries from imposing tighter barriers. Existing bilateral arrangements circumvented GATT rules; and there was some virtue in substituting formal, multilateral commitments that limited the use major importing countries could make of their bargaining power. Some such aims can be read into the guarded language of the preamble, but they are hardly evident in what may be regarded as the hard core of the agreement: The determination of whether there are "disruptive effects in individual markets and in individual lines of production" is to be made by the importing countries themselves.[5] And that, of course, is the other side of the picture—and one that is undoubtedly clearer than the larger vision of an orderly shift of production.

The effective drive behind the agreement was for protection. The demand came from the American industry (including labor) and was supported by much of the European and Canadian industry as well. The decisive response came in the first instance from the American political process and then from the international community; the producing countries were pushed into a position in which assent to an undesirable result seemed safer than risking the alternative. The new rules permitted more protection than the old ones, modified only by the rules concerning the size of quotas. The standards for determining when "disruption" existed were very loose; its threat alone justified controls; the arrangements for challenging an importing country's actions were weak. The only feature of the agreement that created any clear pressure for adjustment was the provision for a 5 percent annual increase in trade after the first year of restriction.[6]

---

[5]The preamble is a model of what results from difficult negotiation among people with strongly conflicting views who regard general statements about purpose as matters of bargaining and concession, even though they cannot alter the very specific and detailed obligations, rights, and procedures provided for in the rest of the agreement. Some of the drafters favored a far clearer and more forward-looking preamble that would have marked the innovative character of the agreement along the lines sketched above. Perhaps what finally came out was less hypocritical.

[6]Considering how many products fell under the agreement, a 5 percent increase in the total could have permitted much larger shifts in some lines of trade and production; but this was avoided by applying the quotas to individual products. If an exporting country agreed to more restrictive arrangements than it was entitled to (perhaps because it was given something it wanted in another field), the prospects of the arrangement's being challenged were poor.

The prospects of adjustment, therefore, depended on what governments or industrialists would do behind the protective wall. In a number of countries there have been major programs to transfer resources into other industries or make the production of textiles more competitive. In the United States the Kennedy administration had announced a program that included a number of measures to help adjustment; but once the agreement was adopted all the emphasis was on negotiating bilateral agreements, and the adjustment issue largely disappeared from the agenda of official business. No doubt there were people in the textile industry who saw that it was in their long-run self-interest to make some changes. A quicker tax write-off encouraged investment. Some people in the labor movement called attention to the kinds of adjustment arrangements that worked well in other countries and stressed the importance of research in products and technology.[7] But there can be no doubt that the dominant aim of all concerned was continued protection, in an almost classical illustration of what liberalizers fear when they are asked to acquiesce in "temporary" measures. Nevertheless, changes did take place in the American industry, largely as a result of domestic competition helped by new equipment and technology, continuing geographical shifts, and changes in taste. The pressure of imports played a part, but probably less than the growing displacement of cotton by man-made fibers and the pursuit of new opportunities abroad.

In terms of international trade, the results of the cotton textile agreement were as ambiguous as the forces that created it. There was neither an orderly transition nor the near-freeze of trade

[7]The outstanding spokesman was Solomon Barkin, then Director of Research of the Textile Workers Union of America. The fullest expression of his views is "International Trade in Textiles and Garments: A Challenge for New Policies," in Carl J. Friedrich and Seymour E. Harris (eds.), *Public Policy*, A Yearbook of the Graduate School of Public Administration, Harvard University, Cambridge, Mass., vol. XI, 1961. See also the *Executive Council Report to the 12th Biennial Convention* of the union, May 7–11, 1962, chap. 4, "The Textile Economy: Restrained Recovery." The former of these, written before the cotton textile arrangement was worked out, includes proposals for a considerably more ambitious international agreement which will be discussed in the next chapter.

patterns that critics of the arrangement feared and its protectionist supporters mostly wanted. In spite of the agreement, sales of textiles and clothing from developing countries to Europe and North America (and a little later to Japan) increased greatly during the rest of the 1960s. In addition to the annual increase specified in the agreement, the products seemed to flow over and around the trade barriers. Detailed agreements limiting, say, blouses led sellers and buyers to turn to shirts; when shirts were restricted there was a boom in pants. In a way that no one had expected, the agreement propagated the production of cotton textiles in the developing world. A ceiling on shipments from Hong Kong, India, the Philippines, and other established sources created an opening for someone else. Malaysia, for example, saw that if it established a cotton textile industry it was almost bound to get a certain share of the OECD market before it was important enough to be subjected to quotas or required to hold back its shipments. The way was further cleared by the fact that in Japan, the giant among the exporters, cotton textiles, though still of great importance, were giving way both to other textiles and to manufactured products with a higher value-added content. This helped make room for LDC expansion without increasing the pressure on the OECD markets.

It also seems likely that limits on cotton goods stimulated developing countries to foster exports of other products which did not encounter so much resistance in North America and Europe—at least for the time being. This seems to have happened, for example, in South Korea, which was actively looking for export earnings and employment. And there can be no doubt that the fact that the agreement applied only to cotton goods stimulated the shift to synthetic fibers, which was already strong. This gap in the agreement had been obvious from the first and the U.S. industry had wanted restrictions on woolens as well. Logic called for the gap to be filled at the outset but that course was resisted by those who were generally unhappy about the new restrictions, and though the American industry might have hoped for a broader agreement, it perhaps did not push terribly hard. The United States government was in a fairly strong position to resist whatever pressure there was on at least three grounds: The import problem for synthetic fibers was not as acute as for cottons; a somewhat different set of suppliers would be involved and the chances of not being able to get agreement would be increased (by, for instance, Europeans worrying about the market for woolens in the United States); the bigger the package, the harder it was to justify as an exception that would not do lasting damage to the trade-liberalizing process. Perhaps the result was simply an illustration of the reluctance of governments to act until they have to. It was hardly surprising, though, that sooner or later the process that produced the cotton textile arrangement should create trouble in man-made fibers and woolens.

That happened before the end of the decade, and again the issue was precipitated by an American election. When Richard Nixon took office in 1969, he had in his electoral record a far flatter commitment to do something about textile imports than the one made by Kennedy. This time there was no serious official effort to study the situation of the American industry. Bypassing the State Department, the White House made it a matter of high priority to force Japan to limit its exports of all textiles to the United States. Since resistance was much stronger than a decade before, it took several years of difficult and rather heavy-handed diplomacy to get results. The process was influenced by a number of factors: the unilateral measures the United States took in the summer of 1971 affecting trade and the dollar; what seemed to the Japanese a breaking of faith on the return of Okinawa; and the threat of congressional action. Japan gave way, and similar arrangements were made with weaker countries, such as Hong Kong, Taiwan, and Korea.

European countries had refused to go along with the American initiatives, in part because they were more important suppliers of woolens and some other clothing to the United States than they had been of cotton. However, they too felt threatened by the Asian producers and on January 1, 1974, a new multifiber textile agreement replaced the older cotton arrangement. It was, by and large, similar to its predecessor and was also lodged in GATT. The minimum annual increase was set at 6 percent instead of 5. The machinery for international surveillance over the bilateral deals was strengthened, but that has not made as much difference as many people hoped. Much of what was said above about the first agreement applies to the broader arrangement. There is no clear-cut change in the balance between adjustment and protection. However, when the time for renewal of the agreement came in 1977, the countries of the European Community demanded a much freer hand to insist on even greater restriction than had been allowed before. They were reacting partly to the recession of the mid-1970s, and partly, it seems, to their slowness in working out bilateral agreements under the new arrangements. For a few years, at least, the situation of the early 1960s was reversed and the import penetration of LDC and Japanese textiles grew faster in Europe than in the United States—in part, no doubt, because the United States had more quickly made agreements with major suppliers. To make up for lost time, the Community insisted on exceptionally restrictive agreements with a number of countries and on measures to keep the Textiles Surveillance Body from questioning them. Fearing that they had little choice, suppliers accepted; and to keep the Community from dropping out of textile agreements altogether, other countries went along with the weakening of the surveillance arrangements. Thus, this time the continuation of a weakened agreement was regarded as preserving at least some international rules and surveillance against the threat of entirely unilateral action instead of being seen as evading the rules by legitimizing forced export restraints.

There is no need to comment further on the multilateral textile agreements in the perspective of trade policy. But how do they look in terms of industrial policy? Less ambiguous. A concept of orderly transference is discernible in principle, but hardly in practice. The rules were very primitive and were never really more than trade rules. There was no effort to provide any objective measure of market disruption. There was no suggestion of when the "orderly transfer" might be terminated or what condition might eventually be reached. That might have been too much to ask at so early a stage. But the most serious omission was that of effective international surveillance or pressures and procedures to bring about adjustment.

Adding all these things together, one has to conclude that the textile agreements fell considerably short of what was set out in Chapter 3 as the desirable target of a revision of GATT's safeguard clauses. Indeed, a useful way of looking at them is as a kind of industrywide application of escape clauses, which, as we have seen, can be made satisfactory only by the building of some sort of bridge between traditional trade policy and the measures of structural adjustment that we are calling international industrial policy.

The textile agreements were not themselves vehicles of adjustment in any formal sense. When one thinks of how long the cotton agreement ran on with no great diminution of the problem, it can easily be rated a failure. Perhaps, however, one should give it credit for containing the problem to some degree, which may be as much as can be said of its successor as well. That view assumes that without the arrangement importing countries would have resorted to more restrictive measures. It is difficult, though, to know whether ''contain'' is the right word. Exports of textiles and clothing from the developing countries to the industrial world increased over 13 times between 1963 and 1976, far faster than if the 5 or 6 percent formula had been an overall ceiling. In 1976, they amounted to about one-third of all manufactured goods sold by the LDCs to the industrial countries, compared to about one-quarter in 1963. The LDC share of world exports of textiles and clothing has nearly doubled in that time, but the value is still less than half that of the exports of the industrial countries in these categories.[8] These figures tell us nothing about what might have happened without the agreement. They remind us, however, that a good part of the competition in textiles is within the industrial world. Japan continues to be regarded as a problem by the others; Canadian textile protection is aimed to an important degree at the United States; in the European Community textile problems are tied up with the entry of Spain, Portugal, and Greece. Though we tend to think of the

[8]All figures in this paragraph are calculated from General Agreement on Tariffs and Trade (GATT), *Networks of World Trade by Areas and Commodity Classes, 1955–1976*, Geneva, 1978, Table A3.

exports of textiles from developing countries as natural, their production is not necessarily the best use of every country's resources, and the textile agreements may have stimulated production in some countries that was less efficient than that of exports cut off from others.

Aggregates conceal too much. What is needed is a far more careful study of adjustment than is possible here. Some countries adjusted a great deal more than others; are we to assume they would have done less, more, or differently in the absence of the agreement? Is the failure to be laid at the door not of the agreements but of the governments that did not take advantage of the time gained? Is the blame to be put on industry? Some American companies say that Federal Trade Commission limits on mergers keep them from reaching the size they need for efficiency. In Germany, significant adaptation seems to have taken place within relatively small companies with government help. This kind of intraindustry specialization retains the value of commercial ties and keeps up activity in established areas. Governments have been especially concerned with employment and much of the pressure for continued protection in the United States, France, Canada, and other countries arises from the location of textile and clothing production in one-industry and often fairly remote areas. In some of these countries prospects for adjustment are bleak. Although the Swedish government is said to have invoked national security as a reason for limiting imports of boots and shoes, the record is not clear that any country has yet felt it should resist further change because it needed to maintain a textile or clothing industry of a certain size for as long ahead as one could see.

To chart a path for further policy one ought to have some idea about what would be a desirable pattern of world textile production. The most common generalization—that the textile industry should move to developing countries because it is labor-intensive—is oversimplified. A wide range of activities and a number of technologies are involved. Raw materials come from plants, animals, wood, coal, and oil. For some activities it is important to be near rich markets, and for others it is economical to pass products back and forth as they are worked on until they have been around the world and back. What happens in one part of the industry affects other parts, and it is difficult to believe that any given pattern of location can be lasting.

It seems likely that most large industrial countries can have a significant textile and clothing sector that pays its way in the world. The industries would have to be flexible and entrepreneurial. But there is also evidence that the textile sector in most industrial countries is still too big; a substantial part of its labor force is paid wages below the average for industry. But when productivity is low, a wage scale influenced by the average becomes an additional barrier to adjustment and a force for inflation as well. The fringes of the textile industry in some countries probably include workers for whom there is no alternative employment except under conditions of great hardship, and then there is a question of social policy as well as of the cost to the whole economy of protection or its alternatives.

As the textile industry is one in which the range of efficiency among firms is likely to be very great, to protect the weakest is to provide windfalls to the strongest. It is also an industry in which there is a very wide range of activities that involve different sets of skills, different degrees of capital and labor intensiveness, and different advantages of location; all these factors are susceptible to changes in technology. There has always been a fair amount of international division of labor organized by the producers themselves; the *Veredelungswirtschaft* of German firms in the nineteenth century was largely a matter of sending clothing to Eastern Europe for sewing and finishing, just as some finished garments, gray goods, unprinted cloth, and yarns and fibers move around the world today. Three members of the Research Division of GATT, using what are still rather broad categories of products, have shown not only how complex and interconnected the trade is, but how difficult it is to single out gains and losses even if one sticks to simple mercantilist views about exports and imports. "Between 1960 and 1974, imports of textiles and clothing by industrial countries from developing countries increased from $0.7 to $8.4 billion. There was, however, also a strong expansion of exports, particularly of textiles, from industrial to developing countries, which meant that the *net* import surplus of industrial countries was only $2.7 billion in 1974 (as compared with an export surplus of about $1 billion in 1960). Even more significant is the fact that this increased specialization led to an increase in the industrial country exports of textile machinery from $0.3 billion in 1960 to $2.4 billion in 1974—an export gain that is clearly related to the increased imports."[9] For the United States, one could also add exports of cotton.

In the face of such complexity it is no criticism of the textile agreements that they lacked a target in the form of a global pattern of textile production to be aimed at. Instead, one must wonder if a reasonable person could have such a target. We are brought back to one of the basic difficulties of industrial policy: determining what pattern to move toward, even if one can be quite clear what to move away from. The deficiency of the textile agreements as industrial policy is their lack of emphasis on insuring that adjustments dictated by economic advantage and technological change take place even if their pace is slowed so as to reduce the impact of the change on the people involved or, for that matter, on the political processes of the importing countries. It is, of course, not at all surprising that this should be so, since the arrangements not only had their origins in a demand for protection but were constructed so as to give only minimal influence to any countervailing force. The only effective opposition to producer interests in the industrial countries—except for the permitted increase in imports and loopholes in the arrangements or their administration—was the governments of those countries themselves. This suggests that an evolution of trade arrangements into industrial policy measures depends on a changed concept of national interest in countries under pressure to make changes. Perhaps, however, different conclusions are to be drawn from experience in other sectors. (The question of what light the textile experience throws on the nature of the sectoral approach is discussed at the end of the chapter.)

[9]Greece, Portugal, Spain, Turkey, and Yugoslavia are excluded from Western Europe in the list of industrial countries for this calculation. Blackhurst et al., op. cit., p. 13.

## STEEL

The experience in the steel industry has been quite different from that in textiles. It started later, has not been formalized in comprehensive international agreements as yet, and is still mainly a matter concerning the industrial countries. However, there are also some significant similarities: Major changes in the pattern of world production are at the root of the matter. Japan's emergence as a major exporter was a key factor in precipitating the issue. Trade barriers and import competition have been central to the dispute. Once more the response of the United States government to the pressures of domestic producers and labor has been a major factor pushing for international agreement. Of course, the economics of the two industries are quite different, the one with heavy fixed costs requiring very large investments, the other far more mobile. However, as in the case of textiles, technological change and large shifts in international trade have played an important part in the steel developments. An expansion of production in the developing world promises to be a major factor in the future. While the political and security significance of steel to major powers may seem obvious, governments seem to have something of the same view of textiles. Both industries have been the subject of much national industrial policy, but what its intercontinental equivalent will be, if any, remains obscure in both cases.

On a smaller scale, however, steel provides one of the rare examples of international industrial policy: the European Coal and Steel Community. Though the treaty that came into effect in 1952 removed barriers to trade in the heart of Europe, it was not just a trade agreement. It did more than change the political and security face of Europe, though it could never have come into existence if the French and German governments of the day had not seen it in those terms. The industrial policy aspects of the Coal and Steel Community lie in the fact that the Treaty of Paris laid down rules about pricing and transport rates, business practices, and investment. The High Authority it created (now superseded by the Commission of the European Communities) raised and allocated funds and helped in closing down coal and iron mines and encouraging labor to move to new steel plants. Although the initial thrust toward integration spent itself and national industries looked more to their own governments than to the High Authority on crucial matters, it was powers derived from the original treaty (which would reach their maximum when "a manifest crisis" was declared to exist) that were wielded by Vicomte Etienne Davignon of the European Commission in the late 1970s as he tried to get the Community steel producers to adopt measures to cope with the recession and then bring about structural change.

Whether it was those powers or the needs of the moment that gave Davignon and his predecessor Henri Simonet their greatest influence can be debated. They were leading and partly shaping a process by which the Commission, the national governments, and especially the steel producers of the Community, nationalized and private, were trying to deal with the recession. Whether all were agreed that they should also work toward a more lasting adjustment is less clear, especially if it meant a contraction of the industry. The short-run measures were of a classic cartel character, but with close public supervision and indeed leadership. Initially the Commission tried to guide the industry by forecasting demand and recommending that producers limit output and shipments.[10] By mid-1977 the guidance extended to prices for most products, and minimum prices were fixed for reinforcing bars because established producers were being undersold by small Italian mills, the Bresciani. To raise prices while keeping production as high as possible was crucial to both short- and long-run aims. This would give the industry the best return it could get in the circumstances and improve the possibility of making the new investments needed to modernize plants that could no longer compete in world markets. Old capacity would have to be retired and excess capacity sterilized, at least for the

[10] Through Eurofer (The European Confederation of Iron and Steel Industries) the producers worked out arrangements to follow the Commission's lead, apparently including agreements on the amount to be shipped from one Community country to another. How strong this "club" or "cartel" was is a matter of some dispute.

time being and perhaps longer. In all this the Commission and the governments could help, but it was not easy to allocate the burdens and benefits among countries or companies. While the industry generally welcomed the approach, any given producer was tempted to gain a larger share of the market by cutting his prices. And they did. "I live in a world without law," Davignon is supposed to have said as he levied fines and tried to prevent misbehavior.

Support was more general for the efforts to check imports of foreign steel. Japan was already applying a "voluntary" export restraint and the amount of steel coming in from other countries was not great. But the low prices were troublesome and the Community set "reference prices" for imports and a quick antidumping procedure for sales below that level. Then the Commission negotiated arrangements with Japan, South Korea, South Africa, Australia, Brazil, and the nonmember countries of Western and Eastern Europe, which in effect limited the quantities and price of their sales to the Community.

The recession added to the Japanese steel industry's interest in exporting, but the bent was already well established. It was practically built into Japan's very large expansion of capacity and particularly the installation of massive plants using new methods that reduced costs well below those prevalent in the United States or Europe. Understanding very well the risk of a repetition of past patterns that would lead to new restrictions, the Japanese were willing to respond to the signals—or specific proposals—from Europe and the United States about not pushing too deeply into those markets. At one point they were in the position of complaining that when they stuck to the agreed prices they were undersold by Community producers who cheated.

In the Third World, Japanese steel made strong headway, displacing the European product in a number of markets. For the future the great question would be how large a market Japan could expect to keep there in the face of expanding production in the developing countries, not only within major national markets but also on an export basis from centers in Korea, Mexico, Brazil, and Venezuela. But Japan could also contemplate a possible future in the markets of the industrial world, since both

Europe and the United States paid it the compliment of recognizing that Japanese costs were the ones that had to be accepted as something like the standard of competition for the future.

This was most explicit in the case of a new device installed at the beginning of 1978 whereby "trigger prices" were set for steel products coming into the United States. Sales below that level would immediately attract the attention of the Treasury Department, which would pursue a "fast-track" procedure to see if dumping were involved, in which case antidumping duties would be imposed (and in the meantime, if experience was any guide, the suspension of valuation for tariff purposes would hold down imports).[11] The new procedure promised to be far more effective than the slow and cumbersome course usually followed in antidumping matters. The major change, however, was the establishment of what would certainly be seen by most people as a minimum price for steel imports (though that was not, strictly speaking, correct). The trigger prices were based on costs in the Japanese steel industry (assuming operation at about 85 percent of capacity and including the return on capital), to which were added transportation costs and some other charges. Neither the basic data nor the calculations were beyond challenge. There were many administrative problems even if it was assumed that quarterly adjustment would keep the prices up to date in a world where not only technology and wages but transport costs and exchange rates varied. Still, to keep Japan tied into the process made a good deal of sense.

What had brought about the trigger price device was a rash of antidumping suits by American steel companies directed against imports from Western Europe and Japan. There is little doubt that a good number of them were justified; not only did the European industry have a tradition of price cutting for exports whenever the market was weak, but the economics of steel production make it reasonable to sell at any price that contributes to covering fixed costs. Moreover, the Davignon Plan—and var-

---

[11]Sales above the trigger price might possibly be dumping as well, and steel firms could make use of normal procedures; but it was made clear that while it was administering the new arrangement the Treasury could not expeditiously handle any large number of normal antidumping investigations.

ious national or industry efforts before it—was made to order for dumping, since its emphasis was on raising the domestic price. However, the American antidumping law is complex and not altogether predictable. At the best of times it is slow; and with many cases pending, the chances of administrative and even judicial channels becoming blocked were considerable. There was substance to the feeling of many businessmen that even legitimate grievances would not be dealt with promptly and that by the time action was taken, foreign suppliers or American importers could shift to other products for which the process would have to start over again. The chances were good, therefore, that the industry would appeal to Congress, where tests of injury would not be as precisely applied as under the antidumping law. Import quotas might well result.

From the point of view of the United States government, the new device—uncertain as its effects might be—offered the prospect of improving the situation in several ways. It would provide some relief from import pressure and weaken the case for unilateral trade barriers. It would do so in a way that permitted import competition to continue so that the domestic industry was not given a free hand in the home market (though it was able to raise its prices somewhat). The new method would provide protection more expeditiously than the antidumping measures and a more predictable situation than would have resulted from a series of piecemeal decisions. One could think of the new system as expressing a rough judgment about the level of prices at which American producers ought for the most part to be able to compete with imports. There could be little serious complaint from Europe that fair competition was being impeded. The Japanese had a better case; but they had encountered such problems so often that they probably did not see much point in making it, especially as they were already trying to find ways of appeasing American concern about their trade balance and the exchange rate of the yen. [12]

The trigger price system was part of a larger program of con-

[12]Whether American officials actually reasoned this way is another matter. I am not writing history, but this kind of analytical approach to the argument has relevance to the future.

siderable interest for the study of industrial policy. Before discussing it, however, a few words should be said about some earlier episodes which remind us that the problems of the American steel industry predate the recession of the mid-1970s.

## A New American Approach?

Once very high, American steel tariffs were substantially reduced throughout the postwar period. By the end of the Kennedy Round, tariffs in North America, Europe, and Japan were similar at roughly 8 percent; this is not negligible, and effective protection seems to be above the industrial average, but tariffs are not regarded as the major determinants of trade. Still, it was almost immediately after the Kennedy Round ended that American imports increased sharply and the industry turned to the government for help. Negotiating directly with foreign producers in 1968, the State Department got commitments limiting Community and Japanese sales to the United States, first for three years and then for three more on a still tighter basis. Japanese and Europeans seem to have agreed among themselves on how to divide the American market and also on the level of Japanese sales to Europe. Even within the Common Market various national measures were taken to limit competition. To a degree, the industries and governments were simply reacting to temporary economic difficulty. With an upturn in demand the formal restraints on sales to the United States were not extended. However, some people thought longer-run factors were at work that made for declining competitiveness of the American industry.

There were a number of aspects to the problem. The European and Japanese industries had been largely rebuilt at the end of the war, but change came more slowly in the United States. Heavy investments in existing plant and the gravitational pull of existing large centers of production slowed experimentation with new technology that was much used abroad and created resistance to shifts in location that had provided important economies in Japan and Europe. It was also not easy to finance new investment, as limited profitability held back both self-financing and the raising of funds in capital markets. Wages were high, and a strong union responded quickly to rises in the cost of living, whether or not they were matched by increases in productivity. The industry's theory of pricing was that all increases in costs had to be passed on to the consumer and would not discourage demand. When any of the leading producers raised prices, others followed suit. At the same time, the industry claimed that government pressure plus imports kept prices too low to permit the level of earnings needed for investment. Occasional strikes and some peaks of demand that went beyond what domestic suppliers could meet gave foreign producers opportunities to sell, which led some of them—and the American importers—to keep a foothold in the market.

It was not very surprising, then, that by the mid-1970s, with demand slack in all industrial countries, imports should be rising again. The Europeans were selling at whatever prices they could get; new Japanese capacity set the pace. The American industry asked for various kinds of measures to check imports and was successful in an escape clause action that led to quotas being put on stainless steel in 1976. In the same year one of its principal spokesmen made it clear that he did not see a permanent solution in trade barriers. Free trade versus protection was no longer the real choice. The role of governments was too strong, and this falsified competition. How could the private, unsubsidized American industry cope with import competition stimulated by foreign governments that helped their industries in a variety of ways? R. Heath Larry, a leading spokesman for the industry, said that what was needed was "an international forum in which government policies relating to steel trade may be kept under surveillance and kept in comparative balance."[13]

To move in that direction, he said, the United States should call a conference of developed and developing producer nations to do three things. First, it could examine the forces that would

[13]R. Heath Larry, "A Trade Policy for Steel: Is There a Problem, Is There an Answer?" The American Iron and Steel Institute (AISI), 84th General Meeting, New York, N.Y., May 27, 1976, 12 pp. (Mimeographed.) Quotes on pp. 114–115 are also from Mr. Larry's speech. Mr. Larry was at the time vice chairman of U.S. Steel Corp.; he subsequently became president of the National Association of Manufacturers.

shape the industry for some years ahead. Second, the conference would "create a consultative mechanism in some form, within the GATT or elsewhere, which would keep steel trade flows under review and which would oversee the application of internationally agreed upon rules and procedures under which nations could employ temporary safeguards against market disruption under agreed circumstances." Third, if sufficient progress in that direction were made, the United States industry would be prepared to move to eliminate tariffs and other trade barriers (including export controls on scrap or other raw materials). A key result of this process would be "some rules . . . which would define when governmental reactions would be proper in the face of interventions by other governments in their economies in a manner which had trade-distorting results." There was no hope of ending such intervention.

A forum, surveillance, rules and procedures, the definition of proper governmental reactions to interventions—these are all the ingredients of an international industrial policy. And that is what the American steel industry has been seeking for some time, though the term is never used. Those speaking for it have not always been as explicit as Mr. Larry or as bold on the freeing of trade; some have wanted quotas imposed whenever imports reached a certain level, or domestic output fell below a certain share of capacity, or some other event signaled trouble. No doubt there is not full agreement in the industry on many other issues as well. As American businessmen must, the steelmasters have said they want no cartel arrangements, only fair competition; but they seem to feel sure that the result will be a strong American industry capable of meeting all or most of the domestic demand. Perhaps that is only natural. The need for such an industry is a cardinal point whenever steel makes its case for one or another kind of public action. Very likely it is taken for granted (and probably correctly) that Europeans, Japanese, Russians, and citizens of other major countries want the same situation for themselves. But how the result is to be assured by international action is not so clear. Nor is it evident how the United States and the other countries can be sure that a more or less guaranteed home market and an efficient and competitive steel industry can be made to go hand in hand.

From 1973 through 1976, imports averaged 13 percent of American domestic steel production. Well above the level of the 1960s, this seemed a period of "relative stability" to Mr. Larry. But by late 1977 the figure was 20 percent, and imports supplied half the growth of domestic demand which Larry had wanted met "in major part by domestic producers." Naturally the industry called for protection and began a series of antidumping actions. The new Carter administration feared that to check imports would lead to higher prices at a time when inflation was one of the most serious problems facing the country. However, there was no getting away from the fact that the closing of several steel mills and the laying off of workers at others were contributing to the country's other big problem, unemployment. An interdepartmental task force chaired by Anthony Solomon, Under Secretary of the Treasury, dug into the matter, conferred with industry and labor, and came out with the trigger-price plan—and something more.[14]

The report of the task force made plain that imports were not the sole source of difficulty, but put the domestic problem in the setting of "the world steel glut"[15] and the damage to foreign relations threatened by the flood of antidumping cases. It stressed the need to act because of unemployment and especially the effects on whole communities of the closing of plants that were major local employers. But it also made some very basic statements that looked beyond the immediate situation and referred to the conditions that created the need for "a special government program. . . . The industry is one of the Nation's largest and is critical to its economy and security. . . . A large reduction in U.S. capacity in this basic industry threatens future problems for the economy . . . . " Some of the plants were closed because they could not be easily modernized, and the industry needed to use new technology and shift locations. The difficulty of getting investment was compounded by uncertainty about future national policies on pollution, energy, and environmental matters. Although it was up to the industry and not the government to

[14]*A Comprehensive Program for the Steel Industry*, Report to the President, Task Force, Anthony M. Solomon, Chairman, December 1977, 35 pp. (Mimeographed.)

[15]Ibid. Quotes on p. 116 were also taken from this Task Force report.

decide what to do, the government must help with certain clear aims: to "stimulate efficiency and enable the industry to compete fairly. . . . To help ease the burden of adjustment to market trends for both industry and labor. . . . To provide meaningful incentives for plant and equipment modernization . . . " and "to expedite relief from unfair import competition, but to do so in a manner which will not preclude healthy competition in the U.S. market."

This reads remarkably like a national industrial policy for steel and an enlightened one at that. The report went on to make a number of specific recommendations in addition to the installation of the trigger-price system. Several have to do with aid to communities where plants are shut and the guaranteeing of loans or other forms of aid that would make other shutdowns unnecessary. A speeding up of depreciation of new equipment was proposed and note taken of a commitment from the industry to use the increased cash flow from the whole program for modernization. Transportation policies and government aid to R & D were to be looked at. The Department of Justice was urged to speed up its procedures for giving advance approval to certain kinds of mergers and joint ventures. Finally, the task force recommended "the establishment of a tripartite committee of industry, labor and government representatives as a mechanism to ensure a continuing cooperative approach to the problems and progress of the steel industry."

Such an agency is probably unprecedented in American government-business relations. It is certainly different from anything now in operation in a major industry. Almost as much can be said about the whole program. Will it work, and if so how? This is not an essay in vaticination, but questions can be asked. It is far from clear, for example, how far the U.S. steel industry is in fact committed to this program. It is certainly not committed to the trigger-price plan if it lets in too much foreign steel. But if times improve and import competition slackens or at least stays at a level the industry can get used to, who can be confident that significant changes will take place in efficiency and investment? As profits rise, statements by presidents and board chairmen suggest that it is not only governments that put off acting until they have to. But it is not to be taken for granted that the government program is bound to be successful. Measures to keep open obsolete plants will not improve efficiency even if they ease the problems of communities; to find alternative activities requires ideas about other sectors of the economy. Is the United States government really in a position to provide significant help in R & D to the steel industry? At inflated construction costs the industry will have trouble financing new investment. If profits increase, what trade-off will the United Steelworkers make between wage increases and the kind of long-run job security that goes with competitiveness? Should the government promise more financial aid or more protection?

### Expansion and Contraction Elsewhere

Questions have to be asked about the future of the European steel industry too. Even if Davignon or another Commissioner in charge of industrial policy succeeds in getting the continuing cooperation of the industry on current problems, there are few signs that it accepts the idea that a sound future requires not only modernization but also contraction (which seems to be Davignon's view). Nor is it to be taken for granted that the public and private steel industries of different countries have a common view of the future. Some people oppose the new approach because they think it will lead to government-enforced cartels. Others suspect that no matter how good Davignon's intentions and ideas, neither he nor the whole Commission will be able to dominate the industry in the end. But the issue is not just Commission vs. industry; the national governments have their own ideas about reorganization and the pattern of production and employment. In the fall of 1978 the Italian government advanced funds to its steel producers while Belgium nationalized firms to keep them from failing. In France the large accumulation of loans to steel firms from the government and the mostly nationalized banks were turned into equity. Changes in management and organization would follow, it was announced, and some obsolete steelworks would be closed, notably in Lorraine. Whether the increased responsibility of the government for the conduct of the industry would really make it possible to carry out these drastic steps or whether brave words would fade before popular pressure remains to be seen. The need for this great change made it look as if past policies had failed, but what kind of steel industry would the government of France—or the rest of Europe—support for the future?

It is less difficult to think what Japan's future steel policy is likely to be. The industry will remain ahead of Europe and America in efficiency and export capacity for some time to come. It will have a major domestic market as its base, and whatever has to be done to adapt to changing home needs will be handled as such things are in Japan. Steel remains, it seems, one of the industries close to and dependent on government guidance.[16] The large question concerns the future of the export market in the Third World (and Australia). In free competition there is little doubt that Japan would beat Europe, but the competition may not be so free if the Europeans try to hold their steel export markets in the OPEC countries and whatever other LDCs they try to work out special relations with. In the long run, however, the larger Japanese question about steel in the Third World will be the one posed earlier about competition in the area itself, protection and intra-LDC trade. Even if Japan could expand production more cheaply than smaller producers, as seems likely to be true for some time to come, it may well encounter new trade barriers. There are a number of ways Japan could or might have to accommodate itself to some decline in these markets. China might provide major new possibilities for a while, though eventually it seems bound to be a competitor. Perhaps by that time Japan may be ready to reduce its own steelmaking on the grounds that it can use its resources more efficiently in some other activity.

Before then the question of Third World steel is likely to have taken on other dimensions. Exports to the old industrial centers already take place; to hold them down was a fairly easy matter during the period described above. Once the difficulties of the

[16]James C. Abegglen and Thomas M. Hout, "Facing Up to the Trade Gap with Japan," *Foreign Affairs*, Fall 1978, pp. 146–168.

mid-1970s are overcome, the question will appear in a new guise: Will Europe and the United States, and eventually Japan, be prepared to accept imports of steel from these countries on any large scale, or will they seek some permanent ceiling—if not to avoid dislocation at home, then to retain a high level of self-sufficiency? Their approach ought to be shaped in part by a view of how the world steel industry is likely to evolve. Is it to be the textile story all over again? At first glance that seems most implausible, and it is easy to make a long list of differences. But there are some interesting facts to bear in mind.

The developing countries' share of world steel production more than doubled between 1966 and 1976. That still left it at only 7.4 percent, versus 60 percent for the developed market economies; but in those years the share of North America and the European Community combined fell from 51.3 to 39 percent.[17] Over half the LDC share came from Latin America (especially Brazil and Mexico) and much of the rest from India and South Korea. There are good reasons to suppose that this shift will continue. Steel is used more at early stages of industrial development than later on, and local producers have an advantage. Since technology is readily available, lower wages count. Capital intensity is high and energy requirements are large, but the skills required—at least for basic steel—are below the average for manufacturing as a whole. (The ratio of R & D expenditures to sales was only 17 percent of the average of German industry in 1970.) Though high initial capital costs present an obstacle, this is an industry that is bound to grow in the newly industrializing countries (not the least developed) and one in which they are likely to have a considerable comparative advantage over the older industrial centers (but not in all activities or when there are major technological changes or capital is scarce).

Without pressing the textile analogy, with all its weaknesses,

[17]Since steel is cyclical, single-year figures can be misleading; but the trend is steady through the 1970s. These and the other facts and figures in these paragraphs come from an excellent study: Frank Wolter, *Perspectives for the International Location of the Steel Industry*, Working Paper No. 60, Institut für Weltwirtschaft an der Universität Kiel, Kiel, Federal Republic of Germany, October 1977. (Mimeographed.)

one can see that there are bound to be long-run problems of adjustment. The story of the last 30 years will be continued, with new actors playing the parts of recovering Europe and expanding Japan, though playing them somewhat differently and probably at a different pace. But for the older industrial centers there are some stages of adjustment to be looked at—as was true for the United States in the early postwar years (when its strong export position was, however, known to be exceptional). To give up exports to local production is common; to give them up to a new competitor is not unusual. Brazil, Korea, and the rest seem likely to supply more of the needs of the developing world. But they will also want to get hard currency by selling to the industrial world. To accept competition in their home markets on any scale can be hard for the older steel industries. But the case for doing so even at the cost of reducing domestic production may be strong in terms of economics and the use of resources. As we saw in Chapter 2, however, efficiency and economy are not the only factors that move governments, and steel is one of the industries in which other considerations weigh heavily, whether their focus is domestic or foreign.

### The Possibilities of International Agreement

In steel as in other things, international issues arise largely from what is done nationally. In turn, the national measures are to a degree shaped by the international ones—or at least by foreign reactions. Measures taken in Europe lent color to the American steel industry's claim of unfair competition; the antidumping cases forced Europeans to see that there was a limit to how much of their problem they could export. There were consultations as the Solomon and Davignon plans took shape; and, of course, there were major negotiations with the Japanese. By mid-1978, when the main lines of approach in each area were discernible, though not firmly set, consultations had led to more formal action. A steel committee was set up in the OECD that automatically brought into play some significant smaller producers, such as Austria, Sweden, Spain, Canada, and Australia. Several key nonmembers, such as India, Brazil, South Korea, and Mexico, were to be invited to participate in the committee's work; none showed an immediate disposition to do so. It did not follow that there would be no more tripartite conversations, but the new forum was interesting.

Like most OECD committees, this one was to study the situation, exchange information, and "develop common perspectives regarding emerging problems. . . ."[18] It was also to "review and assess government policies," an activity that could be highly meaningful or pro forma but lends special interest to the invitation to the developing countries—and to their response. Going beyond the ordinary arrangements for OECD committees was an agreement to follow some guidelines in the shaping of policy: All actions affecting steel and steelmaking materials are to be reported, and countries agree to consult with the others whenever asked. Measures should be as limited and temporary as possible and avoid severe disruptions of trade even if they are domestic measures taken to deal with serious difficulties. Price guidelines should conform to the antidumping code, be exceptional (some circumstances are described), be limited regarding high and low prices, and be dropped as soon as they are not needed. The participants are to establish programs to transfer steelworkers affected by readjustment to other activities and to exchange information on these matters. The earlier OECD agreement on adjustment policies (see Chapter 3) is invoked to stress that "domestic policies to sustain steel firms during crisis periods should not shift the burden of adjustment to other countries. . . ." In general, plants that "cannot become commercially viable within a reasonable period of time" should be closed.[19] Export credits should not lead to "destructive competition." Participants are not to violate GATT rules, the validity of which are reaffirmed.

No one can tell what such agreements will amount to before they are tried out or what the OECD committee will prove ca-

[18]"Problems of the Steel Industry . . . and a Search for Solutions," *The OECD Observer*, no. 95, November 1978, pp. 27–29. This is the annex to the decision setting up the committee.

[19]OECD Press Release, June 15, 1978, op. cit.

pable of doing. If vehicles were policies, drafters and administrators would ride to success. Even if the committee becomes a permanent fixture, much will depend on how the European Community, the United States, and Japan see the steel problem and how they treat one another. The international steel policy that could be produced by the three centers could develop in at least three possible ways.

The first is that they would try to have as little to do with one another as possible. This would be possible only if each decided to focus on the domestic economy and made believe the others were not there. This does not seem very plausible and would probably really turn out to mean that there were sporadic difficulties of the sort there ha've always been in the past. Perhaps the existence of the OECD committee would significantly alter the way these problems were handled, but not if the channel had been allowed to silt up, as the hypothesis suggests.

A second possibility is that Europe, Japan, and the United States would try to reach some understandings about their trading relations. If the trigger-price system were continued and the Europeans stuck to their arrangements for negotiating import prices, the effects of these measures and perhaps even the prices themselves (the formulas are not sacred) might be involved. For Europe as well as the United States there would be an advantage in having some foreign competition to keep the domestic industry performing well and to take its measure, so to speak. One cannot have too much confidence in this device if the amount of competition is also to be limited. A ceiling on trade or the occasional use of export restraints might come into play. It might even be possible that the governments would agree on some price ranges or sets of products in which a fairly free play of competition could take place. At the other end of the scale lies market sharing of a traditional cartel sort.[20]

In the same category, a rather different kind of trade understanding would establish conditions for fair competition and the boundaries of government intervention, in the manner suggested

[20]Frequently called for in Europe, this was considered but rejected by Washington in favor of the trigger-price system. U.S. Department of the Treasury, *News*, January 27, 1978, p. 13. (Mimeographed.)

by Heath Larry. This kind of thing is very close to the arrangements about nontariff barriers and trade-distorting practices worked out in the MTN and the principles set out for the OECD committee. The question arises, then, whether fuller, stronger, or more specific agreements might be made for steel than for trade generally. Or might the opposite be true, because countries attached too much importance to steel to trust to competition? Another issue that runs through all these questions is whether the three steel centers would establish special relations among themselves or, as in normal trading arrangements, apply all measures more or less equally to other countries.

The third possibility is that Europe, Japan, and the United States might recognize that trade rules are of secondary importance if each is pursuing a steel policy that must serve other purposes than simply permitting international competition. They might then see whether there were ways of defining their objectives that would permit cooperation or even mutual assistance. If, for example, they accepted the idea that in each of the three centers the steel industry must be sufficiently large to meet most of the domestic needs most of the time, they might negotiate about the necessary percentage of self-sufficiency and leave the remaining margin for trade. (Something like this has been proposed for dealing with agriculture; the analogy is fairly good.)

While a marginal amount of foreign trade (20 percent of the market?) would create some pressure for efficiency, every country would probably need some internal arrangement that moved in the same direction (it might be competition). Otherwise, each risks being saddled with a high-cost steel industry that will damage the international competitiveness of the rest of its economy. Or, to retain the competitiveness in, say, automobiles, a government may find itself subsidizing automobile production to offset the higher price of domestic steel or providing automobile producers with compensatory tariffs against imports.[21]

Some combination of all these possibilities would fit perfectly

[21]Both these devices were once used in American trade policy. The woolen industry long got part of its protection to offset the higher cost of protected wool. Cotton goods exporters were once subsidized because support prices made their raw cotton more expensive than that of competitors abroad.

well with the idea of an international forum to deal with steel. Another dimension of the problem is that governments may have to keep an eye on their own industrialists lest they try to carve up what pie there is for themselves by cartel arrangements, thus further frustrating the task of generating efficiency. Since new investment is going to be important at least in Europe and the United States, international discussions might concern this activity. Though steel industries have tended to be quite "national" in the past, a certain amount of European investment in the United States and American investment in Europe has developed. Obviously this affects national steel policies, since policy makers have to consider what may be the results of growing internationalization of the industry or the emergence of multinational firms producing steel in several different areas. Import control often gives an impetus to investment from abroad. Would it further the aims of an American steel policy if Japanese steelmaking processes were introduced into the United States by Japanese companies? Would there be a United States preference for joint ventures with American firms? As the example suggests, still another issue that in one way or the other enters into an international policy is the flow of technology and the related questions of patents and processes, their freedom or control, and the stimulation and financing of the research and development behind them. Some thought also needs to be given to the tendency that has appeared (at least in the United States) for steel-producing companies to diversify their activities into other fields, often related lines of machinery and equipment.

No countries have yet taken giant strides toward an international industrial policy for steel. But what they have done on a national basis (or the Community basis in Europe) has made it just a little easier—and perhaps even more important—to raise such questions than it would be for other industries. Our analysis has not yet gone far enough to warrant offering very clear opinions about which of the possibilities it would be best to pursue, though it is not hard to see what is not so desirable about many of them. It is also quite likely that a more probable line of development is suggested by what the Solomon report says of the future of the trigger-price system:

An expansion of the world economy in future years will gradually eliminate the ''overhang'' of excess steel production capacity. As a result, pricing practices in world markets will return to more normal patterns and the need for a special program for dealing with import prices will recede.

This program will be reviewed from time to time to insure its consistency with the original concerns. . . . When conditions warrant, the system will be terminated and the more traditional procedures restored.[22]

The intent is clear; to foresee perpetuation of an emergency measure is neither wise nor prudent. Because the protection given to the steel industry against imports was the most visible part of the program, the Carter administration did not want to encourage other industries to see steel as an example. But the future can be no more visible in Washington than elsewhere.

## OTHER SECTORS

No other sector arrangements require quite as much attention as textiles and steel—which is just as well, considering how little we may learn from summaries. A word or two about a few other industries will, however, suggest some of the kinds of industrial policy questions that can arise.

Shipbuilding has been a chronically troubled industry subsidized in many countries. The recession of the mid-1970s forced it dramatically onto the agenda of the European Community and Japan. (The United States is of secondary importance in this matter since it builds ships only for the sheltered American market; but that protection narrows the world market.) It became clear that the efforts of each to deal with its own problem worsened that of others so that all were spending to offset the spending of others with no great amelioration. Efforts to limit subsidies provided an approach that had very little success as capacity kept pressing on demand. Proposals to eliminate or sterilize ''excess capacity''—as judged by current needs or according to estimates of long-run future demand—precipitated several clas-

[22]Solomon, op. cit., p. 20.

sical disputes. Were all to cut equally, regardless of efficiency? Was the base to be capacity, even if it had been unused, or would actual recent production be a fairer standard? How could cuts be carried beyond a certain point when shipbuilding was the only activity in certain areas? Did it make sense simply to spread the cuts over a number of regions so that the capacity of each to support its people in the future was reduced? Political sensitivity made governments want to keep a free hand in cutting back, but that was hardly compatible with an effective international agreement. And then there was South Korea. Increasingly, that country was taking away orders from Japan, the most efficient of the other producers. It was also not interested in measures to reduce its sales and was expanding, not cutting back, its capacities. If Japan or the Community kept their nationals from buying Korean ships, how would they compete with operators based in Greece, Panama, Singapore, or Hong Kong?

The building of ships is antediluvian; the building of aircraft is of the twentieth century. But there are similarities: Both activities have to do with security as well as economy; almost everyone wants some capacity in the field, usually more than can be sustained by ordinary commerce; the market is international but much of the employment local. However, a distinctive characteristic of the aircraft industry is that a relatively small number of very large orders, both civilian and military, can spell the life and death of firms which governments are rarely willing to see fail. The ability to produce the most modern aircraft is limited, and not to have the most modern products can be damaging. A government may wish to go all out to support its domestic aircraft producer by insisting that the national airline buy from him; but if the product falls short, the airline will suffer, and prestige as well as profits will be affected.

Increasingly, the tactics that governments employ (and manufacturers respond to) is to insist that substantial portions of the aircraft they buy be produced at home and sometimes by their own nationals. Subcontracting, joint ventures, and investments are involved. The contractor may buy local products for use in its other work. Governments are often after much more than just local sales and employment; they want the foreign (usually

American) firm to provide them with new industrial and technical capabilities. Another approach is for several countries to pool their efforts in research or production so as to share costs, get the gains of size, and establish a position to compete (again usually with the Americans) that would be beyond what could be done by one country alone. Long highly touted in Europe, this approach continues to have both validity and advocates, though its reputation is somewhat marred. Some failures have been spectacular and costly as in the case of the Concorde. Others are registered in inefficiency, poor performance, and the absence of the expected advantages. In part this is because the principle of the *juste retour*, which says that everyone should have a share in production, research, etc., commensurate with his investment, is not often the formula for efficiency.

That there are national industrial policies about aircraft production is clear, even though they are not always so clear or consistent themselves. This is one of the sectors in which industrial policy is especially concerned with the preservation of specific companies as producing units and repositories of technology. It is almost equally clear that the international element in the industry is so strong that in different ways and to different degrees there are elements of international industrial policy in what is done, even when there is no formal joint venture or shared production. When, as he did in mid-1978, a Prime Minister of Britain devotes a major part of a visit to Washington to discussions about aircraft procurement and the implication of alternative possibilities concerning the production of certain kinds of equipment or engines in England, and then all this has to be weighed against another set of conditions involving European instead of American firms, we understand how important this kind of industrial policy is.

Not only are national decisions affected by international considerations; what each country does shapes the international industry. For that reason, the appearance fairly late in the Tokyo Round of an American proposal for an international agreement on aircraft production was not as implausible as many people first thought. While simply the elimination of tariffs or rules about government aid was unlikely to prove satisfactory, the interest

127

of many countries in having some national capacity and the cost and difficulty of anyone (outside the Soviet Union) duplicating American capabilities meant that ways might be found of recognizing a common interest that both increased efficiency and shared its benefits. But the willingness to follow through remained to be demonstrated.

To juxtapose ships and airships is to point to another sector, arms production and trade. Although its primary concern is chiefly (and always should be) security and politics, private and public economic aims shape much of what is done. Pentagon officials making their case to Congress have stressed the contribution of arms exports to the balance of payments; all over Europe the employment resulting from exports of machine guns, tanks, and munitions is noticed; even nominally disarmed Japan has thought of exporting unarmed naval vessels from its empty shipyards. It is a field dominated by government procurement, where the economics of comparative advantage takes second place and surpluses do not press on the market (or the price) in quite the usual way. There is an after-market, since military forces have to be kept up to date and in repair, and a secondhand market of accordionlike characteristics. To keep a capacity for arms production in an emergency, it is helpful to sell abroad when domestic opportunities are exhausted. When the new money in the oil world was turned into power in very old-fashioned ways, the significance of arms exports as a way to pay fuel bills grew in the East and in the West. As the recession dragged on, it struck an increasing number of people in Europe that arms expenditures created jobs, a demand for products that did not have to be used, and a flow of public funds for uses that were politically more acceptable than many others. A full picture of industrial policies can no longer leave aside the state's role as producer as well as consumer in the old traffic once conducted by private entrepreneurs who were sometimes called merchants of death.

One could not say that there is anything resembling an international industrial policy for chemicals, unless it is the policy of the companies themselves. A relatively small number of giants dominate the chemical world, in contrast to the thousands of producers involved in the textile industry (which is very important to these giants and they to it). In contrast to steel, these are highly international companies; most of them operate all over the globe. Like the textile and steel industries, the chemical industry was much affected by the recession of the mid-1970s—to the extent that many people believed international action was needed and some was taken. As in the case of the other two industries, it is clear that the chemical industry's problems are not all cyclical; analysis and sensible action both have to be put in structural terms.

Only the problems, not what might be done about them, can be sketched here. The most obvious and general is excess capacity. The recession and the delayed recovery would be enough to explain that, but there is more. Before the oil crisis there was a boom, with expanding markets for many chemical products. Technology was changing, so there was always a need to start something new, even when the old plants were still producing well. Oligopolistic competition makes everyone do what everyone else is doing or is thought to be about to do. Consequently the chemical industry and particularly its petrochemical branch invested and expanded greatly.[23] Economies of scale and the elaboration of interconnecting processes make it attractive to build enormous installations, and it has been common to create capacity far ahead of the world's needs for the next few years. For what seemed to be good and sufficient reasons, many of these new installations were in the industrialized countries near their greatest markets.

Then came the quadrupling of the price of oil. The costs of producing petrochemicals rose with it, throwing doubt on the economic viability of much that the industry was committed to, including plants that would not come on stream for several years. A second consequence of the rise in oil prices was that for many of the oil-producing countries a sound, natural, and wise step in their own development seemed to be to establish industries built

[23]It is awkward to have to generalize about an exceptionally complex industry, but there is no alternative. Thus all the statements have major exceptions; many refer only to certain parts of the industry; companies are differently affected according to their mix of activities.

on oil and gas (which they were flaring at an extraordinary rate), i.e., petrochemicals. It is quite posible that the importance of saving transport costs by producing near the raw materials was exaggerated. The cost of establishing complex industrial centers in areas with little infrastructure or few ancillary industries and services is clearly high. After several years of activity the results were less striking than they were expected to be. Nevertheless it seems inevitable that a considerable addition to world capacity will result from this activity; and if capital costs are ignored, cheap raw material will give the OPEC countries a marked advantage. Though the existing producers may be uneasy at that prospect, they have not thought it wise (or possible) to stay out of these new developments. They are providing technology and expertise and will sometimes have a continuing commercial interest. But how much control they will have in the end, especially over marketing, and how they will use it, remain matters for debate. However cautious and restrained they may wish to be, one blunt fact that cannot be burked is that in a competitive market for petrochemicals a country (say, Saudi Arabia) that offers them in sales tied to the oil that everyone needs has a distinct advantage.[24]

A second rather special set of circumstances has added to the worries of the chemical industry. A very large expansion of chemical production is under way in the Soviet Union, especially in fertilizers and basic chemicals. The plants are for the most part being built by Western companies who, by Soviet practice and their own wish to have the business, are required to take part of their payment in the product of the plants. Calculations made in good times about what could be absorbed created problems when demand in the West fell and threaten to be even more burdensome in a period of general oversupply. Even so, when the Western taker is Courtaulds or ICI or one of the big German or French companies, they are often able to internalize the strain so as to avoid cutting prices or upsetting their own production

[24]On these issues I have relied heavily on the excellent studies on Saudi and Iranian petrochemical developments that Louis Turner and James Bedore were making at Chatham House during the time I was working on this book (see the Critical Bibliography).

schedules more than they have to. But when smaller companies, or firms that are not chemical companies at all, have to take Soviet products in part payment of their earnings, they are mainly anxious to turn the barter into money, even if that means throwing supplies on an already weak market. Even bigger companies may have problems if they have to take large quantities from the East. Eventually, Soviet capacity will be very great in some lines; the many Western partners will have been paid off and the Soviet government will surely try to see how much hard currency it can earn by selling to the West.

It is not at all clear that this problem is as serious as a number of people in the European chemical industry feel it is. For one thing, European governments have a good deal of experience in keeping out communist products they do not want, and they have mechanisms that work fairly well to make sure they are sold at the going domestic price in the West. A hardening line and tighter controls ought to be able to deal with much of the trouble—it will be called Soviet dumping, whether it is or not. But there may be some opposition from Western exporters interested in keeping up their sales to the communist countries and from bankers who want to collect on their large credits. There is also the possibility that the Soviets will divert their chemicals to third markets where people who do not produce the same things at home are rightly always happy to get bargains, dumped or not. However, there is little chance for the Russians to earn hard currency that way, and they may even find themselves competing with OPEC petrochemicals or other Third World suppliers of some products. Beyond that, the Russians are interested in maximizing their earnings and have been quite willing to sell at going prices during most of the postwar period. One can imagine their changing under pressure, but it is certainly not to be taken for granted that they will do so.

Still, it is understandable for Western companies to worry when this problem comes on top of all the others. Even without any significant Soviet dumping, the recession stimulated the formation of cartels in Europe in the late 1970s. The industry has a history of such practices which, though not altogether successful, did somewhat better in the 1920s and 1930s, from their members' point of view, than the steel cartels did. There was some official sympathy for this approach, especially in view of the threat of long-lasting surplus capacity; and the industrial policy part of the Commission of the European Community helped to organize a cartel for synthetic fibers. There was, however, a sharp reaction, and a majority of the Commission overruled the plan. No doubt further efforts will be made to devise international measures to deal with the problems of the chemical industry, and if they fail there will be national measures. National or international, these measures will have to deal with the same sets of problems: capacity greater than demand; competition among major producers; import controls, especially in Western Europe but perhaps in North America as well; the extent to which these import controls will favor supplies from OPEC and other Third World countries over those from the Soviet Union or Eastern Europe; and how much a government should give preferred treatment to the foreign ventures in which its own chemical companies are involved.

The electronics industry lends itself not at all to a thumbnail sketch, in part for the reasons that make it an exceptionally fertile field for the study of industrial policy. It raises all the basic questions. Can one speak of a single industry that ranges from pocket gadgets to the greatest computers? At one end there is mass production par excellence. One product after another is becoming a household object in large parts of the world: transistor radios; television; cheap pocket calculators, derived from sophisticated tools of statisticians and space engineers; a new watch industry with practically nothing in common with the old one except the customers. The communications industry requires all kinds of mass-produced equipment that works through an assortment of highly sophisticated devices that are practically hand-crafted, such as satellites. Moreover, a key characteristic of the electronics industry has been the size and speed of change in its technology. When they first appeared, the microcircuits, transistors, and other devices that go into computers were identified with the technological lead of the United States. But in half a decade a *cause célèbre* of the "export of jobs" was the shift in production to Taiwan, Singapore, and other places where cheap skilled labor was to be found. Then in another few years parts of the activity moved back to the United States as a new degree of automation of the production lines was introduced. The process goes on: Japan gives way to Korea in black-and-white TV production but has to sign an Orderly Marketing Agreement (OMA) with the United States limiting exports of color TVs and looking forward to Japanese investment in their manufacture in the United States, which has taken place on a large scale.

Thus we find problems of adjustment somewhat comparable to those in textiles. But much of the electronics industry is carried on in great multinational firms, producing and marketing around the world. At the same time, invention and innovation in this high-technology industry are said to stem more from smaller firms. What the giants do is provide the economies of scale in production and, above all, distribution. One close student of the subject judges that "the primary causes for the decline of the European computer industry were not technological but commercial."[25]

While the industrial importance of advanced electronics technology seems obvious, the reasons almost every European country tried to develop a computer industry lay as much in the identification of the industry with modernity and power.[26] But a good case could be made for the view that the failures lay less in lack of power to support the symbols or in a "technological gap" than in the economics of the industry. A close study of what happened in France, where major efforts were made for years to build an independent computer industry, led one American scholar to say, "The French experience suggests the limits on a government's ability to shape the growth of a domestic

---

[25]Nicolas Jéquier, "Computers," in Raymond Vernon (ed.), *Big Business and the State*, Harvard University Press, Cambridge, Mass., 1974, p. 199.

[26]"Rightly or wrongly, computers have come to symbolize the essential power of the second industrial revolution; and the efforts of countries . . . to preserve a national computer industry in the face of immense technological and economic odds are not so much a fight against the apparent rationality of industrial specialization as an attempt to retain some form of real power by preserving the symbol of power. The less the real power, the more important the symbol." Ibid., p. 195.

industry that forms an integral part of an international marketplace."[27]

Perhaps as much as any other industry, electronics in its various manifestations has been the object of national industrial policies, defensive, initiatory, and occasionally adaptive. For the devising of a reasonable international industrial policy it presents almost all the problems dealt with in earlier pages and those yet to come as well.

Of considerable importance for industrial policy is the growth of a sector that is not truly a sector: services.[28] A worldwide phenomenon, it is particularly marked in the most highly developed industrial countries, for which reason some people rather oddly call them "postindustrial." Measured by jobs, the expansion of services has been particularly marked compared to manufacturing, mining, farming, and other activities. The contribution to national income is less clear, partly because government services, education, and other major segments of the service "industries" have a product that is not easy to quantify. One reason the "postindustrial" label seems wrong is that much of the demand for services stems from the production of goods (research, designing, distributing, marketing, advertising, selling, financing) and not as a substitute for it. The generalizations into which people who know better frequently slip have produced a great deal of nonsense about services. After all, few propositions apply equally to barbers, bankers, bailiffs, singers, stockbrokers, and streetcleaners.[29] Emphasis is often put on the supposed lack of international trade in services, though in fact there is much;

[27]John Zysman, "French Electronics Policy: The Costs of Technological Independence," in S. J. Warnecke and E. N. Suleiman (eds.), *Industrial Policies in Western Europe*, Praeger, New York, 1975, p. 245.

[28]For an extended discussion of the international service sector see Ronald K. Shelp, *Beyond Industrialization: Ascendancy of the Global Service Economy*, McGraw-Hill for the Council on Foreign Relations/1980s Project (forthcoming).

[29]Perhaps the trouble lies in what Flaubert called *la rage de vouloir conclure*, the compulsion to draw a conclusion, which can distort the reasoning process. For this fine expression I am indebted to Albert Hirschman, who quoted it in a stimulating article, "The Search for Paradigms as a Hindrance to Understanding," *World Politics*, April 1970, pp. 329–343.

on the built-in inflationary tendency because productivity does not increase, in the face of massive automation of clerical work; on high skills, in the face of the need of most industrial countries to import labor for the hotel trades; and so on. There are problems in definition and concept: Movies, records, and books are traded as goods, but what is really bought and sold is the services they embody; the management of a plant is a cost of industrial production, but consulting about it is a service. The service account in the balance of payments is mostly about transportation, tourism, and the return on investments while a good bit of insurance and banking activity escapes the statistics.

Nevertheless, services have to be thought about in shaping and analyzing industrial policies, and they deserve much more attention than they have been given in this book. There are two main reasons. First, some services are particularly well suited to countries with high incomes, high levels of education, and a sophisticated industrial and scientific base. They are remunerative, they generate new opportunities, and they are often less vulnerable for longer periods to the rapid growth of production in the developing world than is industry using established technology. Second, for these services (in contrast to shipping and aviation, for example) there are relatively few international agreements about fair competition, but there is often much national regulation of a sort likely to give rise to the kinds of difficulties that occur in other spheres of industrial policy.

## SECTORS SUMMED UP

Not textiles, steel, or the other cases are the focus of this chapter's conclusions. It is the sector or industry-by-industry approach as such that concerns us. The "lessons" of the two main cases have for the most part been drawn as they were discussed. The textile issue shows the limits of what can be done if trade policy alone is relied on with no real provision for measures of industrial policy or structural adjustment. Though it is conceivable that governments would use the time gained for such purposes, the chances of their doing so are reduced by the protectionist drive that lay at the origins of the step. It is also conceivable that in a different situation the countries whose exports were hit would be in a position to retaliate or force some better bargain—a possibility that needs to be considered in the future.

The steel measures lack the formal international agreement of textiles but move much further toward being real industrial policies. Whether they will continue in that direction is unpredictable. Both in the United States and in the European Community the combination of those who fear what would be done and the industry groups that would like to go their own way could bring matters to a stop. However, if one of the major steel-producing centers undertakes substantial restructuring, the others will be affected; and in any case there will either have to be an understanding about foreign trade or there will be a series of clashes. Moreover, unless there is a substantial change in attitudes toward steel as a basic industry, no major country will be satisfied to let trade liberalization be its primary policy if the result threatens whatever level of steelmaking capacity is regarded as adequate.

Something like this may also be true of textiles, though it is rarely made so explicit. If, as seems likely, minimum capacity is also demanded in other industries held to be "basic," then we are bound to see a multiplication of cases in which each country's industrial policy limits (but does not eliminate) the potential market of more efficient foreign producers. To the international problems there will be added those of the burdens on the efficient parts of any national economy of carrying a large number of inefficient producers for the sake of their capacity rather than their productivity. However, to the extent that different countries see different industries as the ones they must preserve, new prospects open up of compromise: I will accept your need to protect X if you accept mine to protect Y, and that may permit more economies of scale that will benefit us both, so we may be ready to permit the international division of labor to work in other instances as well.

The concept of needing to have a minimum capacity in a sector for the indefinite future opens two major possibilities for thinking about international industrial policy. The first arises from the fact that for each center there is a cost, if sustaining the capacity entails an uneconomic use of resources. A certain pooling of effort, permitting larger-scale production and more specialization, could improve the trade-off. Second, all the old industrial centers are pressed to make adjustments to cope with the growth of production in the developing world in many major sectors, including steel. Though resistance in the manner of the textile arrangements may often seem the easiest course, there are advantages in more ambitious kinds of international measures (to be explored in Chapter 5).

Our case material does not cast any doubt on the view that difficulties result from applying the sectoral approach only to industries in trouble and that it is impossible to confine the effects of what is done to a single sector. Still, it is not wise to ignore another dimension of these issues. Adjustment within a sector is sometimes easier than if broader segments of the economy are involved. One of the reasons the removal of tariffs within the European Common Market was not as disruptive as was generally thought likely, even though there was a very large increase in trade, is that much adaptation took place within major industries. Shifts in trade produced intraindustry specialization so few enterprises went out of business; they mostly altered the patterns of their activities. Even in meeting textile competition from LDCs, some adaptation of this sort has been possible—for instance, in Germany. A possibility considered in Canada is that some small textile enterprises could stay alive by giving up most manufacturing and becoming importers and making use of their expertise in the market. Producing and importing at the same time is quite common and may help adaptation. In Germany in the 1960s, typewriter and sewing machine companies brought simpler machines from Japan while making more complicated models at home. In Japan, in turn, simpler processes were yielded to Korea, Hong Kong, and Taiwan while the Japanese developed newer and more complicated products. Of course, this is a shifting process, not a once-and-for-all change. It also cannot be taken for granted that there will not be significant dislocation in the labor force, but that depends to some degree on company policies and national habits.

The sectoral approach is not incompatible with the idea that governments may act before they are forced to. At the end of the Kennedy Round, Sir Eric Wyndham White recommended the selection of a few key industries as the best way to push ahead with trade liberalization. Where there were relatively few producers and much modern technology, he argued, it ought to be possible to eliminate tariffs more easily than in industries like textiles. In such industries one could make reasonably good judgments about the consequences of liberalization; one could also deal more easily with nontariff barriers, and one can imagine balance being retained even while adjustment takes place. For these reasons, we may see this aspect of the sector approach reappearing; there was an echo of it in the idea of free trade for aircraft, put forward in the Tokyo Round. However, Wyndham White's suggestion was not pursued when it was made; and when the sector approach next made an appearance, its implications were more disturbing.

In the 1974 Trade Act the U.S. Congress told American negotiators to assure themselves that any new agreements provided a balance of advantages for each American industry affected. This was a response to the fear of some industries that they would be "sold down the river" to benefit some politically more influential groups and the widespread feeling that past negotiations had left Europeans and Japanese in a preferred position in a number of key industries. Negotiators are uneasy about the concept because of the frequent difficulty of making a balance within one sector and the normal practice of making up packages in which gains in one sector are balanced against losses in another. If the congressional mandate were to be pursued rigorously, that would in itself dictate a kind of industrial policy for the United States. That is to say, the existing structure of industry would be "ratified," and its relation to other countries as well.

A generalization to all trade and industrial policy of the concept of intrasectoral balance could make for a good deal of rigidity. Long-run structural change must involve running down in some fields and expansion in others. It is doubtful whether a highly controlled process can be managed internationally, but there is little doubt that countries by and large will not enter into agreements with others unless they expect to get their fair share of

138

the benefits and something like reciprocity from the others. The bargaining that assures such results and makes agreements possible is very likely to affect the interest of countries that are not part of the agreement. Countries may be outsiders because they have been excluded, stayed out of their own accord, or became relevant producers only later on. In any case, the effect of agreements on outsiders, the implication of trying to include the outsider even if that might make agreement impossible, and the consequences of these alternatives for the economic and political structure of the world are central problems for our subject.

A particular form of the problem raised by the industry-by-industry approach is the inescapable tendency of a sectoral agreement to resemble a cartel. It is true that most international cartels have not been very successful and that what people thought they saw did not always exist (as in the case of a number of Americans who saw the creation of the European Coal and Steel Community as a revival of the old steel cartel). Still, when governments and industry work together they can do a lot of damage as well as a lot of good. And the question is not just what happens to outsiders. The worried and suspicious reaction of some Europeans to the speed with which other Europeans concluded that cartels were a proper response to the recession of the mid-1970s was warranted. It is also true, of course, that there are some things that cartels can usefully do and some circumstances in which cartel-like practices are at least temporarily necessary to secure desirable results. It seems quite clear that when the sectoral approach is used in industrial policy, an objective observer ought to look carefully for the cartel-like features, and interested parties ought to do what they can to ensure that there is room for competitive pressures to make themselves felt, sooner or later, from inside or outside. It may be that weaknesses in enforcement mechanisms and the tendency of participants to cheat are among the better safeguards of most sectoral industrial policy measures.

Finally there is the question whether the industry-by-industry approach might not snowball. Special treatment is contagious in a democracy. If you have done something for the other fellow, why not for me? It is not just a matter of log-rolling but of equity, whether that is treating like cases alike or compensating for the damage caused by the first step. The difficulty of working out industrial policy measures may slow this process. The pressure could also be reduced by requiring both adjustment and burden sharing. But there is no doubt that ''me too'' is often a politically compelling argument for protection.

# FIVE

# International Innovation

As we have circled around the subject of structural change and the international industrial policies it has evoked, we have here and there cut in with questions not about what has been but about what might be. This chapter, without predicting or prescribing, gives imagination a little freer rein in speculating on some new approaches to problems which are not being adequately dealt with by the old approaches. It asks what people might do if they were willing to treat some familiar issues as parts of a continuing process of structural change in the world economy and if they were willing to look ahead and take action before they were forced to.

It follows that there will be less stress than in earlier chapters on the defensive reactions that have dominated industrial policy. The emphasis is on what might be called a "positive" approach, one that looks for ways in which countries can join together to avoid the undesirable results of purely national and mainly defensive measures. While current difficulties cannot be ignored, the main focus is on what today's problems will look like tomorrow. Consequently, doubts about the feasibility of some approaches because governments and electorates are not ready to accept them can be put aside. For the time being, the prior questions concern what could be accomplished by acting in advance to deal with foreseeable problems. Good demonstrations of that kind of feasibility—which cannot be entirely mechanical—may themselves contribute to the ultimate willingness of governments to try new approaches.

People have thought in these terms before. No sooner had the Nazis invaded Poland in September 1939 than people in many countries began working on plans for the kind of postwar world order they hoped could be created. Like us now, they could foresee problems that were never adequately dealt with in the past and tried to work out new methods, even though they could have no assurance that governments would adopt them. Many contemporary problems are different from those faced by the wartime planners; but one important set of issues is remarkably similar: those concerning the structural change in the world economy resulting from industrial growth in the less developed countries.

Not ignored in past chapters, this subject is central to this one. It is looked at first in terms of what might be done to link development finance with structural change and what should be avoided. Then, in an even more speculative mode, some thought is given to how the automobile industry may evolve in the years to come. In both these sections private activities are taken into account and not just government policy. Neither is treated simply as a North-South issue, for two good reasons. First, structural change involves relations among the industrialized countries and not just between them and others. Second, the North-South dichotomy and its variants (rich-poor, industrialized–less developed, etc.) are too crude. Some of the countries of particular interest for the problems of structural change are those with industries far more important than those of other developing countries, such as Korea, Taiwan, Brazil, Mexico, Hong Kong, and Singapore. Others are countries that it was never proper to group with the rich industrial world, such as Spain, Portugal, Yugoslavia, Greece, and Turkey.

## CLEAR PROBLEMS, CLEAR SOLUTIONS, AND NO ANSWERS

On the whole, the postwar planners underestimated the development issue, partly because they did not foresee the extent of decolonization and the emergence of so many new nations. However, they anticipated a great deal of industrialization and aimed to foster it by strengthening the international financial system and increasing the flow of both public and private capital, particularly the latter. They understood the importance of education to economic development and the need for technical assistance and other forms of help. Agriculture and mining would continue to be important to developing countries (as they were sometimes called even in those days), but it was clear that industrialization was also necessary to provide the "ever-rising standard of living" that was the general target of these approaches.

The planners had to reckon with a somewhat different point of view that was fairly widespread in the general public and among some political leaders as well. If the backward countries (as they were often called) began manufacturing, what would happen to the export markets of the industrial countries? Did not international trade involve the exchange of food and raw materials for manufactures (as with Ricardo's wine and cloth)? It would dry up! One of the major studies published by the Secretariat of the League of Nations during its exceptionally fruitful period in Princeton showed how incorrect this view was.[1] Trade increased with industrialization, at least in part because industrial countries were richer. It did not follow, to be sure, that everyone simply sold more of what he had sold in the past. The makeup of trade would change and with it the structure of production. To show how these shifts, within and among countries, would produce advantages for all if the right policies were followed was the aim of Eugene Staley, a prescient American economist, in a report published in 1944 by the International Labour Office (then in Montreal).[2]

---

[1] League of Nations, Economic, Financial and Transit Department, *Industrialization and Foreign Trade*, 1945. The principal author was Folke Hilgerdt. This and a half-dozen other volumes produced by the League group during the years it was at Princeton epitomize the collective wisdom of liberal internationalist economists as to the meaning of the interwar experience and its lessons for the postwar period. Most of the volumes carry "Geneva" on their title pages but were in fact produced in the United States.

[2] Eugene Staley, *World Economic Development: Effects on Advanced Industrial Countries*, International Labour Office, Montreal, 1944.

Staley's book contained a great deal of factual material about patterns of production and trade and some estimates of what might happen under the most likely postwar conditions. A major element in this picture was the expected growth of China as it fulfilled the plans built on Sun Yat-sen's principles. Staley's main argument, however, was made up of three contentions. The first was Hilgerdt's message that economic development would increase international trade, not throttle it. The second was that the demand of the developing countries for manufactured goods, and especially for capital equipment, could be linked to the reconversion of the industrial countries from war to peace economies and to the efforts they would have to make later on to offset business cycles. Staley suggested a variety of ways in which these links could be established so as to increase stability and maintain full use of resources. Ideas of this sort are coming back into fashion as the OECD countries contemplate a period of slow growth, but for present purposes we leave this matter aside to concentrate on the third major argument of the book:

> The key to the problems which will face advanced countries as economic development proceeds in other areas is *industrial adaptation* — that is, shifting of the uses of labour and capital. Progress elsewhere in the world will mean economic gain for established industrial regions if there is sufficient mobility of labour and capital into those industries where the new conditions create better prospects, and out of the industries where opportunities are less good. . . .[3]

Staley's development of this thesis is highly relevant to the present day. He suggests a number of concrete instances of adjustment with both national and international elements. He stresses "that *internal* production structures within the various countries, and especially their flexibility, have an enormous *international* importance."[4] He shows that policies to resist change ("likely to be entered upon piecemeal in response to pressure from particular groups of workers or employers") will "throttle opportunities for expansion in other and more promising indus-

[3] Ibid., p. 175.
[4] Ibid., p. 199.

tries.''[5] He explains why market forces alone are unlikely to bring about the changes although businessmen will be major agents of the change. "It is not industries as such that we want to protect, but people. In order to protect people it is sometimes desirable to liquidate a particular industry in a particular locality.''[6] Policies of economic expansion and full employment are essential to the success of those measures but will not by themselves bring about successful adaptation.

This remarkable book is a well-argued treatise on industrial policy as an international issue by a strong and eloquent advocate of a national and international adaptive strategy. It is tempting to quote whole sections, but our aim here is to focus on ideas for positive international action, of which there are a number in Staley's book. In considering them we can take advantage of decades of development experience that still lay ahead when he wrote and with variations on his ideas that suggest themselves. Since only governments could provide the positive intervention needed for adjustment, the "international interest in national adaptiveness" created "a new field in which international consultation and agreed action might well be sought.''[7] Adaptation is easier when it is gradual than if it has to be made suddenly; if absolute contraction is required in some lines, the costs are higher than if a series of relative shifts would suffice. Therefore "agreements might be sought with the newly developing countries in which they would undertake to take such considerations into account, as applied to established suppliers of import goods, when framing their own programmes of industrial promotion.''[8] Their own infant industries might even make out better that way than if they got into "bitter and costly struggles with established industries. . . ." To encourage this cooperation (and the adoption of relatively liberal import policies toward other manufactured goods) advanced countries should "(1) make capital and technical assistance available to the newly developing countries on reasonable terms, in considerable amounts, and regularly over

[5] Ibid., pp. 175–176.
[6] Ibid., p. 191.
[7] Ibid., pp. 198–199.
[8] Ibid., p. 203.

a period of years; and (2) permit increased imports into their home markets of goods produced in the developing countries."[9]

In addition to agreements to coordinate the shift in industrial production and increase the complementarity of the structural changes in developing and older countries, Staley proposed that development financing should be guided in the same way. Avoiding organizational detail, he called for an International Development Authority (IDA) "of some kind." It would mobilize funds from around the world, provide technical assistance, improve the security of private investments, avoid the troubles of bilateralism by stressing multilateral aims and methods. It would study the problems of economic development in a long perspective so one could see what was likely to happen next. All these things have become familiar in the postwar world as desirable aspects of development financing; they have been provided with some success and some failure by national and international agencies, notably the World Bank and regional development banks. But none has done the next thing Staley wanted his IDA to undertake. It should "propose coordinated programmes of action on the important problems of economic adjustment which developmental activities would raise." It would "point out that current plans of various countries will lead to a world over-capacity in some industries and under-capacity in others."[10] It would indicate in which lines the developing countries were likely to acquire a comparative advantage fairly soon.

And what then? Would all the world take heed and act accordingly? Would IDA deny support to the "wrong" activities and provide it for the "right" ones? Would that suffice to shape the future of development? Staley did not spell out any of the range of possible answers, perhaps to keep the focus on the basic problem. This book, too, is not looking for specific organizational prescriptions; but we can underline Staley's central argument, which is (in the terms of this chapter) that positive international action on industrial policy should be taken through development finance.

[9] Ibid., p. 204.
[10] Ibid., p. 86.

It is investment that brings about industrial change. Perhaps if we start with the source we can achieve results that elude us when we try to deal with the consequences. But there is no single source. Even if we think of the World Bank, its "family" (including a different IDA from Staley's), regional banks, and all other international agencies concerned with development finance as the latter-day equivalents of Staley's IDA, we can see that they do not control the financing of industrialization. National aid agencies are very important, and so are private investment decisions made by corporations based in the rich world but operating anywhere. These last may have a disproportionately large influence on the kinds of manufacturing growth in the developing world that produces exports to the industrial countries. Within the developing world there are two more financial agents of development, governments and local private enterprise. The latter has too often been dismissed but in quite a few countries, especially some where industrialization has proceeded furthest, such as Korea, Taiwan, Hong Kong, and Mexico, it is a very real force that not only shapes the choice of activities but is able to finance it—if not from domestic resources, then from the capital markets of the world. Governments too have learned that most of them and their state corporations can borrow from banks in many countries and, outside national controls, in the Euromarkets.

It is no violation of the restriction that feasibility should be played down in this analysis to say it is not worth considering the possibility of establishing an effective single control over all these sources of finance. But to consider how some of the flows might be used as instruments of positive international adjustment measures is not that foolhardy—at least at first sight.

## GUIDED DEVELOPMENT?

It may seem the merest common sense that the world should not waste one of its scarcest resources, capital, in expanding industrial capacity beyond what is clearly needed and so making some of it redundant and unprofitable. Public spending or public guarantees of private investment could certainly be limited along those lines. This has in fact been done, for more selfish reasons. For years, American aid agencies were not permitted to help foreign countries expand the production of cotton, which might reduce the market for one of the most traditional American exports. But the Ellender effect, as it was called after the Louisiana Senator who laid down the rule, was frustrated in the end because American farm policy kept the price of cotton high enough so that Mexico, Pakistan, and other producers were encouraged to expand their output. In the latter 1970s a comparable effort was made by the United States government to keep the World Bank and regional development banks from financing the expansion of palm oil production in tropical countries on the grounds that it would narrow the market for soybeans. Throughout the postwar period people in the industrial countries took a condescending view of the penchant of developing countries to treat steel mills as if they were attributes of sovereignty and tried to limit the use of development funds for these purposes. The economics of the steel ventures were, indeed, often very faulty—but some paid off.

Sometimes the expansion of capacity in LDCs is firmly linked with the assurance of a market in the industrial world. Major new mining developments are sometimes based on the contractual obligation of groups of partners to buy the output over a long period of years. Sometimes foreign plants are established by a multinational corporation that wants to use the output in various parts of its worldwide operations, including the home country. These steps do not guarantee that there will be no excess capacity in the world; they simply assure that the particular new capacity will not itself be redundant. Some Japanese foreign investment has been in labor-intensive manufacturing in other Asian countries to supply Japan with products it formerly exported. Then a shift in location rather than a duplication of capacity takes place if the investing company adjusts its domestic production. Kiyoshi Kojima correctly argues that this kind of investment promotes structural adaptation in both the investing country and the host country and will be trade-creating. The pattern is very different from one in which the firms in the labor-

148

intensive activity in an industrial country are too poor or too unenterprising to invest abroad and so call for protection against someone else's expansion of capacity. It is not evident, however, why one pattern should predominate over the other unless the government takes a hand, either by fostering or hindering investment or refusing to impose trade' barriers.[11]

Perhaps a case could be made for the rather traditional view that if all investment were private, the problem of excess capacity would take care of itself. To be sure, there are a number of reasons why a private entrepreneur might deliberately add to world capacity beyond what he thought demand would justify. Simply to do a better job than an established producer or to keep up with his competitors might explain such action; but if the calculations were wrong, it would be the investor who paid for his mistake. And if they were right and a competitor suffered, the decline in the latter's profits should help bring about adjustment. Reasonable as all this is, it does not present a good enough answer, or we would not have so many adjustment problems. On the one hand, the market does not work that well, either in guiding new investment or in bringing about the balance of supply and demand when "excess capacity" (in some sense) has been created. On the other hand, governments and societies are not prepared to let market forces work even as well as they might if they do not like the results.

Knowing this, governments of developing countries might be expected to hesitate to establish plants producing for export without feeling sure that they had markets. But in spite of protection, almost no one has found all foreign markets closed to

[11]Professor Kojima contrasts Japanese and American patterns of direct investment along these lines in an interesting fashion. He explains the difference largely in terms of the existence of a dualistic structure in the United States economy, where large firms make the trade-destroying investments for oligopolistic reasons. This raises the question of future patterns of Japanese direct investment. There is also the question of trade barriers in both home and host countries. A key point for our purposes is Kojima's suggestion that American firms would act differently "if they were conscious of national economic interests." Kiyoshi Kojima, *Japan and a New World Economic Order*, Charles E. Tuttle, Tokyo, 1977, p. 81. The analysis referred to is in chaps. 4 and 5 of this book and in some of Professor Kojima's other writings.

him. The world economy has been growing; competitive sellers have found customers. Sometimes foreign investors could be made responsible for exporting as part of the privilege of entering the domestic market. Even when several countries move into the same lines of production at the same time, the results do not seem to have been disastrous. Countries with only one major raw material may have no choice; when prices go down they try to sell more. That can happen in manufacturing, too. Private banks do not appear to have exercised a general restraining influence and have certainly not imposed any sense of order on the process.

The future may be somewhat different if growth is slower or people are simply more worried, but it is hard to believe that the result will simply be balanced adaptation. The government of a capital-providing country might decide to refuse aid for projects adding to excess capacity and to put pressure on private investors to the same end (which it might do informally or by taxation and regulation). It would find its investors and lenders—and its aid policy, for that matter—outflanked by other countries that did not impose such restrictions. And if all the capital-providing countries agreed to act together, would they be able to agree on what industries should be expanded and which contracted and where? It seems as unlikely as that total control could be established over all sources of finance.

Still, to say that everything cannot be done does not mean that nothing can be done. Suppose Staley's IDA had a policy of refusing funds for development that would be redundant and a fairly respectable mechanism for passing judgment that would not simply reflect the interests of the donors of aid. Would this not discourage others from financing the same activities—even though governments of the developing countries might persist in their aims? Financing decisions would have to be made case by case, but as time passed a pattern would emerge that created a presumption in favor of some activities and against others. Lists of approved or disapproved investments of the sort mentioned in Chapter 3 as guides to national regional policies would begin to take shape on a global scale, but would change as time passed (otherwise they would create excess capacity).

A simple stop-go signal for new investment will only occasionally be valid. Excess capacity may exist or be foreseeable on a global scale, but the needs of some area may be better served by expanding local production. There is also the perennial question of how long concern for excess capacity should be allowed to block, or at least hinder, the creation of new plants that are more efficient than the old—or, even if only equally efficient, create employment and stimulate activity in some part of the world that badly needs this help. To make excess capacity or the avoidance of too rapid a rate of expansion the dominant motif for "guided development" is clearly unacceptable. It has far too great a bias in favor of the status quo and in favor of the position of the "haves" versus the forces for change in the world.

There is, however, a case, from a global point of view, for putting a brake on processes that hasten expansion without regard to need, that throw into doubt the efficiency of the plants to be created, and that let one country's needs set a course of action that ignores the problems it presents to others. Such considerations strengthen the case for the kinds of rules on subsidies discussed in Chapter 3, both in general and specifically in connection with measures to induce foreign investment by making financial concessions but insisting on exports. The flat banning of such practices is unlikely, but they could be made more onerous in fields where excess capacity was regarded as a serious problem. If a country ignored such warnings, countries toward which the new products were channeled might be entitled to try stronger countervailing measures. Financing might be made more difficult. The lists of approved and disapproved industries hypothesized above could be taken as guidance by international bodies authorizing the use of safeguard clauses. Again, it would be vital to have a way of arriving at a global view and not simply a biased judgment favoring established producers.

If there is to be an innovative and constructive international effort to deal with structural change, concern about excess capacity has to be balanced and frequently overriden by a sense of the need to break down the barriers to adjustment in the established centers of production. That, after all, has been more of a problem for longer than has excess capacity, and it is also

151

undoubtedly a continuing burden to the global economy. Earlier chapters have made it clear that to do a good job of promoting change one must be concerned not only with contraction but also with expansion and the location of new industry. An IDA on the Staley model or any other effort to guide investment should be concerned with developing new capacities as well as closing down or avoiding the duplication of old ones.

Without trying to spell out how all this might be done, one can see several basic requirements. First, ideas about what lines of activity should expand would have to take account not only of global aggregates but of changing patterns of needs and capabilities in specific parts of the world. Otherwise it would be hard to arrive at a conclusion as to how a country that was phasing out of the production of certain things could usefully shift to more profitable lines. Second, there would have to be an understanding about the kinds of policies governments would follow. If the expansion of production in LDCs only substitutes for what used to be imported, the older centers have one set of problems. But if the new producer is to export, its survival may depend on access to the older market. This might be assured at one rate of increase but not another. While it would be too much to expect that a "compensating" export from the older country could be guaranteed, it is not unreasonable to suppose that the rate of adjustment at home would be influenced by such possibilities. Though bilateral balancing would only rarely make sense from a global point of view, at least some of the rationale for adjustment is based on the prospect of the older centers supplying capital goods to the new producers.

A third requirement for the positive international function is that the burden of this shift in productive structures ought to be shared among the countries involved. The shift in trade patterns would provide some of that, especially if the rate of imports from the LDCs were geared to the pace of adjustment in the industrial country. There might be some sharing of the financial costs as well. Though it is hard to imagine actual costs in the better-off country, such as those of job retraining, being paid for in any direct way by the poorer one, it would be sensible to have an international fund that would supplement national expenditures.

Some industrial nations are a good bit poorer than others. Help may make it easier to agree to adjustment, and some international supervision of funds may play a part in speeding up the process. If there are adjustment costs in the developing country (say, writing off unwise investment in plants that make equipment that will now be imported), they could suitably be financed in this way or by a direct contribution of development funds. If a richer country adjusted more slowly than expected, it might pay a penalty to compensate the poorer country or pay into the international fund. Again, the prod might speed the process.

Another kind of burden sharing that might come into the picture would be among a number of older industrial countries. It was part of the argument for the cotton textile arrangements that Continental Europe as well as the United Kingdom and the United States should pursue roughly similar courses so that no one of them became the sole target of intensified exports from the LDCs. Still other possibilities will appear—and difficulties as well—when trade patterns are examined to see how increased exports of manufactured goods from developing countries will affect trade among the industrial countries as well as each one's domestic adjustment. For most products, not excluding textiles, there is significant trade among these countries, which is bound to be affected by either the imposition or the removal of barriers to imports from developing countries.[12] If there is to be a global view of the lines into which it is desirable for industrial countries to move as they adjust, that too is bound to affect trade among the industrial countries. Moreover, adjustment to changes in production among the developed countries themselves in fields in which there are no significant LDC producers remains a large and unresolved problem that a global approach cannot ignore.

There is in addition the whole question of the trade practices of the developing countries. Extreme and unselective protectionism is one of the principal causes of the maldistribution of industry in the world. Not all industries are equally good choices

---

[12]The favorable tariff treatment granted to developing countries under the General System of Preferences has been blamed by Spain and other ineligible countries for shutting some of their products out of European and American markets even though the Spaniards claim to have lower costs.

as infant industries entitled to protection and help. There has, without much doubt, been a great deal of waste of investment, and many of the difficulties some countries have had in developing competitive industries have stemmed from saddling themselves with high costs of production through more or less generalized protection of all kinds of manufacturing. In contrast, LDCs that were selective, built up industries able to compete in world markets, and let them acquire their inputs at competitive costs have done well. Awareness has grown, but the problem is not easy to deal with.

The issue is too broad to be dealt with here, but it clearly has to be part of any global approach to structural change. Improved national selection of infant industries is one key, but wisdom and toughness in these matters are hard to come by. So is the willingness to admit mistakes and abandon protection after it has failed. The ideas already discussed for checking the use of subsidies and other special arrangements to foster exports could, to a degree, be linked to this problem. So could the improved international supervision of safeguards and any related arrangements for gearing adaptation in older centers to exports from developing countries. Ideally there ought to be some kind of international surveillance over the protection of infant industries. The long-delayed effort to work out a suitable set of trade rules for developing countries should explore this possibility. One stimulus to some improvement in these matters is the growth of trade among the developing countries, which creates a certain peer pressure for rationalizing protection. There is also the fact that the first wave of industrialization in the Third World is giving way to a second, in which lower-wage, less-developed countries are challenging some who have made the greatest progress in the past. The example of Japan works backward as well as forward, so to speak.

Two simple observations will underline points that have emerged in earlier chapters: Whatever guidance is feasible has to take account of relations among a number of countries, not just a pair, and probably of a whole range of products as well. The more complex the process, the less reason there is to expect that any agency could work out a convincing picture of what patterns of production and trade the world ought to be moving toward and how it could get there. And yet at least some ideas along these lines are indispensable. One may wonder, however, whether a prescription for what ought to be done, even if it rises above questions of feasibility, can properly say that there ought to be measures to enforce the judgment of the authors of so ambitious a scheme when one has to doubt the ability of even the brightest and most global-minded to provide an altogether satisfactory road map.

How much might be accomplished simply by information? Suppose the lists, the analysis of the problems, the clear indications of where adjustment was needed, and even reports of performance, whether good or poor, were simply data provided publicly (and in ways that could not be overlooked) by those who might otherwise have thought it sensible to move in a contrary direction. Would this accomplish a great deal—for instance, by influencing investors, banks, and national or international aid agencies? At a minimum they would have to be ready to explain to the world or their stockholders or legislatures or ministers why they had acted in a contrary fashion.

Some people put great stock in improved information as a means of preventing mistakes. My own feeling (it is not much more than that) is that ignorance is not the most basic problem. Governments, international agencies, multinational corporations, and banks know most of what would be "discovered" by the process suggested. If they act in ways that create or perpetuate adjustment problems, it is for some other reason than ignorance. An exception to this statement, however, may well be private groups in many countries who lack the data on which to judge their own true interests and are taken in by the conventional wisdom about national interest, especially in its mercantilist version, as well as by the special pleading of the nearest interest groups. There is also no doubt that data are lacking on many specific issues and that not everything known is available to government officials, much less international organizations or the general public.

When they are expected to have an influence on policy, the preparation and publication of reports (and indeed the collection of the data going into them) are likely to become corrupted and highly politicized. That is widely recognized and discounted where private and national interests are concerned, but the problem may be especially acute where international agencies are involved. It is no accident that international organizations are often mealy-mouthed and otherwise try to serve many masters. A possible remedy would be to entrust this work to a small group of well-thought-of and largely independent people. They would ensure the quality and objectivity of the staff—and defend it. Their own judgments about the implications of the analyses for policy might come to have an influence on at least some national governments and perhaps some international agencies as well. Jean Monnet once suggested a similar device for guiding the industrial countries in dealing with their greater-than-national issues.

One could also think of the guidance for adjustment being provided on a less than global basis. The OECD is already doing work on structural relations among its members and while an expanded approach might not secure complete agreement in developing countries, it would not be without meaning if it were regarded as serious advice to the OECD governments. Then if there were another such set of estimates made in, say, UNCTAD, and perhaps a third by a board advising the World Bank, the competition of facts and analysis might promote competence and deepen understanding. Even if one has doubts about how effective such methods may be, it is hard to take a stand against learning more. There is a good case for any promising method to focus attention on global adjustment problems. Few people have this perspective, and it would be of value to alert them not only to the problems but to both the cost of following traditional policies and the opportunities offered by change.

One predictable result of putting these issues into focus would be to disabuse people of the common view that structural adaptation is primarily a North-South issue. It is true that LDC exports of manufactured goods to the OECD countries have been among the most rapidly growing segments of world trade. They increased in importance for the non-oil-producing LDCs until by the late 1970s they amounted to about 40 percent of their exports to the OECD countries. But in 1976 the LDCs still supplied only 8.2 percent of the industrial world's total imports of manufactured goods (compared to 7 percent in 1970 and 6 percent in 1963).[13] Far from negligible overall, this share is naturally much higher in certain products and some markets. Sales can expand rapidly; and their impact is stronger if the domestic industry is weak, as is so often the case. Nevertheless, the amount of employment that is lost to the competition of LDC imports is a good deal less than one would guess from listening to debates in the national parliaments of almost any Western country.

A study for Western Germany estimated that between 1962 and 1975 increases in labor productivity in manufacturing equaled ("displaced") 6.5 million jobs. Import growth displaced 1.7 million, but imports from developing countries accounted for only 133,000 of these. Estimates put the possible figure for the decade to 1985 at 850,000, a substantial increase but not an alarming amount in view of the expansion of other industries, new lines of production, and increased exports (those to LDCs would create 400,000 jobs).[14] While Germany has one of the more open European markets, the experience of other countries does not seem to have been drastically different. Summing up a series of studies, a report prepared for the ILO said that the contribution of imports to the rising unemployment of industrial countries in the 1970s "was so small as to be virtually insignificant. . . . There is no denying that imports from LDCs do have an adverse effect on employment in industrially developed countries. But the evidence is clear that those negative effects are a much smaller cause of job losses than the normal functioning of dynamic economies and the growth of intra-trade between DCs."[15]

[13]Calculated from GATT, *Networks of World Trade*, op. cit., Table A1.

[14]Frank Wolter, "Adjusting to Imports from Developing Countries," in Herbert Giersch (ed.), *Reshaping the World Economic Order*, Institut für Weltwirtschaft an der Universität Kiel, Symposium 1976, J. C. B. Mohr (Paul Siebeck), Tübingen, Table A-6, p. 129.

[15]Santosh Mukherjee with Charlotte Feller, *Restructuring of Industrial Economies and Trade with Developing Countries*, basic working document, Tripartite Symposium on Adjustment Assistance and Employment Restructuring in Industrialized Countries due to Increased Trade between Developed and Developing Countries, Geneva, May 3–5, 1978, World Employment Pro-

As the German study cited indicated, the problem will be larger in the future, especially if industrial production in the developing world grows faster than in the older centers, as is widely expected. Moreover, aggregate totals conceal much greater problems in particular lines where LDC imports are concentrated. Still, it would be strange if anyone could face such an analysis and go on acting as if the main adjustment problem stemmed from LDC competition. But what are the implications for the global approach to structural adjustment that we have been exploring if "guided development" of the LDCs is not enough, since the sources of change are to be found all over?

Is the choice between global planning and doing nothing? Is the task too great, or are the problems less serious than people have thought in the light of the changes we have lived through without having had to do very much about them? An in-between answer would make the case for better adjustment policies that will ease adaptation to pressures that must be taken as given. Quite a different reaction is to say that the all-or-nothing dichotomy is foolish; one acts where one can if there is a problem. Little can be done to block change from increased productivity or most other internal factors. International trade *can* be dealt with; relations among industrial countries may give rise to new kinds of measures applied to imports from the developing countries as well. Or, finally, one might conclude that whatever else was done, the LDC dimension ought to be dealt with on its own terms, for several reasons: the foreseeable increase in its impact, the bargaining power of the rich countries, the leverage they gain from LDC needs for capital.

The argument brings us back to our starting place in exploring ways of using a global perspective to devise positive measures to guide structural adjustment. Interestingly enough, there is one other set of developments that pushes in this direction. Though

---

gramme, ILO, Geneva, p. 2. (Mimeographed.) In addition to the studies for Britain, Germany, and the United States cited in this work, there is another report with comparable results: Commissariat Général du Plan, Groupe de travail sur l'appareil productif français face aux changements des economies du Tiers-Monde, Rapport d'Etape, August 1977.

the analogy with the situation Staley was writing about is not too close, there are some common features that may suggest to people in the industrial world that they ought to think in his terms, perhaps for the first time since the 1940s. Essentially, the point is that the developing world is looking more important to the industrial world.

The evidence is everywhere: newspapers, speeches, government documents, company reports, the travels of businessmen and bankers. It is more than a matter of energy imports, growing dependence on raw materials, Arab money, and the sense that opportunities to lend or invest are growing. Expanded exports of capital goods take the central place in the new picture, not just to pay for energy and other imports but because slower growth at home is a threat to employment and profits while faster growth abroad creates opportunities that can be expanded in ways that stagflation has made impossible at home and in other industrial countries. Since the rich countries are not anxious actually to give away their capital goods (though government credits and highly liquid banks sometimes make it look that way), they have to be prepared to buy things that will help the developing countries to pay. That points toward the Staley formula: Adapt your industry to the importing of labor-intensive goods; gain by expanding the sale of capital equipment to the developing countries. If that conclusion is accepted, the next step is to recognize the need for the kind of global linking of trade and development Staley called for, since the problems of adjustment are no easier than they ever were and there are common gains from handling the changes well.

There are, unfortunately, some strong forces at work that may produce a less benign result. Export competition is strong among the industrial countries. More is involved than separate orders, however big. There is planning, construction, training, patent licensing, repair parts, modernization, future expansion, and the reputation and contacts that bring more business to the successful firm or country. Each will seek a preferred position for itself in LDC markets, if possible on a long-run basis. Financing industrialization projects is one way. Opening the home markets wider for imports will help, but the resistances to making adjustments are still there. Bilateral arrangements can reduce them. The richer country can buy competitive goods from its partner by letting him displace those from other LDCs. Commitments to take imports may be linked to contracts for building new plants. The industrial country can make long-term contracts for agricultural products or raw materials from the developing country and, if it takes manufactured goods as well, can control their marketing so as to create the least domestic disturbance.

There is more to be said about these forces for bilateralism: They can involve groups of countries instead of just pairs, and they touch East-West relations as well. The issues are central to what is said in Chapter 7 about the groupings of different countries for industrial policy purposes. Here the prospect of a division of the world into North-South slices looms as a highly unattractive alternative to a broader and at least potentially global approach. It adds to the arguments that one should try to find innovations to permit a truly international approach to structural adjustment. It underlines, too, the desirability of going beyond the support for adaptive policies, compared to defensive ones, to try to find positive measures to initiate industrial change on an international basis. The difficulties are at once apparent, but before coming to a conclusion one should explore one more set of possibilities that may shape change in a single global industry.

## THE CAR OF THE FUTURE

"Cars and refrigerators may prove to be the cotton textiles of tomorrow." When he said those words in a lecture at the London School of Economics in March 1954, Professor Donald Mac-Dougall (as he then was) was criticizing the view that the United States would continue to have an export surplus because its productivity would always remain so high that it could export in spite of its high wages. "It must always be remembered that American techniques are generally available to other countries. It may be, too, that the industrialisation of new countries will hit the United States as it has hit Britain in the past.''[16] As yet, however, no American President has come into office with a promise to get an international agreement to restrain trade in automobiles. But the industry has undergone large structural changes in the postwar period and some future changes seem reasonably predictable, at least to one with no expert knowledge of the industry. The question is whether steps can be taken in advance to avoid the waste and trouble that would be entailed if automobiles did indeed follow in the pattern of textiles.

At the time MacDougall was speaking, the United States and Canada produced about 80 percent of the world's passenger cars and two-thirds of its commercial vehicles. By the mid-1970s both figures were about 35 percent; Western Europe's output of passenger cars was greater than that of the United States, but in commercial vehicles it was well behind. However, nearly 45 percent of the world's cars were produced by the big three American companies, over one-third of them outside the country. American exports of cars to Europe had fallen to very low levels; the flow the other way had become large, especially in small cars that American producers had for years alleged were not to the taste of the American consumer. In the mid-1970s, about 25 percent of American demand was met by imports. As their American market grew, the European producers began assembling cars in the United States and then producing them there. The investments were stimulated by the fall in the exchange rate

[16]Donald MacDougall, "A Lecture on the Dollar Problem," *Economica*, vol. 21, no. 82, 1954, pp. 185–200. As I was preparing the final draft of this section, I came across a reference to this quotation in Charles Kindleberger's Harms lecture of 1978. Unfortunately, MacDougall did not expand on the theme, even in his subsequent book on the dollar shortage, but I was delighted to discover that a question on which I had been speculating for some years should have been raised so early. In the course of my investigation, I have found that several people have been thinking along some of the lines sketched in this section, but there is little written about them. Other people think the whole idea of major shifts in the location of the industry is highly implausible. Since my focus is industrial policy and not automobiles, I have kept the discussion general, ignored the need to qualify some rather broad statements, and provided no detailed data. It is not a close analysis but a speculation.

of the dollar, but the process was similar (in reverse) to that which had led the American producers to Europe from the 1920s on. By the mid-1970s over one-quarter of the new car registrations in France, Italy, Germany, and Britain, taken together, were of cars produced in Europe by American companies.[17]

In the automotive industry, Japan was a later arrival on the world scene than in other major branches of manufacturing. From 5 percent of the world's output of cars in 1966, Japan moved to 18 percent 10 years later, ahead of any of the Western European countries. Exports increased 17 times, much more than production. Whereas Asian, African, and Australian markets had taken more than half of Japan's exports in the earlier year, only a quarter went to these markets in 1976; half went to the United States and a quarter to Western Europe. In Western Europe, as had happened with other products, Japanese autos and trucks encountered greater resistance than in the United States; still, the rapid growth set off alarmed reactions, even though in 1976 Japan's share of the four largest markets was less than 4 percent (with a maximum of 9.4 percent in Britain, which became a ceiling, at least for the time being, as the result of Japanese agreement to limit sales). In smaller European countries where there was little or no home production and the Japanese had started selling earlier, their share was often a good bit higher. Part of the strain felt in Europe was recession, part the annoyance that Japan imported so few cars from the West. Clearly, one foreseeable set of adjustments in the automobile industry was the by now familiar one of fitting Japanese producers into a pattern formerly dominated by Americans and Europeans.

Another foreseeable development cast a longer shadow. His-

---

[17] André Gabus, Otto Hieronymi, and Pàl Kukorelly, *Japanese-European Trade Relations: Restrictions or Cooperation? The Case of the Automobile Industry*, Top '70 Study Group, Geneva, January 1978, p. 42. (The study was done by Battelle-Geneva Research Center.) The 1976 figures for Britain and Germany were 41.8 and 37.5 percent, respectively; those for France and Italy, 17.4 and 14.3. The other figures in this paragraph come from a variety of sources drawn together in an unpublished study (not by Battelle) that I have been allowed to use. Unattributed figures later in this section come from these two documents.

torically the pattern of demand had, in the end, shaped the location of automobile production. Europeans had done the pioneering in the development of automobiles. Their inventions were applied on a large scale in the United States, where the assembly line, low prices, distance, roads, and relatively cheap energy created a mass market. After the Second World War, rapid economic recovery helped Western Europe catch up on the American lead, and so did the production of cars better adapted to European conditions than those imported from the United States. The use of cars has grown more slowly in Japan but is catching up. Though the American, European, and Japanese markets are certainly not fully saturated, it is hard to imagine that they could continue to grow as rapidly as in the past few decades. The great areas of potential expansion of demand are clearly in the developing world and the socialist countries, where the use of cars per capita is about one-twentieth of that in the OECD countries and of commercial vehicles one-tenth.

By the mid-1970s some 10 percent of the world's automobile production was outside the OECD area, about half of it in the Soviet Union and Eastern Europe. That fairly modest figure had been reached after a good deal of effort. A number of developing countries, especially in Latin America, had for long required those who wanted to sell cars there to carry on a certain amount of local production and to procure parts and supplies, such as batteries and tires, locally. More and more domestic content was insisted upon. Costs were high, and for years much of the production was highly uneconomical; but as markets expanded and the domestic production grew, the picture improved in a number of countries, especially those where there was a general expansion of manufacturing, such as Brazil, Argentina, and Mexico.

American and European companies were heavily involved in both production and distribution in the developing countries and it seemed likely that Japanese companies would follow. To a degree they could expect to meet the needs of the developing countries by exports from the OECD bases, but the local governments would press to have as much produced at home as possible. As time passed, economics too seemed likely to encourage a substantial movement of the industry. The technology

163

of automobile production seems to fit well into the product cycle theory of foreign direct investment which says that as new processes are introduced in industrial centers the time comes when their standardization makes them eminently exportable to areas of lower wage costs. Moreover, the assembly line that for Henry Ford, Charlie Chaplin, and much of the Western world epitomized the modern age of industrial production has become the symbol of the alienation, boredom, and anomie that beset industrial civilization (hardly postindustrial in this case). The interesting efforts made to change the method—almost to put kinks in the line—seem to have their limits. If quality and productivity both fall because workers in Detroit, the British Midlands, and other places greatly dislike their work, something will have to change. The jobs may fall into the category of poorly regarded work to be done by immigrants. But if Renault can produce cars in Paris with a heavily Algerian labor force, could it not produce them in Algeria with French-made tools?[18] It was striking that the biggest investment in new production in Western Europe was in Spain, which by the mid-1970s had become the tenth largest producer of automobiles in the world. Important as the link with Europe was, one could be excused for wondering whether the next step would be farther southward.

Two major changes could alter this estimate. Some significant innovation in the technology of making cars might regain for the industrial centers an advantage that they do not have now and overcome the disadvantages of the assembly line. The other possibility is a radical change in automobiles themselves, perhaps to conserve gasoline, use another fuel, or end pollution. If the entire fleet of internal combustion engines in the OECD world were to be replaced quickly, that would create markets in the industrial countries far outstripping those in the rest of the world for a long time to come. Failing such developments, however, it seems clear that the areas of growth in production and con-

[18]Professor Galbraith has suggested that "one of the less noticed causes" of the continuing troubles of the British automobile industry "is that Britain has been trying to make automobiles (though by no means exclusively) with Englishmen." J. K. Galbraith, *The Nature of Mass Poverty*, Harvard University Press, Cambridge, Mass., 1979, p. 136.

sumption of cars and trucks will be mostly in the developing countries, the Soviet Union, Eastern Europe, and China.

The pace will be determined largely by the economic growth of these areas, and that will set one dimension of the adjustment problem for the OECD countries. Another will depend on whether, in addition to meeting their own needs, the new centers of production also export to the industrial world on any scale. Will the heralded Korean car be a major factor in trade? With whom will it most compete? It requires entrepreneurial judgment and an expert ability to forecast costs in manufacture and transportation to have any real sense of either the impact of such change or the economics of the whole issue. Given the growth of past international trade in automobiles and trucks, the possibility certainly exists; the exchange among the industrial countries in 1976 was 32 times the 1955 level, about twice the increase of trade in manufactured goods as a whole.[19] Any careful assessment would have to take account of the scale of automobile plants. For some time to come only a few developing countries are likely to have large enough markets to accommodate several domestic producers. From the entrepreneur's point of view, at least for some time, exports will often be needed, and governments will want to promote them. Exports might be directed to other LDCs; but the larger markets of the industrial countries will be tempting, and governments interested in hard currency will throw their weight in that direction. There can, of course, be a division of labor that provides economies of scale, permits the development of new centers of production, and lets a country export as well as import. Quite a few developments of this sort are already taking place, usually conducted by the large companies themselves. Some stress regional ties among developing countries, but there is also trade among countries fairly far apart and shipment of engines and parts from some developing countries to North America or Europe.

[19]Calculated from GATT, *Networks of World Trade*, op. cit., Table A3. Between 1963 and 1976 the increase was 11.5 times for "road motor vehicles" compared with 7 times for trade in manufactures as a whole. Trade within the Common Market and between Canada and the United States makes up much of the total.

It is not altogether clear how much these developments are motivated by the economic advantages of specialization and how much they are the product of governmental requirements that foreign investors export. It is, of course, to the advantage of the companies to make the transactions pay; they may therefore make a virtue of necessity and try to build a rationally internationalized industry. There has been some increase in the same kind of exchanges (parts, engines, etc.) and therefore more specialization among the OECD countries themselves, especially within Europe and across the Atlantic, but with a Japanese-American dimension as well. If the standardization required for this kind of specialization is carried to 100 percent, we will arrive at the "world car," identical wherever made or sold. So long as the production of the standardized items and interchangeable parts is spread among a number of plants, there is also flexibility in meeting needs from whatever center has excess capacity at a given moment.

Pushed far enough, this integration of production could alter some major features of the pattern that had emerged in the OECD world by the mid-1970s, with its emphasis on a large automobile industry in each main center—North America, Western Europe, Japan. Though there is a substantial trade among them, each still depends primarily on its home base for both its market and its economies of scale (though this is more true of the United States than of Europe). Within that pattern there is, however, a different kind of internationalization of production resulting from the presence of the same producers in all or most markets. Most developed by United States companies and least evident in production within Japan, this line of development is being pushed further as European and Japanese companies invest in North America, the Japanese follow the Americans into Europe, and American and European companies create partnerships for special purposes with Japanese producers. This tendency toward global production—not nearly as far advanced as this sketch may suggest—is potentially a very important element in the problems with which this book is concerned. Itself a major structural factor, it could be an important means of facilitating further structural change, since shifts in the international (indeed, intercontinental) division of labor would take place partly within each large company that is present in more than one producing area and market.

The situation regarding the socialist countries is different, but related. Western automobile producers have played a large part in the expansion of production. Fiat's work in the Soviet Union and Poland has resulted in some competition for the Italian company in Western European markets; other companies may have similar experiences, even though they initially see little trouble and even some value (older models otherwise unavailable have some uses, create some demand for parts and engines, etc.). When the possibilities of the Western company's controlling the situation have passed, the problem, if there is one, has to be treated by governments along with other cases of import competition from the state trading countries. The size of the Eastern market assures a continuing interest: a Bendix proposal for a spark plug plant in the Soviet Union that will also supply Western Europe; the East German purchase of Volkswagens so long as the West German company buys substantial amounts of equipment in East Germany. If these parts are used in the general Volkswagen line, there is integration comparable to that taking place in other parts of the world. How far this can go depends largely on the Eastern governments. Two sources of additional problems are heavy reliance on payment in kind for Western technical assistance or the competition of the automotive products of the socialist countries in the Third World.

Leaving the East-West issues aside, we are concerned here primarily with the question whether, if it were generally accepted that something like the constellation of forces suggested here would exist for the next few decades, ways could be found to make international structural adjustment relatively smooth and as beneficial as possible to all concerned rather than waiting for difficulties to arise of the sort that have plagued textiles or steel. If there are such possibilities, what part in them is to be played by governments (and which governments), by international agencies, and by private business?

The present structure is not simply the result of entrepreneurial activities in a free market. Governments have played a large part in shaping the automobile industry from the beginning. "The

167

automobile of the 1920s and 1930s in many respects occupied the place of the computer and the aircraft in the 1970s, as far as governments were concerned."[20] Tariffs not only protected domestic production but encouraged the foreigner to invest. In the postwar period Americans complained bitterly that European automobile taxes favored small over large cars and thus limited American exports. A rich growth of nontariff barriers is to be found in national regulations regarding the equipment of automobiles, safety standards, and pollution controls.

Furthermore, direct governmental involvement in production has been important in Europe. The Volkswagen company was founded by the Hitler regime but only produced the first "people's car" after the war. Though its ownership and ultimate disposition were in doubt, it grew mightily; its "privatization" in the 1960s left the federal government and the *Land* government of Lower Saxony each with 20 percent of the shares and in a position to control (or veto) actions if they chose to do so. In France, Renault was nationalized at the end of the war, perhaps as much to direct its operations as to punish collaboration. However, in both the Renault and the Volkswagen cases, concern for international competitiveness was allowed to limit governmental intervention aimed at other objectives. Competitive weakness was largely responsible for the British government's measures to nationalize British Leyland and later bail out Chrysler. The maintenance of national firms was made more difficult by the opening of frontiers in the Common Market and the presence of American companies which were among the largest producers in Europe. International mergers were on the whole discouraged, and many people felt that Europe probably had a somewhat larger number of companies than was wise in the conditions of the late 1970s. Peugeot's taking over of the Chrysler interests in Europe (including the heavily supported firm in Britain) opened new prospects already hinted at by some cooperative arrangements between American and European producers. If the reaction to Japanese competition continued to be a demand for trade restraints after the mid-1970s recession (instead of primarily an

[20] Louis T. Wells, Jr., "Automobiles," in Ray Vernon (ed.), op. cit., p. 229.

attempt to bargain for access to the Japanese market), then a renewed emphasis on protectionism would pose new questions about the future of the European industry.

In the United States, the government's part in shaping the automobile industry was less marked and less direct. Tariffs on cars came down to 3 percent in the Kennedy Round (higher on trucks); later agitation for quotas when imports became very challenging was turned aside. The fall in the exchange value of the dollar subsequently gave domestic producers a considerable advantage. As foreign companies began to produce in the United States, the market for imports was narrowed, and some observers thought that that process would continue as domestic companies gave increasing emphasis to producing smaller vehicles that consumed less fuel. Consumer interest weighs more heavily in the automobile industry than in many other cases. Energy, safety, and environmental policies have a major impact. Since it is one of the largest American industries, affecting a wide range of suppliers, transporters, distributors, and communities and serving as the base for one of the most important and politically active trade unions, the automobile industry's welfare is bound to be a matter of governmental concern. Therefore, how the industry copes with the domestic and international pressures for change that seem bound to grow in the latter part of the century may well involve Washington in more industrial policy than it is used to.

The United States is also a party to some international industrial policy in automobiles. The Canadian-American Automotive Agreement of 1965 grew out of a dispute over Canadian export subsidies. It took the form of a trade agreement, abolishing tariffs on trade between the two countries in new automobiles and trucks and their parts. The result was supposed to be increased efficiency, since plants in either country could produce for the whole continental market. Since the Canadian producers were almost entirely American-owned, the basic competitive situation was not changed, but productivity in Canada seemed bound to improve as specialization replaced the more fragmented production that had grown up behind the tariff. Nevertheless, the Canadian government insisted on commitments from the companies regarding future investment and production in Canada. Originally looked on as temporary, at least by the Americans, such promises have come to be seen by many Canadians as continuing necessities, since the main pressures on the companies—from the market, from labor, and from federal, state, and local governments—lie in the United States. Naturally, a very large increase in trade followed on the reorganization of production, and there is a tendency in both countries to judge the agreement by the export-import balance. This seems too narrow a view; but it is not altogether surprising, since there has been too little analysis of the agreement from the point of view of industrial policy.

For a number of reasons, there has been a fair amount of dissatisfaction with the agreement (it is, of course, much more important to Canada than to the United States) and many proposals for altering it, usually by expanding it to include replacement parts and secondhand cars. One side or the other has always had a good reason to postpone any serious negotiations about change, but an increase in disputes that bear on the effect of the agreement without falling under its provisions suggests that the time will come when Ottawa and Washington will have to confront the question of what results they really want from the agreement.[21] It will then have to be looked at more clearly than before as an instrument of industrial policy and not just as an adjustment of trade barriers. It may also have to be viewed in a broader international setting.

It is in a broad international setting that all governments have to view the future of their automobile industries if they are to shape sensible policies. They cannot be indifferent. More is in-

---

[21]The results of the Tokyo Round would provide a multilateral rather than a bilateral method of dealing with such disputes as the Michelin tire case referred to in Chapter 3 and the 1978 argument about the subsidy to Ford to locate a plant in Ontario instead of the United States. But are not such issues better examined in relation to the whole pattern of Canadian-American automobile production? Another kind of issue concerns the ways in which European or Japanese automobile companies in Canada could become eligible for tariff-free entry for their cars in the United States, a factor that could presumably influence the location of their North American plants.

volved than just the production of automobiles and the employment of auto workers, important as these are in modern industrial economies. Auto makers are major purchasers of the goods and services of many other industries, ranging from simple products like steel, textiles, rubber, glass, and paint to custom-made machine tools, electronics, precision instruments, and chemicals. Engineers, designers, advertisers, Teamsters, finance companies, and bill collectors are all involved. There are security considerations. The coming of the automobile industry brought great changes; so would its departure. But nothing so absolute is involved, any more than that major industrial countries will stop making steel. Transportation and other factors seem sure to leave some competitive producers in the old centers, even if the advantage of other parts of the world grew. Moreover, the large industrial organizations that the major producers control seem well adapted to carrying out a variety of functions within the industry. Still, large changes are likely to take place in what is made, how it is made, and how it relates to the whole industrial process of which it is a part.

There will be consequences for the number and nature of jobs, for exports and imports, for the demand for the output of other domestic industries, probably for tax revenues, and perhaps for location and transportation. All these matters may pose issues of public policy, and so will more general questions of dependence on foreign sources and, for some countries, the foreign presence in the domestic economy. Though companies will be differently affected, it can be assumed that the largest will take part in these global shifts and may be able to gain from them. Probably they will be able to handle some of the adjustment problems so as to limit the impact on their industrial organization at home, its labor, and the communities in which it is located. It is to their interest to minimize trouble there because serious labor difficulties or major disputes with the public authorities can affect the firm's ability to compete all over the world.

Labor has fewer alternatives, less ability to adapt, and fewer opportunities to influence the whole process. The international cooperation among automobile workers' unions is more highly developed than in most industries, and there has been some success in coordinating the activities of employees of the same company in different parts of the world. Still, it seems unlikely that this kind of action will give labor a controlling voice in what companies do. But the companies can hurt themselves if they do not take serious account of labor reactions, and they might find it advantageous to develop cooperative methods of working out adaptive arrangements. The unions can frequently bring their weight to bear on governments to take actions against the companies. Even so, automotive workers of Europe and North America, if they are not to become trapped in the false security of jobs in a declining industry, may have to be prepared to move into somewhat different kinds of activity, perhaps along with their employers.

To put all these factors together is not the task of this book. We are only asking whether, if some such view of the future is realistic, it would not be possible to take steps in advance that would make the changes more acceptable and more advantageous. A number of possibilities suggest themselves. Can a willingness on the part of the old centers to accept the need for change be translated into policies in the developing countries (and perhaps the socialist countries as well) that avoid the most uneconomic measures for encouraging local production and reduce the pace of forced exports? Would a link with financing encourage acceptance of these terms? If enough countries agreed to them, the odd man out who insisted on developing an uneconomic domestic industry would very largely pay for his choice in higher domestic costs. Unless he were in a very good bargaining position, he would have fewer opportunities to unload part of the cost on big foreign companies anxious to get into his market. Instead of the new centers simply decreeing that so much must be exported, patterns of trade and production could be developed that provided for some specialization with long production runs, gains for all, and less (or at least slower) dislocation. An approach emphasizing these factors would open the possibility of financing and investment patterns that encouraged and speeded up changes instead of postponing them until they were inevitable. For some countries, at least, that would be an inducement to cooperate in the process instead of trying to do better on their own. The expansion of LDC production to fill growing LDC needs reduces the scope and pace of adjustment required in the older centers (in contrast to the textile situation). Japan, as the latecomer, may have the largest adjustment to undertake if its exports to North America and Europe remain limited so as to ease domestic adjustments there.

Many issues are worth thinking about. Ought one to contemplate a formal general agreement among governments to bring about the desirable changes? Might it be better to envisage a process that is more piecemeal and pragmatic, taking its sense of direction or purpose from the widespread realization of what is needed? Should some international agency be created to oversee the process, possibly one to which representatives of industry, labor, and consumers belonged along with those of governments from different parts of the world? In any of these cases, the possibilities of agreement would be affected by the relative importance countries attached to employment, exports, value added in production, self-sufficiency in some line, or other things. If one factor dominates, a government will have a set of aims different from those if it sees the gains in one field offset by losses in another. Compromises may also be easier to arrive at if different governments have different priorities.

Though one thinks in terms of governments, the companies have a key role. The great importance of there being a relatively small number of large and increasingly multinational companies has already been made clear. This is a major difference in structure from that of textiles or, for that matter, of steel. There are potentially great advantages to the adjustment process in this situation; and governments would be foolish to overlook them, even though they cannot sensibly leave the matter entirely to the companies. But if the effort to control what the companies can do leads to a series of measures blocking change, the ultimate price is likely to be high. There is also a troubling underlying dilemma. Some international coordination of public and private action seems essential for an orderly process. But a competitive industry is essential for both economic performance and the entrepreneurial flexibility needed to bring about major changes. Most of the time governments, like consumers, should favor competition even if that means they sometimes end up holding a bagful of problems resulting from some lack of coordination. The history of the industry suggests that single companies regarded as national champions will only rarely be the weapon of choice, at least for the industrialized countries. Even with narrower markets, foreign competition, whether through trade or investment, is likely to be more blessing than curse.

## WHERE WE ARE

This chapter began with a question about how countries might act together to improve the process of bringing about desirable structural changes in the world economy and avoiding the waste and friction that go with delayed, defensive reactions. To explore the possibilities, two routes were followed. First there was some speculation about "guided development," linking finance and trade, the expansion of output in developing countries, and its contraction in older industrial centers. Then we looked simply at the great changes that have taken place in the world's automobile industry in the past few decades and contemplated what may be the next phase or phases. Neither exploration produced a prescription, but both suggested some possible answers to the basic question.

It will have seemed to some readers that we were led—perhaps inevitably—to the brink of global planning. The vision will have been enough to cause many, perhaps most, people to draw back. "Won't," "can't," and "don't" will have marked the reactions. "Nations will not accept these limits on their freedom of action. Even if they would, governments, no matter how well advised, cannot know enough to make the right choices. In any case, do not try for this kind of result, for it will suppress the advantages of competition and free choice and impede, not improve, structural change." These views may all be right; the question is what else to do. "More modest steps to deal with parts of the problem (the most urgent, the easiest, whatever can be managed?)" is the most likely answer, and there is a good deal to be said for it. There is no need to expand on the subject here; it runs through the whole book. So does the accompanying question whether the problem is as large as the opening chapters made out, and whether a willingness to explore new paths might increase with more analysis—or more fear of the consequences of doing nothing.

A different kind of reaction is that the explorations went too far in favoring reliance on new, cheap sources of production while ignoring other values. To be sure, it was assumed, more or less explicitly, that the efficiency criterion as laid out in Chapter 2 was the dominant one and that departures from it were bound to exact a price that could be justified only if a society knew what it was doing. But as Chapter 2 made clear, efficiency is more than cheapness; and we have paid a good bit of attention to slowing change, making it more acceptable, and finding alternative jobs and sources of strength in adjusting economies. If, however, other values are to be preferred, it remains sensible to ask whether international action to foster them would not be desirable. One would still be looking for an international industrial policy, but it would be oriented differently.

Usually, efficiency in the broad sense does play an important part in getting what a society wants, and the question is one of combining it with something else that is also wanted. Often enough this takes the form of establishing certain conditions that limit the area within which international competition is allowed to play more or less freely (on the assumption that free trade serves the ends of efficiency, which is not unconditionally true). The possibility was mentioned of a steel agreement assuring each major power a certain level of production. The probability that industrial countries will keep an automobile industry (if not the one they have now) even without special protection was raised in this chapter. The agricultural policies of industrial countries work in somewhat the same way. The same principle was embodied in the proposal for an international textile agreement put forward by Solomon Barkin in the early 1960s.[22]

---

[22]"International Trade in Textiles and Garments: A Challenge for New Policies," in Friedrich and Harris (eds.), *Public Policy*, op. cit., pp. 366–400. Other aspects of this paper were discussed in chap. 4.

Barkin proposed "an international textile coordinating body" that would keep people informed about textile demand, world trade, and the possible problems arising from the expansion of capacity and exports. "The international financial bodies particularly should be guided. . . by such information." [23] Up to this point, the prescription is similar to Staley's with its emphasis on permitting the older centers to adjust. But there are also overtones of the late 1970s in the wish to discourage the construction of "excess capacity." Barkin argued that LDCs would often do better to develop industries other than textiles in their own long-run best interests, especially if they had adequate advice and technical assistance from the industrial countries. The other part of the argument was that not only would adjustment in the older centers take time, but it was reasonable for them to retain textile and garment industries even if they had to "forfeit the advantages of maximum international specialization." [24] To reconcile conflicting aims and interests, Barkin proposed: First a level of self-sufficiency in textiles and garments should be set for each country, based on historical factors. Second, there should be a period of modernization and reorganization of industries to make them more competitive. Third, the pace of import expansion should be geared to the ability of the older countries to shift resources. Protection for longer periods would be needed for plants in areas where there were few alternative job opportunities. However, the importing countries would be committed to programs of adjustment. Fourth, the developing countries, which would "enjoy a rising volume of world textile and garment trade," should undertake to "promote higher labor standards for textile and garment workers."

Barkin painted with a broad brush. One could imagine an international agreement that satisfied the wish of all major countries to have some minimum capacity in textiles (or in anything else for that matter) but also to get as much efficiency as possible by accepting a measure of international specialization within the

[23]Ibid., p. 397.
[24]Ibid., p. 398.

industry. It is not easy to see how to blend efficiency with a limitation on market forces, but that some approximation of a reasonable international division of labor should be possible by negotiation is not altogether unthinkable. The *juste retour* can be a damaging doctrine, but it need not always be fatal or the worst outcome if the alternative is unilateral protection or even the international textile agreements we have known.

Different blends of efficiency with other values are to be found in some of the ideas being discussed in France in the late 1970s. A former Gaullist minister proposed that the European Community establish a "new protectionism" that would not shield inefficiency but would permit a stable and orderly social and economic life by cutting off disturbing or rapid changes coming from outside, especially in the form of disruptive imports. [25] Little was said in that book about the rest of the world, but a global system with a family resemblance was proposed by an academic economist who had proffered them to a working group of the Commissariat du Plan. [26]

The key argument here was the rather familiar one that competition among countries at very different levels of development caused an excessive amount of trouble and that development was essentially an internal process. Self-development by countries in the Third World would be healthier and serve their purposes better if it were not as strongly export-oriented as it had come to be. Trade among the regions would be limited to what each needed from abroad and what it had to export to pay for its imports. Protection would be provided more for industries that were to expand to meet growing needs than for those that should be shrinking because demand was going to fall. Rich countries and international financial institutions would help finance a reorientation of Third World production along these lines.

[25]Jean-Marcel Jeanneney, *Pour un nouveau protectionnisme*, Editions du Seuil, Paris, 1978. Efficiency is assured by competition within the Community.
[26]André Grjebine, "Vers une autonomie concertée des régions du monde," *Revue D'Economie Politique*, vol. 8, no. 2, Paris, Mars-Avril 1978.

One can imagine still other kinds of international industrial policy measures intended to maximize different values from the ones we have called "efficiency." But what all these examples underline is still another question: What countries are most likely to be able to agree with one another about what kinds of industrial policy issues? Some answers leap to mind—but as Chapter 7 suggests, they should be approached circumspectly and in part through a detour in Chapter 6, which reminds us that not all countries have equal capacities in conducting industrial policy.

# SIX

# Aptitudes and Obstacles

In order to carry out a sustained industrial policy, particularly a comprehensive one, a government must be capable of many things. The political, economic, social, and administrative conditions that define its ability to formulate and carry out a policy can be as important as what kind of policy it is. These conditions vary considerably from country to country, even among groups of countries thought to be in many other respects similar. It is the aim of this chapter to call attention to some of the factors that have to be taken into account and to suggest how national differences affect the kinds of industrial policies an individual country can best pursue. This inquiry provides a basis for the next chapter's consideration of the factors that draw some countries together into international cooperation on matters of industrial policy and push others apart.

Perhaps even the most limited kind of government can provide rudimentary protection against foreign competition. But if the industrial policy is more complex than that and the government has to see to it that there are shifts in the use of resources, balance conflicting interests among its citizens, and adjust what it is doing at home to fit with its international position, then it needs many skills and the means of acting on broad and narrow issues. Adaptation to structural change is rarely rapid, and efforts to initiate change are also likely to take time; therefore, continuity of policy over a considerable period may be required. A certain suppleness is also needed as circumstances change and unforeseen conditions arise. Words and ideas have to be translated into action with a fairly high degree of efficiency and consistency. All this has to be accomplished in a setting in which, at least much of the time, substantial parts of the population are critical of what is being done and, if the political system permits, will oppose and resist it. And at the same time, people in office will look to the next election, which is likely to come sooner than the end of any given process of structural adaptation.

That democratic governments are not always able to meet these standards hardly needs to be demonstrated, but that very factor has to be taken into account in deciding what is wise industrial policy. Nor is the problem confined to democratic countries. The weaknesses of nondemocratic governments in developing countries are well known. And in the Soviet Union and the European communist countries, where the undemocratic governments are strong and have what can be thought of as a total industrial policy, the ability to get results is not always apparent. The old aspiration to let the governance of men give way to the administration of things is not sufficient, it would seem. Nor does the ability to get results seem to correlate very highly with the firmness with which some central governments have held power, versus the modest decentralization introduced in other communist countries.

Examples of the differences in political systems among democratic countries that influence their ability to carry through industrial policies come easily to mind. The separation of powers in the United States creates many complications avoided by countries with the relative unity provided by a parliamentary system. The extent of provincial power in Canada and, less markedly, in other federal states does much to shape what the central government can do. Regional differences, the political power of the agricultural interest (going beyond the farm vote), and the conventional wisdom about what governments should and should not do are all familiar factors that shape administration as well as political decisions. It has been suggested that the more democratically controlled governmental decisions are, the more likely it is that industrial policy measures will lean toward the defense of labor-intensive industries (one man, one vote). Or it may simply be more difficult to formulate and carry out any industrial policy at all. Sir Andrew Shonfield sees a major distinction between the United States's insistence that purpose and expected performance be carefully worked out in advance and the French willingness to be satisfied with holding authorities to account afterward, when the results can be seen.

Behind political authority and the distribution of power is the nature of the society and how it responds to a situation. The clarity with which the French saw the need not only for reconstruction but for reestablishment of France's place in the world was crucial to the ability to pursue a national industrial policy, at least for a time. Similar elements worked somewhat differently for Germany. Social solidarity in Japan makes a contrast with the divisiveness in British and American society that undoubtedly explains something. But perhaps those last two countries were more influenced by the focus on the internal sharing of power and redistribution of wealth and income once the imperatives of war, which had created great solidarity, were removed. Developing countries are frequently an extraordinary mix of strong nationalism and great internal division and of a common will to progress and disagreement about how.

A broad historical study would be needed to deal adequately with these matters. All that is possible here is to comment in very general terms on a few fields in which a country's institutions and practices may greatly affect the ability to formulate and carry out industrial policies. For simplicity's sake the discussion is largely confined to democratic, market-oriented economies; and even then the survey must remain selective and impressionistic. The fields are government-business relations, government-owned companies, the financial system, how labor is organized, and the handling of science and technology.

## GOVERNMENT-BUSINESS RELATIONS

A key factor in all economic policy in a mixed economy, government-business relations are vital to industrial policy. Often the organization and functioning of business enterprises is itself one of the objects of policy. More often than not, business is the modality for dealing with structural change—or failing to do so. Governments change, but much of business remains and so provides some of the continuity that industrial policy requires. A great deal of industrial policy requires knowledge that officials have to get from businessmen. Though governments can coerce, they also have to persuade and much industrial policy depends on some degree of cooperation between government and business.

In complex societies there is no natural uniformity of business opinion except on a few points. In many countries machinery exists for establishing the business view on many public issues, and official responsibilities are assigned to such bodies as the German *Handelstag* or the French chambers of commerce. In the United States, in contrast, there is no single body that could properly be regarded as the authoritative voice of business, though there are many different business groups that are highly effective on a variety of issues. Adequate channels of communication are clearly essential to good industrial policy, but the basic question is what the "voice of business" represents. A valid spokesman for a single industry or sector cannot be expected to bring out all the conflicts of interest between that industry and others. Yet a keen awareness of how competitors, customers, and suppliers are affected is essential to shaping a sectoral policy; then the execution of that policy may depend largely on cooperation from the sector itself.

While the microeconomic aspect of industrial policy makes close government-business relations crucial, the public is naturally suspicious of the influence of businessmen on officials and legislators. Moreover, officials whose work involves them heavily with a certain industry are likely to develop views similar to those of its managers (unless they constantly oppose them, which is also a defect). Those responsible for a protected industry are sympathetic to its troubles; those who have had a hand in fostering a new activity—perhaps in high technology—are more likely to see a need for prolonged help than others. Such men are dangerous if the aim of policy is to make an industry competitive, which, if it is achievable at all, requires toughness in

182

cutting off subsidies and reducing import barriers after a reasonable time. But if officials are too far from an industry's point of view, they will also make mistakes in industrial policy. The knowledge, technical competence, and even statistical data on which much industrial policy depends may exist only within private firms. It is rare for government to be able to hold many people whose specialized knowledge of an industry is as great as that of people in the industry itself, who are almost always better paid. The movement of people between government and business can sometimes help but is a limited resource. It seems well suited to strengthening business access to government, but when safeguards against biased action by businessmen in government reach the level of those in the United States, they make it costly to be an "in-and-outer" in lower or middle levels of business and government.

In the United States, at least, it has been common knowledge that close links develop between the mining industry and the Department of the Interior, between defense contractors and the Pentagon, between shipping companies and the Maritime Administration. Perhaps inevitable, these ties make it essential that the same officials should not be able to settle the matters for which they are (if at one remove) advocates. The world over, finance ministries have been major policemen, for obvious reasons; but for the shaping of industrial policies something more seems needed to take adequate account of a wide range of approaches to the public interest. Labor representation in the process, and perhaps in the councils of the industry itself, may be desirable to make adjustment effective; but it is not equivalent to representation of the public interest, since labor and management are likely to have very similar views on the place of the industry in the economy. Public, nongovernmental representation on industry boards, said to be useful in dealing with environmental issues, race and sex discrimination, honesty, ethics, and public relations, does not seem a promising device for industrial policy. However, governmental representation on boards of firms that are receiving direct government support or that have an obligation to accomplish some significant changes in a given period of time seems rather natural. Its effectiveness is not altogether clear, however, and the device may be inferior in most cases to reliance on external pressure (reduced protection over time, scheduled reduction of subsidies, etc.).

The common expectation that ministers of agriculture will serve the farmer's interests and that some other ministers (in the United States, the Secretary of Labor and the Secretary of Commerce) will speak for labor and business can be thought of as a loose form of functional representation. Proposals to divide seats in a legislature by interest groups rather than by geography once attracted a good deal of attention; and the idea survives in the ILO, the Economic and Social Committee of the European Communities, and some national bodies, mostly advisory. There may be a place for such approaches in shaping industrial policy, as is suggested by the Solomon committee's proposal for a tripartite committee made up of public, labor, and industry representatives to watch over adaptation in the American steel industry, mentioned in Chapter 4. Whatever the value of such bodies may be, they cannot be expected to deal with all the issues that have to be dealt with in day-to-day relations between government officials and businessmen.

Continuity in industrial policy—even the success of individual measures of adjustment—is jeopardized if what is done depends entirely on which political party is in office. In most democracies one major party is usually thought to stand fairly close to business and to favor its interests. The other parties need not be really antibusiness, but they have fewer direct ties and will probably have a stand on some issues contrary to those of business circles. Wrongly handled business-government relations can make it hard to avoid an on-again, off-again sequence. If a given piece of industrial policy is perceived as helping business at public expense, or in another case bureaucrats and politicians are thought to be exploiting business, that activity will draw fire when there is a change in administrations. To reduce the risk, the handling of industrial policy should take full account of public and business interests and be regarded as, if not above suspicion, then fair and open. It would be even better if the presumption developed that existing programs should not be upset except when they themselves exemplified real major differences among the parties.

In the United States, where different parties can control the executive and Congress, the situation is in some respects worse and in others better. Having to live this way for so long, the country has developed a variety of devices to preserve a certain amount of continuity. This works best when power is delegated to the President or a partly independent body to work freely within a legal framework. Business has ties with both parties, and candidates often need support outside their own party to get elected. Kennedy and Nixon both tried to give the textile industry what it wanted. The more troublesome side of the matter is that the division of authority means that business (or labor or any other interest group) will be active at both ends of Pennsylvania Avenue and may get support from Congress that upsets a policy in which the executive branch is trying to balance all the interests involved (not just those of the industry in trouble, which is likely to be the one most heard in Congress). No doubt the balance sometimes tilts the other way, and Congress can be a valuable corrective; but regardless of the merits of any case, the more complex the matter, the more difficulty, since legislation and appropriations will be involved. Congress is so constituted that the legislators are much more responsive to certain interests and issues than to others and have to make bargains among themselves that often involve considerations extraneous to the real issue. The combination of pluses and minuses may not add up to the true sum of the public interest, especially if a concentration of pressures makes one issue predominate in shaping congressional action. Continuity is just part of the problem; uncertainty is another. As experience with the energy program proposed by the Carter administration in 1977 and 1978 shows, the shaping as well as the conduct of industrial policy in an American-style democracy can be exceptionally difficult.

It is hard to carry out successful industrial policy *against* business. Government can establish conditions business dislikes or refuse to do what it wants; it can control some things and prevent others; but it can only rarely perform the functions businesses do. Thus the proper choice of incentives becomes important, along with the creation of situations in which it is to the interest of a substantial number of the relevant businesses to move in the "right" direction. There are major differences

185

among countries in the extent to which government can bring pressure on business or would find it wise to do so. In addition to sticks and carrots, there has to be some degree of basic agreement about where the country or industry ought to be going (even though people accept the aim for different reasons). If a few businesses are willing to do things that the rest of their industry will not, possibilities are opened that should be taken into account in designing industrial policy. The pressure to conform should never be allowed to prevent innovators from going their own way. The maverick is one of the saviors of capitalism.

A key element in government-business relations is the approach of different countries to competition. A strong and fairly unconditional antitrust emphasis, as in the United States, contrasts sharply with European practices, where antimonopoly laws exist against the background of traditions of permitting and sometimes encouraging close cooperation among firms in a given industry and the formation of cartels in some circumstances. In Japan, too, antitrust laws introduced under the American occupation, which also broke up the Zaibatsu concentrations, are modified in various ways; there is a good deal of competition, but there is also a framework established by consensus between the government and industry. Neither the American nor the foreign system is wholly predictable in its results; each is modified to some degree when circumstances warrant (or even when they do not, if exceptions have been written into law or policy in general terms). But each produces a characteristic set of difficulties for industrial policy. In the American case these concern the limits to intraindustry collaboration created by the antitrust laws and the question whether ways can be found to make exceptions by executive discretion rather than by requiring legislation. The most serious problem for countries that are easily disposed to permit agreements among producers is how to maintain the degree of competition that efficiency requires. The issue takes on a special edge when the only way to establish a national capacity for some product is by what amounts to a guarantee of monopoly or the singling out of a "national champion" to break new ground with the help of public funds and government procurement. Foreign competition is eliminated or reduced in order to permit the creation of an enterprise that will become internationally competitive—not the easiest feat of public policy.

The list of government-business issues could be made longer, but the loose generalizations of the last few pages are enough to show that there are very considerable differences among countries in government-business relations and no common standard in these matters that applies to all advanced capitalist countries. No doubt some of the contrasts are simply different ways of doing much the same things, as Andrew Shonfield showed so well in *Modern Capitalism*, a book that has much to say on many other aspects of industrial policy as well.[1] The similarities are strongest in Europe. Japan is different and so, for the most part, is the United States. Both are changing; the Japanese are clearly weakening some of the government-business links; whether the Americans are strengthening them or still just groping for new expressions of old attitudes is not at all clear.

Whether differences among countries in government-business relations are obstacles to international cooperation in industrial policy is the topic of later sections. What is clear, though, is that the ability of different countries to conduct industrial policies of one sort or another is greatly influenced by their differences in laws and custom regarding government-business relations. The United States government, for example, cannot work with business in the same way as most European governments do, let alone Japan. The offsetting characteristics and especially their implications for other kinds of economic policies need closer analysis than this book can provide. An alternative not to be forgotten is that when disadvantages in these matters become apparent and troublesome, that in itself becomes a pressure to develop new forms of government-business relations.

[1]Andrew Shonfield, *Modern Capitalism: The Changing Balance of Public and Private Power*, Oxford University Press for The Royal Institute of International Affairs, New York, 1965. Much has changed since the book was published; happily, Professor Shonfield is examining the changes in a work which will extend the comparative analysis to the 1970s.

## GOVERNMENT-OWNED COMPANIES

Nationalization—or socialization at some other level than that of the national government—was once an article of faith for socialists and has often been a practical resort for pragmatists in difficulty. In both capacities it has lost much of its magic, largely as the result of experience. Nationalization becomes a live ideological issue from time to time, as in the Socialist-Communist common platform for the French elections of 1978. It is also still advanced as a solution for certain specific problems, such as increasing the processing of asbestos in Quebec, raising Saskatchewan's returns from potash, or saving a failing firm. For the most part, though, a more sophisticated set of calculations has replaced the old assumption that public ownership made it certain that the public interest would be served.

Front and center are efficiency and cost, matters in which the performance of many publicly owned corporations has been abysmal while that of others has been quite good. Prescriptions for this malady are limitations on funds, independent management, and the expectation of profit. But emphasis on accountability to a parliament goes the other way. So does the simple thought that there is no point in having a publicly owned corporation if it simply does the same things a privately owned one would do. To buy out owners in a declining industry may ease the process of adjustment; it may be sensible to turn past loans into equity as a way of gaining the authority to restructure an industry, as the Barre government argued with regard to French steel in 1978. But neither of these things will happen if governments succumb to the pressures that have often made nationalized industries havens of inefficiency, concealed unemployment, and low productivity.

If a national company is created as the only way to avoid foreign control, it should presumably meet some economic standards of efficiency. But if the reason for having a government corporation is to carry out activities that are unprofitable by ordinary business standards (or at least too risky), other interesting questions arise. Should the government's money be seen as venture capital that might be lost? Should the accounts make

188

distinctions between activities that are supposed to pay and those to be subsidized as social costs? The risk is considerable that without a strong government and a clear public purpose, nationalized enterprises will develop into "a system of public industry that has as its principal characteristic anonymity and a lack of transparency in its decisions that make all forms of political control impossible."[2]

Nationalization may have little to be said for it as a method of control over private business to prevent abuse and assure a socially desirable performance. Most governments have other means at their disposal, and, as a Swedish socialist has argued, "the formal ownership of the means of production is a secondary issue . . . . What is of prime importance is the distribution in society of the economic and political functions which are hidden beneath formal ownership."[3] These functions, Gunnar Adler-Karlsson pointed out, can be and are regulated and controlled in innumerable ways, and it is the intelligent handling of these matters that makes for social welfare and democratic control of the economy. Interestingly enough, this "functional socialism" is quite comparable to the traditional regulatory approach to business in the United States, where socialization has never had wide support.

In both cases, however, there are limits to what regulations can do to bring about positive action if business is reluctant. Sometimes that becomes an argument for nationalization but not necessarily for a monopoly. Government-owned corporations can perform a variety of functions in an otherwise private industry: yardstick, catalyst, source of information, assurance of a public presence, training ground for specialists who can then better supervise the industry, pioneer in difficult technology, and vehicle for reducing the risk and financial burden of activities private firms would not undertake alone. Developments of this

---

[2] Bruno Amoroso and Ole Jess Olsen, *Lo Stato Imprenditore*, Laterza, Rome, 1978, p. 204. The authors apply this description to Italy.

[3] Gunnar Adler-Karlsson, *Functional Socialism*, Prisma, Stockholm, 1969, p. 7. The Swedish original appeared in 1967. It is perhaps significant that when Swedish socialism ran into difficulties in the mid-1970s, there was an increase in nationalization.

kind have been particularly noteworthy in oil and mining, especially in countries that wanted to avoid complete dependence on foreign multinational corporations. A national company may not be able to perform all these functions at once, but the situation is completely different from that of a public monopoly. A further dimension is added if, either to perform its home functions better or simply because its managers act as entrepreneurs, the public company goes abroad, buying, selling, and investing in foreign countries.

It seems likely that the dominant view in the OECD world is coming to be the one set out by two young French officials after much study of the mixed experience in their own and other countries. "Because of the difficulties inherent in it, nationalization should be regarded as a last resort to be undertaken only when the other means at the disposal of the government have been exhausted without results."[4] This is probably not true of the developing countries. The atmosphere, psychology, and politics of control are entirely different; even though the power of foreign corporations and the supposed impotence of LDC governments to deal with them have been often exaggerated, there is enough in the idea—and enough in the history of past concessions to foreigners that would not be made today—to make it likely that governments will continue to expropriate for what they think are good, defensive reasons. Several factors may help change the situation in the future: the disadvantages of this course for the expropriating government; its frequent failure to produce the results expected; the steps investors can take to defend themselves; the proper posture of their home governments; and, perhaps most important of all, the evolution of forms of business-government relations in the LDCs that will produce better results and less friction. For some time to come, however, one has to reckon with this kind of state enterprise, and another as well: the government corporation created because there was nothing there, or so little as to be obviously unable to bring about the degree of industrialization wanted.

[4]Christian Stoffaes and Jacques Victorri, *Nationalisations*, Flammarion, Paris, 1977, p. 400.

It has long been recognized that in developing countries the state's major role will be different from that of the governments of the older industrial countries (though not always so different from the parts they played earlier). A shortage of strong entrepreneurs, the reluctance of local capital to take risks, and a whole series of political and psychological factors push in the same direction. State companies as such may not always be necessary, but there is no reason to quarrel with the view that they sometimes offer the best or only course. That they often fail or provide results at very high costs, and that they may be judged by political, not economic, standards, and staffed likewise, is well known. Some LDC governments have learned these lessons, but their alternatives are not always the simple private enterprise ones laid down by somewhat ideological Western businessmen. There are problems. The interests of multinational corporations and host governments are not identical and, while not beyond compromise, will not be automatically brought into harmony by some law of nature. Nor are foreign businesses necessarily the best alternative when domestic businesses are too few or too weak. In rapidly developing societies without adequate domestic risk capital (or large enough accumulations of private funds) it is not unthinkable that a Schumpeterian entrepreneur should make his mark and improve the country by using government assets and an official position. Even if the emphasis is just on efficient management, managerial skill is to be found in various places in the LDC world (often including the army and foreign enterprises), and management can be hired. There is no need to argue the merits here; the point is only that the state-owned corporation is not bound to wither away.

Whether they are in industrial or developing countries, state-run corporations present some international problems highly relevant to industrial policy. Fair competition is one. Although private entrepreneurs are sure that they are more efficient than socialized companies, they also feel that they are always at an unfair disadvantage in competing with socialized firms at home or abroad. A realistic approach to subsidies (as Chapter 3 pointed out) has to take account of the financing of public enterprises, but that is not the end of the matter. The general idea that state corporations should for the most part apply "commercial considerations" in the conduct of their affairs makes a good deal of sense for some activities but not for those intended to serve broader public purposes. And if the public corporation is a monopoly, the injunction to act as a private monopoly would hardly solve all the problems of other people, as Jacob Viner pointed out long ago.[5] The GATT rules on state trading based on these ideas are inadequate, and the practice that has developed around them is of very limited value. The older rules of international law that distinguished between the government's immunity when it performed the functions of a sovereign and its susceptibility to foreign law when it was engaged in commercial functions hardly holds water any longer. Is it less a sovereign act to shape an economy than to regulate traffic? The chances that state trading will increase in importance are substantial; distinctions between public and private activity become blurred as the government interests itself in the results, whether for so-called political or so-called economic reasons. Trade policy and foreign policy have been the perspectives in which state trading has been mostly discussed in the past; to them has to be added the effect on industrial policy, national and international. Nationalization, or the creation of state-owned companies by other means, often thought of largely in terms of industrial policy, has to be seen as affecting trade and foreign policy as well.

## NATIONAL FINANCIAL STRUCTURES

The French government's ability to make industrial planning work depended to an important degree on its ability to direct the flow of investment capital from the *Caisse des Dépôts* and the

---

[5]"If 'discrimination' . . . is given its usual meaning with reference to trade barriers, or its meaning in economic usage with respect to monopolistic practices, it is evident that any agency having monopoly power would be acting in conformity with, rather than be departing from, 'commercial principles' . . . if it carried out skilfully the practice of 'discriminating monopsony'. . . . *Trade Relations between Free-market and Controlled Economies*, League of Nations, Geneva, 1943, p. 77.

*Crédit National* and to influence the flow from both private and nationalized banks. In Britain, in contrast, there was what John Zysman calls a "double trench," between the government and the banks and the banks and industry. That was not the only factor hampering British industrial policy but it was a major one, as Zysman makes clear in some pioneering analysis that has laid the groundwork for a larger comparative study.[6] Nevertheless, argues Stoffaes, French banks are not close enough to their industrial clients and lack the will to take risks, the ingenuity, and the flexibility that make German banks so helpful to the competitiveness of small as well as large firms.[7] All observers have long agreed that German banks knew far more about the industrial problems of their clients than did their counterparts in other countries and made use of it in their active participation on the boards of many enterprises. The pattern goes back a century or more. The small number of large banks, their role as both underwriters and trustees for stockholders, and their practice of advancing relatively short-term loans that had to be rolled over frequently to serve long-term purposes have all led foreigners to see a coordination of activities that amounts to an "industrial policy"—perhaps on the part of the banks—in spite of the German emphasis on laissez faire. Andrew Shonfield cites some examples of bank influences on investment, for example in the steel industry in the 1960s, and argues that the *Kreditanstalt für Wiederaufbau* was particularly effective in the 1950s because it provided public funds to be distributed through the private banking mechanism.[8]

Japanese often say that Westerners see a closer governmental control over banks than really exists in their country. There is no doubt, however, that the Japanese practice of accepting a much higher ratio of debt to equity than Westerners think proper makes industry highly sensitive to pressure from the banks. Be-

[6] I have had the privilege of reading unpublished papers by John Zysman. The OECD study of French industrial policy (cited in the Critical Bibliography) puts the share of specialized bodies in bank lending to industry at 40 percent; the nationalized banks accounted for much of the rest.

[7] Stoffaes, *La Grande Menace Industrielle*, pp. 109, 110, and passim.

[8] Shonfield, op. cit., pp. 246–258, 276–282.

tween 1950 and 1970 the ratio of equity to invested capital fell from 31.4 percent to 19.9 percent for manufacturing firms and from 26.9 percent to 16.1 percent for industry as a whole.[9] The banks, in turn, depend to a substantial degree on the Bank of Japan. Most Japanese would argue that the central bank's pressures have been used primarily for macroeconomic and especially balance-of-payments purposes. Still, the "fit" between financial structure and industrial policy is very real in a positive sense: The Bank of Japan made sure the commercial banks had adequate funds to lend to the recognized growth industries. One of the factors giving rise to the view that Japan's future industrial policy will have to develop some new methods is the degree of financial independence achieved by a number of large companies. What is less clear to outsiders is what significance to attach to the banks affiliated with the large industrial groupings in Japan. Whether intimate involvement with the manufacturing and trading "family" improves the ability of the bank to estimate risk and shape its lending accordingly, or whether its job is only to supply money for purposes others approve, is not altogether clear.

In the United States the government certainly takes a back seat to the banks in financing industry; but the banks sometimes have to take a back seat to other lenders and to providers of equity capital in various forms through the securities exchanges or by private placement. The separation of commercial and investment banking provided by the Glass-Steagall Act adds to the divisions, but these distinctions are being circumvented by a variety of measures. Whether bankers and investment analysts are really well informed about the workings of the industry behind the balance sheet is a matter for debate. Perhaps a greater weakness is the pressure on American chief executives to be so concerned about quarterly returns and the current price of their shares on the stock exchanges that they do not always give adequate priority to long-run needs except when their resources for self-financing are high.

[9] Richard E. Caves and Masu Uekusa, *Industrial Organization in Japan*, The Brookings Institution, Washington, D.C., 1976, p. 39.

None of these patterns is immutable. While some businesses may become less dependent on banks, some banks will become more concerned with exactly how industries use borrowed funds, not just with general creditworthiness. Insurance companies, pension funds, and other large accumulations of private capital are increasingly important to industrial borrowers. Views vary on the choice between credit and equity for different purposes: Sometimes large stockholders are content to provide funds while refraining from using their votes. Government bond issues in foreign markets have a new lease on life; foreign bank lending plays an increasing part in the industrial policies of developing countries. The internationalization of banking brings new lenders into old preserves where they may behave differently from the natives. It gives banks a wider reach than before, which affects their attitude toward familiar connections. Perhaps most important of all is the enhanced ability of large enterprises to borrow on world markets. Governments have probably lost some of their ability to control national markets unless they are prepared to go quite far in interfering with the freedom of international payments that has grown up. With it they may have lost some of their ability to use financial means to guide industrial policy.

Though denial may be more difficult, there is no question that the ability of the government to provide funds, directly or through influencing what lenders or investors do, remains an important factor. Sometimes this is a matter of providing access to funds that would not otherwise be there, but more often the key question is likely to concern favorable terms, such as lower interest rates or longer maturities (which may in turn provide access to private funds on normal terms). Such devices have been used for years by many governments for housing, small business, export promotion, and a variety of special purposes. They have a key part in most regional policies and are being used to help develop additional energy resources. The problems for national policy lie in determining why financial markets have not reflected the true needs of the economy, which competing purpose has the greatest claim for help, and whether the provision of funds is the most effective instrument the government could use.

An international issue of some importance is what forms of

195

financial aid should be treated as subsidies. Another is whether the clear advantages some governments have over others in providing capital make an important difference to what can be accomplished internationally. A government less able than others to influence the flow of credit through the banking system may move toward direct government financing. This encounters resistance because of views that the amount of GNP flowing through the budget should be limited, and also because of the difficulty of keeping direct government financing from being turned into a pork barrel. It also produces international subsidy questions more quickly than the indirect method of induced bank behavior. A subsidy rule that checked lending at low rates might encourage a government to provide financing through equity, thus leading to all the questions about government-owned firms raised in the last section.

One further international issue is the role of national financing for measures of international industrial policy. Here what happens in one country is linked to what is done in another; contraction in one place, matching expansion in another, and expansion in a different activity in the first place all have a part. Whether much of this can be done by international financing or whether the best method is a combination of national financing is one question; the forms are another. Ordinarily one would suppose that a combination of direct government aid with financing that is supposed to yield a return would make sense, and here the place of the banking system can be crucial.

## THE VOICE OF LABOR

The greatest impact of adjustment is usually on workers. As an interested party in a threatened industry, labor is likely to stand with management in resisting change—but workers in other industries are in the same situation as any other citizens, who lose by resistance to a more efficient use of national resources. Effective adjustment programs can hardly be imagined without the cooperation of workers and labor organizations. The content of such programs and the way arrangements for participation work will depend to an important degree on how the workers involved see their own interests. That, in turn, depends to an important degree on how labor is organized, something that varies a good deal from country to country.

Labor's interest in the whole range of national economic policies is obvious. Industrial policy is no exception, since macroeconomic policies and other measures are not adequate to assure jobs, security, and income, the basic goals of any labor movement once its ability to organize and operate is assured. No doubt labor as a whole and in the long run has a large stake in seeing that industrial policy is conducted on sound principles but in concrete cases it faces a problem: how to reconcile the general interest of working people with the particular interest of those workers directly affected. In industrial policy issues, almost by definition, a partial interest has to be weighed against the interests of the whole, and this cuts across the lines of labor.

With that focus, there is no need to say what difference it makes whether labor unions are affiliated with political parties or not; whether there are one, two, or more federations or other groupings; and just how they are related to one another. Any of these conditions may override consideration of the real interests of workers affected by adjustment. It is, however, very easy to see how important it is whether the major labor groupings include substantially all workers and all industries. Although unorganized workers are not powerless, they are likely to be treated differently from those in unions; and if they are foreigners, their position is likely to be especially weak. Our main concern is with organized labor grouped, at the national level, into one or more federations that include unions in both protected and other industries. Then the key issue is how decisions are made in the federation.

When industrial policy is ambitious, positive, and forward-looking, its immediate labor effects are benign: job creation, increased productivity, and improving skills. Labor may be divided on some questions: Who shall organize the new plant or the workers in novel jobs? Is it fair to keep wages for old jobs lower than for the more productive new ones? But these disputes seem less troublesome than those in declining industries, where

197

the basic question is likely to be whether organized labor as a whole should support the natural resistance of some of its members to change even though the result is to impose costs on the economy (and therefore on other workers). The alternative is to favor, or accept, change so long as the adjustment policy cushions workers against the worst blows of dislocation, provides financial support, and gives what help is possible in finding new jobs. It could be argued that labor's main concern should be with the adequacy of adjustment assistance of this sort and the assurance that it will be provided. But a strong labor movement should be interested in additional steps that could improve the position of its members so that they did not need adjustment assistance. Moreover, positive steps in industrial policy that expand productivity or introduce new industries may contribute to the decline of other industries. To leave each case to the unions directly involved runs against the idea of solidarity among workers. It may also risk weakening labor's influence in important areas of public policy.

In the United States, the tendency has been to have an AFL-CIO position on trade, with a little freedom for a union to diverge in its own interests. When the position favored liberal trade policies, some relatively small unions in protected industries regularly supported their industry's case for tariffs or quotas. After the strong swing to protection took place, there was little public deviation from the main line, but not every union worked equally hard to lobby for import restrictions. In determining the national position the size and wealth of unions make a great deal of difference, but so does the intensity of feeling; those who are hurt carry more weight than those who suffer little or no damage from imports and would benefit as consumers or taxpayers from trade liberalization. In the United States this has meant that unions in the older industries such as textiles and steel did more to shape the views of the AFL-CIO than did the most rapidly growing parts of the labor movement, which are in services of various kinds. The construction unions, which have only a secondary concern with import competition, go along with the majority in these matters. The United Automobile Workers, who used to be an important influence favoring freer trade, are no longer part of the AFL-CIO and shape their views according to what seems to them the needs of their industry. Also unaffiliated are the Teamsters, some of whom might be thought to benefit from any increases in trade, whether import, export, or domestic. That may make it hard for them to see their true interest in trade matters (except when they move out of the transportation business, as they sometimes do), though any particular set of disturbances may seem bothersome. Moreover, they may have a very great interest in other structural policies that affect location and the competition of road, rail, and air. They are presumably well placed to make compromises with unions that have a greater stake in foreign trade issues.

Nothing in this analysis suggests that the position of American labor, or even the AFL-CIO, is immutable. The interests of particular unions may alter with economic changes and shifts in the position of their industries. Change in the balance of power within the labor movement, more open and democratic examination of the interests of workers, and the development of more complex concepts of solidarity are all possible. The domestic political situation is not irrelevant; labor's support for the Hull trade agreements program of the 1930s was heavily influenced by an allegiance to Franklin Roosevelt that had quite a different basis. Perceptions of the economic needs of the country and of the significance of structural change could play a part, and these could be influenced by the kinds of adjustment policies that are developed and the extent to which the needs of labor are met in general and in particular industries.

How labor interests are seen depends in part on the pattern of collective bargaining. Industrywide collective bargaining, such as exists in Germany, undoubtedly provides a vehicle for consolidating the position of labor and management against the government (or anyone else) as to what the interests of the industry are. It may therefore strengthen the natural tendency for labor to identify itself with industry claims for protection. But it could also be helpful in working out constructive measures of adaptation if leaders on both sides were persuaded that that was desirable. Through industrywide arrangements, unions could be assured that adaptation would cost their members no jobs or pay cuts, and employers could get assurances that the union would not strike or otherwise interfere with changes in employment on an agreed schedule. Something like this took place in American coal mining in the 1940s and 1950s when John L. Lewis had built the United Mine Workers into a strong enough union to make a favorable bargain with the operators on the terms on which the industry was to be mechanized.

In the American automobile industry the employers bargain separately, but the United Automobile Workers is effectively the union for the whole industry. There is a relation between what is worked out by Ford, General Motors, Chrysler, and others and a tendency toward homogeneity in wages and conditions, but with some allowance for the particular problem of firms and plants (as there is in the German system as well). Among the questions that need looking into is how these bargaining patterns might influence policies aimed at structural change, because it seems unlikely that competitive relations within the industry would not be affected.

Far removed from these relatively simple cases is one, common in Britain and the United States, in which the firm has to deal on a companywide or plant-by-plant basis with a number of unions. Though there may be committees to coordinate the position of the different unions for collective bargaining, this prescription offers particular difficulties for adaptation and change. The division of labor within the plant and the union membership that goes with it are at the heart of the matter. Rules agreed on by management and labor are likely to decree that anyone who performs a certain activity has to be a member of a specified union. Adaptation means change, and the workers who stop doing one thing cannot do another without changing unions. The process is not automatic and even if one union is glad to receive members, the other may be unwilling to lose them and with them dues and votes. This concern may be directly tied to the position of the national labor federation on adjustment. While in principle that body gains its strength and health from the number of organized workers, no matter which affiliated union they belong to, the head of each union gains his strength and influence from the size of his constituency. Belief in labor solidarity extends to supporting other unions, but not to the point of losing members to them. This is a feature of democracy, not the dictatorship that labor leaders are often accused of; but it helps to create a conflict between the ability of a company or industry to adjust and the willingness of the unions to go along with the process. Unfortunately, the result may be to hurt the workers. If a company feels forced to close down because of inflexibility among the unions and if the cost of firing people is too great (more common in Europe than in the United States), it may go on doing what it has been doing but let the process run down.

The Japanese collective bargaining system avoids this difficulty. One company, one union is the rule, so the union represents all the workers. The industrywide federation of unions sets some targets for wage rates and the like, but within the firm there is a good deal of flexibility, coupled with the firm's need to live up to the conventions of the Japanese employment system and keep the workers on the payroll. Thus it is not too difficult to reorganize, adapt, and at the same time keep everyone more or less happy. On the whole it appears that the collective bargaining pattern is less important in these matters than the job and wage security provided by the so-called lifetime employment system.[10]

The prospects of transplanting the Japanese labor system to North America or Europe are dim. Whatever labor might think of the matter (it suspects company dominance and cooption), businessmen regard with horror the idea of having to keep people on the payroll and raise their pay as they age, not according to what they do. Some Japanese businessmen chafe under these requirements but some Western employers do very well with practices that emphasize security (such as IBM), though labor sees the results as paternalism, especially if no union is involved.

---

[10]"So-called" because the term exaggerates. It is neither universal nor infallible, but for many employees of big firms it works; their part is to learn new jobs when necessary and accept assignments that are not necessarily as prestigious or attractive as they would like—but their pay goes on rising with age, regardless of the work they do. Some smaller firms do the same thing, but the workers can lose if the company fails.

There is little doubt, however, that improved job and wage security plus greater flexibility on the part of workers is something to be sought in working out satisfactory adjustment policies.

One place to look for ideas that are even more venturesome than adapting the Japanese system to the West is something quite common in Europe and North America, the company that works in several industries. Adjustment, as we have seen, involves expansion as well as contraction. A company anxious to improve earnings or even simply to stay in business wants to reduce its stake in weak industries and expand it in strong ones. If in doing that it could hold its labor force together, keeping their jobs and wages while altering their work (and probably increasing their productivity), it would have done a public service by internalizing the process of adaptation. Geography and differences in the kind of work will often make this difficult or impossible. Conventional business thinking rejects the whole idea as too costly; control of the payroll is essential to efficiency. But if society is to provide social security, education, and all the rest and has to tax business to do it, and if the costs rise with the pace of change, it does not follow that business might not sometimes be better off fending for itself in these matters. (Many countries already penalize firings heavily enough to make alternatives worth considering.) Here, though, we are concerned with the organization of labor, which would often fit into this kind of change only with difficulty. A craft union would have less trouble than an industrial union if the same work were required in the new industry, while a company-focused union would be able to cope only if its members enjoyed a high degree of flexibility in attitude as well as skills and if in making the changes they did not run afoul of the jurisdiction of other unions with which they were allied.

A possibility worth thinking of is the multi-industry union. These already exist. The *A* in UAW stands for aircraft and agricultural implements as well as auto, and there is no particular reason why it should not come to mean "allied activities." The steelworkers are strong in aluminum and mining. When John L. Lewis was in charge of the United Mine Workers, he set up

District 50 expressly to organize workers in other industries. The Teamsters are to be found in many different activities, and various service industry unions cover a wide range of jobs and establishments. Some of these developments owe their origins to jurisdictional or factional strife and the efforts of competing unions to build strength. None of them needs to be taken as a model for the future, and no doubt other countries have other devices that may be more useful. It is not unreasonable, however, to suggest that a union with one foot in an expanding industry and one in a declining industry would be a far healthier organization and better able to serve the interests of its members, as well as the public interest, than those that must rise and fall with individual industries. Even if it were not possible to make the shifts within a company or plant that the Japanese are capable of, there would be fewer reasons for union officials to see every adaptation as a challenge to their authority. As they lost members in one field they could gain in others. Mergers between unions in different fields suggest themselves as a stabilizing device. They would obviously have problems—for instance, how to choose the right match and then equilibrate interests is not clear—but it is not beyond all conjecturing, as Sir Thomas Browne said of the song the sirens sang.

Another subject that cuts across all these issues concerns giving labor a voice in running the affairs of companies and industries. The traditional view in democratic, capitalist countries is that labor and capital belong on opposite sides of the table and should not mix. In recent times the chief supporters of this position have been the AFL-CIO, the Communists, and American and other businessmen. At the other end of the scale there is self-management by workers who own enterprises, exemplified by Yugoslavia but used to some extent in Peru and Algeria and tried locally in various parts of the world to keep an enterprise alive when its owners want to close it. These last efforts may also involve local governments and whole communities. Between the extremes are the various formulas for direct participation of workers in the management of companies. The principal examples are the *Mitbestimmung* (co-determination) laws of West

Germany and different devices in other countries for giving union workers a say in the affairs of their own plants, such as works councils.

The relevance of this complex set of affairs to our subject can be reduced to two main points: the usefulness of such arrangements in working out adjustments, and how participation in management could affect labor's perception of its own interest. The key organizational question is which workers are given a voice in management: those in the plant, whether unionized or not; the unions in the plant; those in the firm as a whole; local or regional labor councils or similar bodies; the national headquarters of a union; or the top labor organization in which a number of different unions take part. (The equally important question of what legal powers the worker representatives have we can leave aside.)

Obviously the attitudes of workers in the plant will be vital to smooth adjustment, but whether they are good judges of the need for it is another matter. In general one would assume that worker representation on company boards would help cement the sense of common interest and put labor on the side of management and owners in either resisting change or seeking government help to bring it about in the easiest possible way. Participation at a high enough level may also help persuade workers of the need for change, but in that there may be a difference according to whether they look only at the company's strong or weak position, the position of the industry as a whole, or the state of the national economy. The geographical dimension stemming from the industry's concentration or the way labor spokesmen are chosen may make a substantial difference. Similar lines of inquiry would apply to whatever kinds of industrywide councils might exist or be created to deal with adjustment problems or the carrying out of other elements of industrial policy.

This kind of inquiry can be carried one step further, to labor's part in shaping the national industrial policy as a whole (if there is such a policy). There can be little doubt that both the effectiveness and the general acceptance of Sweden's "active labor market policy"—almost everyone's favorite example of how to do things right—came from the fact that the unions were involved in the process of determining at the top what should be done as well as in working out the results lower down. Though there was deliberate contraction in some industries and a displacement of workers, there was also expansion, help in making transitions, and something like income security in between. Naturally, the recession of the 1970s put a strain on this system, and so did the rise of a malaise among the Swedes about their way of life; but how these factors affected and were affected by the labor market policy is more than I know.

Though they are essentially national in their organization and action, many unions have a more or less international ideology; and most belong (at least indirectly through national federations) to one or another international labor organization. Perhaps the influence of these international factors has increased in the past two decades, partly through the widening of economic areas, as in the European Community, and partly in response to the increased internationalization of business. Facing multinational corporations, unionists have felt the need of an international alliance to deal with an adversary who could otherwise play off workers in one country against those in another and move operations around the world if the territorially bound unions were too successful in pressing their demands. In some major industries international trade secretariats have sharpened unionists' awareness of worldwide issues. International union committees focused on specific international corporations have provided information and an exchange of views for the union workers. Ad hoc measures have been taken in some difficult situations, and a degree of coordination of bargaining has been managed in a few cases. A major growth of international labor actions along these lines would have considerable importance for national industrial policies, but that is on the whole an unlikely development. As Robert Cox has shown, the case is strong for labor's seeking its ends through national governmental action, thus underlining the issues discussed here.[11]

There are, however, two aspects of the international affiliations of unions that may be of special importance to industrial policy

[11]Robert Cox, "Labor and the Multinationals," *Foreign Affairs*, January 1976, pp. 344–365.

issues.[12] One is educational—or psychological, or political—whatever one calls the result of international contacts which cause unionists in one country to see that the troubles of their industry are not entirely the result of unfair competition or labor exploitation abroad and that the effect of a protective policy is to try to keep their own gains at the expense of workers in other countries. That this is not by itself enough to revolutionize the thinking of unionists is obvious, but perhaps it may have some effect, especially when reinforced by the second aspect. This is the possibility that a certain amount of international coordination of union action could be developed to help the adjustment process. Even without any elaborate international agreements, the existence of a reasonably strong union movement in a foreign country is evidence that minimum standards are likely to be set, which has a bearing both on the concept of unfair competition and on the moral position of the unions in protected industries. Insofar as anything approaching the kinds of arrangements we have called international industrial policies were to be undertaken, it would be necessary to see what place unions would have in them in terms comparable to those discussed here for national industrial policies.

This long catalogue has omitted such important questions as unionization versus nonunionization, especially in developing countries where unions often operate very differently from the way they do in Europe and North America; the difficulties stemming from the uncertain authority of the union leadership in some countries and the fairly widespread tendency (most notorious in Britain but perhaps not really any worse there than elsewhere) for workers in a plant or area to refuse to abide by a settlement made at a higher level; and the effect on cooperation of political

[12]Some unions with headquarters in the United States are truly international in the sense that they have Canadian members. So far as I have been able to discover, there is little evidence of any but sporadic influence of the Canadian affiliates on the position of the American union on trade policy or other matters affecting Canada. This may well be because of the small portion of the total membership usually found in Canada. In turn, the Canadian affiliates seem to be quite autonomous in taking positions on Canadian policy that might clash with those of headquarters.

or ideological issues among unions. No attention has been given to specific kinds of adjustment arrangements, such as collective bargaining contracts covering the terms on which companies will treat their domestic workers when they make new investments abroad. Nothing has been said about immigration and emigration, temporary or permanent, two traditional and direct methods of labor participation in adjustment and a factor affecting the strength of unions. The emphasis on how labor is organized may have scanted other factors that have influenced the willingness or unwillingness of labor movements to cooperate in pursuing national goals, such as recovery in Germany and Japan, the degree to which workers accept the broad lines of national economic policy, party affiliations, and the supposed "bread and butter" attitude of American unions, stressing benefits, not politics.

The labor issue is central to the shaping of industrial policy. Workers, organized and unorganized, are the groups most exposed to injury through structural change not accompanied by proper adjustment policies. But they will also suffer if structural change does not take place. The political strength of organized labor in many countries makes its assent and probably its positive cooperation essential to the working out of any effective adaptation. In most countries labor operates as a predominantly national interest group, so the international elements with which this book is primarily concerned reach it only through government policies and international business. In these circumstances, organized labor in the older industrial countries could easily become a major force for the kind of conservatism that says that people have a right not only to a job and a living wage but to the kind of work they have always done in the places they have always lived and at the income levels they have achieved, whatever their productivity. Perhaps a caricature, this description is near enough to the reality of much labor practice and it is a formula for economic disaster. If accepted, it would assure the continued use of resources in an increasingly costly pattern. To maintain some industries on this basis would be to throw a burden on workers in other industries as well as consumers. It would give the protected workers only the assurance of lifetime employment in declining industries at declining real wages.

It is the weakness of this kind of "protection" that is for the most part overlooked. An American labor leader said to me with perfect candor and the best intentions in the world, "I don't mind being called a protectionist; protecting my members is my job as a labor leader." Of course it is, but by itself the protection of the status quo can only temporarily provide for the welfare of his members. And since it does so at the expense of other workers, the concept of solidarity becomes strained. In the long run, not necessarily in the immediate future for everyone, real security and improved incomes for workers depend on adaptation, not resistance to it. If a conflict of interest is not to develop between union organizations and the real interests of the majority of their members, new ways will have to be found of providing security and flexibility. It is not hard to see how to move toward security, partly by perfecting and extending adjustment assistance arrangements, but also by greatly broadening the kind of support society will provide to everyone. It is much harder to see just how to achieve a much higher degree of flexibility; but some combination of education, incentive, and security itself must be workable. It will be better if labor can play a part in looking for the solutions.

## THE HANDLING OF SCIENCE AND TECHNOLOGY

Few aspects of national behavior bearing on industrial policy are more complex and frustrating to study than the issues surrounding research and development, public support for pure and applied science, and the ability of a country to adapt to its own industrial and commercial needs new and old technology, whether produced at home or abroad. Even the vocabulary is confusing when *innovation* by common consent means something like the effective application in production and distribution of inventions that may have been made long ago by others. Working through the constant flow of studies of these subjects— national and international, public and private—the layman is faced with a series of basic disagreements, contradictions on fundamentals, divergences in emphasis, and conflicting answers to puzzles about the connection between what governments have done or left undone and the results achieved by their national economies.

For long the main controversies centered on the United States. Did its strong position in the world economy in the 1950s and the early 1960s stem primarily from its technological lead? Or was the technological gap between it and the rest of the world really a management gap? Did that come down to saying that management was a part of technology? Either way, such a lead seemed natural, given the way the war had not only left the United States less damaged but had stimulated great technological progress. Though the focus had been on the means of bringing death and destruction, much of what had been done in atomic energy, electronics, and other fields could also be used for peaceful purposes. After the war other countries were able to get the benefits of these results quite quickly and without paying the full costs of development. One could expect that by the time they had arrived at the point where the United States had been in 1945, American laboratories and factories would have new products and processes to export. But what did it matter if Europe, Japan, and the rest of the world never altogether caught up—at least so long as there was not a permanent brain drain to the United States? All would gain economically, and without its technological lead, the United States, with its high labor costs, would lose its ability to export anything except food and raw materials. Or so it seemed to most observers at the time.

There was no doubt, however, that to catch up and then keep pace, even a step behind, other countries would have to make major efforts. Analysis and compilation set in on a large scale, measuring the amounts of public and private funds spent on research and development and debating which measures were correct, given the widely different situations of countries. Educational systems came under scrutiny and were differently judged by those who saw the need as educating scientists and those who emphasized training technicians. Governmental measures of different kinds were advocated and resisted, along with ideas about the proper division of labor between governments and business. Though few doubted the need to import technology from the United States, there was great controversy about how best to do that. When to cooperate with other countries in new projects and how to develop domestic capabilities posed questions of the highest long-run importance.

Results were mixed, and the explanations of them even more so. Japan's expenditure for research was not particularly striking; it kept out American investors but bought patents and licenses. A higher proportion of technically trained people in the Japanese labor force than was found in Europe (but not in the United States) may have had something to do with the impressive record in adapting imported foreign technology to domestic and export needs. (Later the fear arose that indigenous capacities were not adequate to do original work in new fields.) Germany and other European countries that accepted American investment along with the technology found that combination compatible with a substantial growth of domestic R & D, much of it helped by government funds. In Canada, however, there was constant worry that the heavy flow of American investment brought so little R & D that it was itself a factor in what some called "Canadian industrial underdevelopment."[13] Britain's impressive record in basic science was not reflected in innovation or productivity in industry; many people saw an explanation in the distance between the universities and business in attitudes, employment, and formal relations (a marked contrast with the United States and Germany).

The postwar American record in these matters itself became a subject of controversy. Though the war was over, defense spending continued to be large and included a flow of government funds to business and the universities for R & D. On top of that, the decision to put a man on the moon in a decade poured billions into invention and innovation in electronics, aerospace, and all manner of other fields. To foreigners, all this translated directly into a massive subsidy to the technological advance of American

[13]To borrow language from a provocative report: John N. H. Britton and James M. Gilmour, assisted by Mark G. Murphy, *The Weakest Link: A Technological Perspective on Canadian Industrial Underdevelopment*, Science Council of Canada, Ottawa, 1978.

business. In the United States there was a greater division of opinion. The spillover of knowledge and products into the private economy was judged by some observers to be much less than some spectacular examples suggested (or than scientists wanted the taxpayers to believe). The concentration on limited purposes seemed to some to shortchange other activities and skew the supply of scientists. A country that spent less on defense (say, Germany or Japan) could get much better benefits for its economy with smaller R & D subsidies—so ran this argument.

A second area of controversy concerned the use American business made of its technological advantages. It was said that the speed with which firms invested abroad or sold technology gave the rest of the world technological advantages more cheaply than the United States, which had paid the cost of development, sometimes with the help of taxpayers. Difficulties with American exports at the end of the 1960s and then again a decade later were attributed by many people to a decline in competitiveness resulting from the loss of a technological lead. A new debate arose about what the government should do to encourage innovation, how much it should spend, how it should be divided between basic and applied science, what the government needed to finance directly, and what should be left to business to decide. Only one step behind were proposals that if the government in fact used public funds for technological development, it should not permit the results to be exported, at least until American business was ready to take the next step ahead. From such a position it was easy to add that whether the taxpayer had subsidized the research or not, American firms should not export technology except on terms that assured a foreign contribution to development costs. One could further expect a renewal of the argument for government scrutiny of private investment on grounds of technological disadvantage as well as export of jobs.

Much of this argument concerned rates of growth, productivity, and the balance of payments—largely macroeconomic matters. Into the same category fell the highly debatable view that something had to be done to bring about a technological breakthrough, without which there would be nothing to buoy up the world economy in the next few decades. Our concern, however, is only with the distinct and major links between science and technology and industrial policy. They hardly need elaboration.

Technological change is probably the biggest single source of pressure for adaptation. The increasingly rapid spread of known technology to new parts of the world moves in the same direction. The ability of established industrial centers to adapt to the resulting changes in trade and competition depends heavily on their technological resources. Some may be applied to making existing activities more competitive, others to finding new lines of production. Much past industrial policy has been devoted to providing a country with high technology and providing better jobs with higher value added and productivity. There is no reason to expect a change in this emphasis. Indeed, continuing movement toward knowledge-based industries requires increased investment in science, research, and development. So does the provision by older industrial centers to the rest of the world of patents, know-how, design, planning, expertise, and other services which make up increasing shares of their exports (along with capital equipment itself). It follows that a country's aptitude in matters of industrial policy will continue to depend to an important degree on its ability to deal with the whole complex of issues involved in the handling of science and technology.

Needs differ substantially from country to country and are likely to change over time. No more than the other sections of this chapter can this one resolve disputes or prescribe for countries or situations. It will have to suffice to point to some of the alternatives and the confusion they often involve.

While interest focuses on high technology, a number of studies have shown higher returns per R & D dollar applied to older industries where OECD competitiveness is waning. Part of the problems of textiles, steel, and the rest may lie in this kind of neglect. Less research because profits are low may be part of a vicious circle. How should targets be chosen? A high rate of failure marks concentration on a single industry or device. But to spread the risk by following several lines at once requires either a much larger commitment of funds or greater risks of waste. It makes sense to choose an activity that is likely to find applications in many different branches of industry (as the British government did it its 1978 decision to invest heavily in micro-electronics—"chips with everything"), but only if it can be done with enough built-in flexibility to encompass the further changes that are almost bound to come. Some thought that the British would have done better to subsidize the development of new applications instead of concentrating on production.

The need for huge resources will require the government to play a large part, but mistakes are going to be bigger as well. Yet who else is to choose? When in 1971 Lord Rothschild proposed a "customer-contractor" basis for much of the British government's spending on R & D, he created an understandable furor among scientists who subscribed to the traditional view that creators should be left free to create. Both activities are vital, as Rothschild in fact recognized, and much depends on how the government's choices are made. To be accountable to a minister or legislator is not the best stimulus to imagination, but the public interest includes mundane needs too.

Comparable questions arise about what a government should determine itself and what funds it should put at industry's disposal. Who in industry should be helped is itself a question. Industrial research evokes a picture of very large firms supporting major laboratories, looking to the long-run future, accepting losses on failures, and making life attractive for scientists whose interests go far beyond what the market researchers have called for. Such activities exist, are of major importance, probably pay off, and get public support through tax laws. But there are also any number of examples of small firms that have generated inventions and made innovations that might have been impossible in large firms, or suppressed as undesirable. Thus industrial policy questions arise about the organization of industry, the fostering of venturesomeness, the provision of capital to small companies, and the proper attitude toward large firms' stepping in when the time comes for large-scale exploitation and marketing. For companies themselves there are problems in dealing with more than one government. They may see advantages in concentrating research or in not letting a laboratory get too large; they may want to put their scientists close to headquarters or to corporate planners or to market analysts or have different scientists in each place. Judgments based on economics or management principles are subject, however, to pressures from the governments of the countries in which they do business. These could be damaging to the companies, might be made to pay off in subsidies or tax advantages, or might be kept at bay by providing what Rothschild called "a reasonable balance of glamour."[14]

The patent system itself is a center of controversy. Does it give enough incentive or too much monopoly protection? Does filing an application signal to others the need to find a way around a problem or encourage pirating in the knowledge that by the time a court case has been fought out the real issue will concern the next stage—and that a weak inventor may go broke defending his rights?

By the late 1970s some businessmen felt that government regulations were making it too expensive to innovate; a favorite example was the tightening of American requirements concerning the introduction of new pharmaceutical products; but no one could seriously argue that new chemicals or drugs should be introduced simply because they were new, and reasonable people may differ about what standards are reasonable. Business resentment about environmental controls led to their being cited as inhibitions on innovation, whereas one would have thought that new standards regarding pollution provided a major incentive to develop new products and methods. Still, it is true that uncertainty, low profits, and increased costs to meet regulations reduce the sums most businesses are prepared to spend on research, with its uncertain payoffs. Still further controversies can be predicted about the use of "technology assessment," i.e., public procedures attempting to forecast the probable effects of significant innovations before they are widely used. It is easy to evoke nightmares about bureaucratic delays, caveats based on disputed hypotheses, and interminable logomachy while rival firms and countries establish a lead in production. As in so many

[14][Victor] Lord Rothschild, *Meditations of a Broomstick*, Collins, London, 1977, p. 65. In a lecture given in 1968 when Rothschild was working for Royal-Dutch Shell, he used this expression to refer to the balance of research between Britain and the Netherlands in contrast to worries about France, Italy, Canada, Australia, and Japan, and uncertainty about Germany.

related matters, the key to sensible policy lies not only in reasonable standards but in a procedure that brings to bear the whole range of relevant issues at one time so that valid trade-offs can be made and that then gives a firm answer in a reasonable length of time, after which debate is only debate.

Like everything else in industrial policy, science and technology issues are much affected by recession. Many observers thought that businesses were cutting down R & D as well as other forms of investment because it was so hard to prove a direct connection between each activity and profits. Expectations of a long-run inflationary future discouraged expenditures on R & D as well as other forms of investment. If one thought that unemployment would be lasting, it was natural to raise questions about the historic emphasis of innovation on labor saving. One heard again the kind of worries about job destruction that had accompanied the first wave of automation in the 1950s. A more considered view was that "technology should in the future become 'appropriate' to the changes in factor proportions (at least in the medium term, surplus of labour and scarcity of capital)."[15] But even then labor saving might be the correct course for some industries. Further changes would be called for in technology if one gave high priority to conservation of energy and raw materials and to the decentralization not only of production but also of decisions about industrial policy. Certainly, slow growth does not reduce the need for innovation, as Colombo points out in the article quoted. What was said in Chapter 2 about the increased relevance of the efficiency criterion applies to technology as well as to other parts of industrial policy. It may also be, as was observed in Chapter 1, that a turn in the business cycle or increased profits, less fear of future inflation, or higher growth would reduce current fears about the future of R & D or innovation.

Such a development would not, however, eliminate the need to see science and technology in the perspective of industrial policy. It may be that certain more or less constant general

[15]Umberto Colombo, "Strategies for Europe. Proposals for Science and Technology Policies: Industrial Innovation in Europe," *Omega*, vol. 5, no. 5, 1977, p. 523. (Colombo was general manager of the Research and Development Division of Montedison, Milan.)

policies will serve most of an economy's purposes and permit easy tailoring to the needs of particular industries. Or it may be that, whatever the general policies, applying them to circumstances is the key to success or failure.[16] Whether as the result of policy or circumstances, a country with a high capacity for technological adaptability and innovation will certainly be better off in industrial policy than one deficient in these capabilities. Although leading examples of success often seem to be independent of governmental action, they may provide clues for what can be done in other cases.[17] Finally, there is the question posed by one approach to the Canadian issue: If the limited capacity to innovate is the result of the structure of industry, measures of industrial policy will be needed to create a technological capability and not vice versa. But will independent Canadian companies succeed or foreign investors consent to do R & D in Canada if broader economic measures cannot overcome the disadvantages of a small home market? Again we come around to the international setting of national policies.

## COMBINATIONS—AND PERMUTATIONS?

What is there to say about these sketches of factors bearing on the formulation and conduct of national industrial policies? No

[16]"I do not believe there is such a thing as a policy for science as a whole, popular as the concept is. We must have a policy about pollution, ocean resources, food supply. . . . And science, engineering and mathematics—and the research associated with them—will and should contribute to the formulation and implementation of these policies. But that is all: science as a whole is not an activity to be carried on in isolation." Rothschild, op. cit., p. 83.

[17]The advocates of an active Canadian government policy to foster R & D repeatedly refer to Northern Telecommunications, a successful multinational in a high-technology field, given its independence by an American antitrust action and made successful by a group of scientific entrepreneurs. It did have the advantage of a sheltered market in the Canadian telephone system and may have benefited from preferential government procurement. It is difficult, however, to judge how important this help was compared with other factors, including continued technological cooperation with Westinghouse and perhaps other American firms. Full elucidation of such cases could be a useful guide to policy.

definitive or altogether persuasive conclusions can emerge from this collection of impressions and passing judgments. Though the evidence on some points is fairly strong, and common sense helps, most of the ideas and possibilities touched on need much closer analysis. Existing expertise may settle some issues; but on most, research seems to be in order as well as some ingenuity to design it.

The dynamics of these issues need attention. How much frustration of efforts to bring about structural change will be needed before people change their ways instead of accepting trade-offs that fall short of what they want? For almost any country it is easier to protect existing interests than to reshape the economy to stay competitive. What kinds of measures would make adaptation to change more attractive than not disturbing the status quo? Would international pressure or a commitment to other countries help reconcile differing views and overcome conflicts of interest about industrial policy? In Japan it is said that one of the new criteria for industrial policy (or at least one that needs more emphasis than ever before) is international acceptability. Moreover, I have been told, this will help bring about a resolution of internal disputes. That does not seem likely to be quite as true of other countries. Is this just another entry on the list of differences in national aptitudes? While scholars and practitioners ponder these questions, the making of industrial policy, good and bad, will go on. And that is where one clear conclusion, and the questions that flow from it, come in.

Variety is greater than homogeneity among industrial countries in the aptitudes we have examined. Nor are the differences likely to be overcome easily, quickly, or uniformly. Even if malleability proves greater than seems likely, we had best assume that the aptitudes of the industrial countries for various kinds of industrial or structural policies will continue to differ greatly. What difference does this make to international action or industrial policy? That question and the alternatives which the answers require us to examine are the main topics of the next chapter.

217

# SEVEN

# Affinities and Frictions

We start, but shall not be able to end, with two related questions: How much harmony or similarity in aptitudes is needed for international cooperation in industrial policy? What difference will it make if some countries move far ahead of others in what they do, at home or in agreement with others? Lest the questions seem fussy, or detached from reality, they can be recast to ask whether it would be a matter of concern if the major countries of Western Europe, along with Japan and Canada, were able to formulate broad national industrial policies and work out cooperative arrangements among themselves while the United States stood aside because it could not carry through measures of comparable scope.

That is certainly a real possibility. Our survey can have left little doubt that the United States has fewer aptitudes for conducting industrial policy and more built-in obstacles than most countries. Its ability to carry through a flexible policy that over the years responds to a changing situation while pursuing a clear-cut set of objectives is limited by the complexity of congressional-executive relations and the need of extensive, detailed legislation for many measures. It is further inhibited by the various factors that make government-business cooperation and labor participation in the process clumsy and usually ineffective. The resistances to change reflected by organized labor are not likely to disappear quickly. The possible exceptions are the handling of science and technology and relatively free competition in industry.

When large problems are pressing and are seen and their character is agreed to, it is not impossible for Americans to pull together and overcome these obstacles. But most of the time industrial policy problems are subtler than this and slower to show their true nature. They have to be dealt with over a long period of time and stir up conflicts of group and regional interests that are more obvious than the common interest. If the solutions involve major shifts of a structural sort, they will require further compromises not easy to arrive at and capable, in many circumstances, of so dulling the cutting edge of policy as to make it impossible to achieve the result originally sought. The American system has sometimes broken out of such difficulties through strong presidential initiatives that put pressure on the most recalcitrant parties and push both Congress and the public toward a clearly stated end. But these efforts are rare and not always successful. The easier alternative is to offer protection to those who claim the greatest need.

One conclusion to which such an analysis might point is that the United States would be better off not to try to pursue complex industrial policies, but to adhere more closely than it usually does to its frequently professed principle of letting market forces work. That course could be combined with doing much more than has been done in the past to help those most damaged by the change. Politically and psychologically the two steps might be mutually reinforcing and might make it easier to limit such protection as proved unavoidable. Strong as the case is for this line of action, one may legitimately doubt that it will be more persuasive than rival ideas. This will be true especially if the rest of the world pursues industrial policies that appear to American eyes to involve governments deeply in the management of their economies to the national advantage and that bring other countries together in activities in which the United States has no part. Again, one need only recast the question to suggest the answer: Would the United States, facing such a situation, be more likely to alter its ways of doing things so as to be able to join the industrial policy club; or would it take the steps in trade policy and other fields that permitted it to protect what it thought was its national interests, strike bargains where it had the power and, where it did not, retaliate for what it perceived to be the damaging actions of others? To businessmen the issue would be one of establishing the conditions of fair trade, not free trade, when faced with the competition of government-aided enterprises abroad.

## WHO, WHOM?[1]

To stress American difficulties is not to imply that other countries can easily do what is needed to carry out effective industrial policies. Dozens of examples show that that is not so. But there is no doubt that when each tries to move in the fields of industrial policy, it has advantages the United States lacks, whether in government-business relations, the ability to influence the pattern of investment, labor's willingness to cooperate in adaptive measures, the absence of a clash between executive and legislature, or the ability to reach a workable consensus about the direction in which to move. But few countries possess all these advantages. The differences among them in aptitudes and weaknesses are striking. And so we are brought to another question: May international cooperation require not so much a similarity of methods as a common need and will to cope with structural problems, each in its own way but with some similarity of aims? Since there is bound to be much interaction among the industrial policies of leading countries, part of the common aims might be to curb the pressures in every country for strongly nationalistic or nonadaptive policies that would stimulate others to the same courses of action.

This last sentence suggests a dimension that goes beyond the

---

[1] Lenin's question was about who could dominate; this question is about who can cooperate. One big omission in this book concerns Lenin's successors. How might the Soviet Union and other centrally planned economies fit into international cooperation in industrial policy? Though not one of the most urgent matters of industrial policy, the question raises interesting issues that cannot be elaborated here.

similarity of aims in industrial policy. It suggests that the interests countries have in cooperating with one another in matters of industrial policy are based on the importance of each to the other. That importance might be defined in a number of ways. The volume of trade and other economic contacts is the most obvious. The particular value of the exchange—say, in supplying energy or raw materials to one and capital goods to the other—may be more important than its nominal share of the total. Common commitments that affect the economic life of each country (as in the European Community or, more loosely, among the signatories of GATT) could make cooperation in industrial policy especially important. Political or security ties that made either or both parties especially sensitive to the affairs of the other might be another form of special relation. It is also to be borne in mind that such relations are not always symmetrical; a small country may attach immense importance to the affairs of a large one that can afford not to pay too much attention to the smaller. Such considerations cover too wide a range of behavior to be conveniently thought of as providing a single motive for cooperation. Without imagining that sharp distinctions can be maintained in all cases, we can conveniently think of a rough division between the positive side—intensity of economic relations or special ties of common interest—and an enforced selection of partners for cooperation because of their bargaining strength.

We have then four headings under which to look at the question of whose cooperation with whom is of greatest importance: similarity of method, similarity of aims, intensity of relations, and bargaining power. As we consider these, we have to bear in mind the implications of cooperation among a limited number of countries for those left outside—the external as well as the internal dimension of cooperation, so to speak. It will follow naturally that one needs also to pay attention to how the shape of the international economic system as a whole is affected by these groupings or pairings or their absence. Which nations are essential for which purposes? If only some countries can be thought of as having a part in managing the system, will the others find their interests largely neglected, or will they be given a free ride, benefiting from the conduct of the others without fully reciprocating it? As benevolence is not the outstanding characteristic of national sovereignty, the discussion of these issues, with which the chapter concludes, returns to an early theme of this book: autonomy and who pays for it.

## Similarity of Method

Enough has been said about this subject to warrant dealing with it very briefly. The OECD countries can be taken as the most similar in terms of political and economic organization and the problems they face in industrial policy. We have already seen how great the differences among them are in three vital matters: (a) Only a few have had thought-through and comprehensive industrial policies; the others have varied greatly in the extent and types of measures they have taken. (b) This is not just a matter of the past; even if all now wished to do more, they are very differently endowed with relevant aptitudes, which would affect their methods and probably their total performance. (c) The industrial policy aims of these countries have been pursued by a wide range of methods, and there is every reason to think that in the future this variety will continue. Thus, if methods were the sole criterion, one would have to dismiss the possibility of international cooperation.

That is not a realistic conclusion, but the differences in method do affect the problems of cooperation. As Chapter 3 made clear, agreements bearing on industrial policy have to cover several subjects—subsidies, government procurement, concessionary financing, etc.—or they will invite evasion. But linkage, balance, the difficulties of judging the equivalence of measures, and the very comprehensiveness of agreements make them more difficult than, for example, setting rules about tariff bargaining. Differences in organization and differences among the aptitudes also stand in the way of agreements. The President of the United States cannot make commitments that Congress will accept in the way legislatures will in parliamentary systems. American businesses cannot negotiate as a group with foreigners. A Japanese high civil servant told me how hard it was to find with whom he should talk in Washington about American industrial policy.

Still, ways can be found to work things out. In the 1960s the United States government made a steel agreement with European producers. In the 1970s, without a formal agreement, American, European, and Japanese measures on steel added up to something like cooperation. Foreign governments cannot negotiate with Alberta about oil and petrochemicals, but they can take the province's views into account when they make a trade agreement with Ottawa. Differences in views about competition and how governments are to enforce it are almost bound to stand in the way of agreement between the United States and other countries on antitrust matters for some time to come. That is no reason, however, not to try to find ways of mitigating disputes and making whatever arrangements are possible in limited areas. It would certainly not be reasonable to conclude that no cooperation was possible before uniform domestic measures were adopted. The opposite approach makes more sense: Since new ground has to be broken, primary emphasis should be on the effect that is wanted, not on the methods.

### Similarity of Aims

If countries are of a like mind about what they want to do with industrial policy, they have a better foundation for finding ways of doing it than if their methods are similar but are used for different purposes. When "like-minded" was used to characterize the countries that were drawing together to form NATO, it meant that they wanted similar results. To have formalized the commitment at that stage or even to have been very precise about the objective would have been either impossible or unacceptable. Discussion and negotiation were needed to define what was possible. Meanwhile all possibilities were open that seemed to serve the common end. Something like this is also true of international understandings about industrial policy, at least for the time being.

As we have cut into this messy and badly defined subject from various angles, we have repeatedly come on several points that are sufficiently similar in different places to suggest that they are part of what most democratic countries with mixed economies (and perhaps others) will be trying to do as they push forward

224

with industrial policy. In most fields, sooner or later, there is a need to stress efficiency; the rough test has to be some degree of international specialization and adaptation to changing circumstances. A second consideration is that because change can be disturbing, especially if it comes rapidly and alternatives are unclear, public policy should often ease the transition for the people hardest hit by change. A difficult problem is how to do this without so slowing or impeding the process that it no longer produces the advantages of adaptation. A third consideration is that in some matters efficiency is not what is most wanted. A society may perfectly well choose to carry on certain activities (or avoid others) even though doing so costs more than an alternative course. Both the consequences of this choice and the way it is carried out are likely to have some effect on others.

Though it might seem unlikely that most countries would put high on the list of the aims of their industrial policy the avoidance of damage to other countries, that may in fact be a significant consideration that a number of countries have in common. If there are two ways of achieving more or less the same industrial policy objective, and one would do a good deal of damage to another country while the other would do little or none, a prudent government would prefer the latter. It would avoid the risk of retaliation and also whatever indirect losses might result from the other's difficulties (for example, a loss of exports if the other country's buying power were diminished). Of course, if the measure that does least damage to the foreigner also causes more internal disturbance than something else, or is simply more difficult to get agreement on, domestic considerations may well govern. But it is a characteristic of international cooperation that it involves domestic as well as international trade-offs both initially and as time passes. Awareness of the connection from the first is superior to the subsequent discovery of the results, which is more typical of national industrial policy action.

Sometimes a conflict of interest with other nations is inherent in what a country is trying to achieve by its industrial policy. Then the question is whether something can be accomplished by bargaining about how to share the costs. There is also the question of seeing each case as part of a larger set of events. In a certain setting, a country would understand that if it came off second best at one time, the situation could be reversed at another time. Each country's industrial policy would take into account not only the immediate effect on neighbors but longer-run questions about cooperative arrangements in a number of fields and in the international system as a whole. Countries that are "like-minded" in the sense of being pluralistic democracies should be particularly aware of the need to take foreign reactions into account since they have a direct bearing on the ability of the foreign government to resist domestic pressures for unwise measures.

An emphasis on the effects of what each country does, rather than on how it achieves its industrial policy aims, might reduce the need to have specific international rules about which measures were acceptable in carrying out industrial policy and which were not. However, it is not necessary or wise to rely entirely on the approach through results; it should supplement the traditional approach through rules, not replace it. (Chapter 3 showed the difficulties and weaknesses of trying to rely entirely on one approach or the other, and the final chapter will suggest ways of combining approaches.) Here the point is only to put like-mindedness in proper perspective as a basis for cooperation. There are essentially four points. First, where there is some similarity in institutions, processes, and values, countries have a degree of common understanding going well beyond industrial policy questions. Second, such countries are likely to be exposed to somewhat similar pressures concerning the ends of industrial policy, or at least the choices they face. Third, this does not prevent serious conflicts among them, but it should make each country cognizant of the problems the others face in economic aims and political processes and how they are affected by what is done in the rest of the world. Fourth, countries pursuing conflicting ends can be like-minded about the desirability of keeping international friction to a minimum and limiting the damage that conflicts in industrial policy can do to international cooperation in general.

When like-mindedness, economic similarity, and the impossibility of living by precise rules are taken together, they bring to mind the OECD. In a field as difficult as industrial policy, a global approach seems hopeless. One may not have much confidence in what can be done by the OECD, but in breaking new ground it is unwise to forgo opportunities. "Just talking" in the sense of consultation and the exchange of information is, we have seen, essential to any cooperation on industrial policy; and that is a key activity of the OECD. Moreover, the wide range of issues considered in that body could help to keep industrial policy issues in a proper perspective (success in macroeconomic measures reduces the difficulties of adaptation, etc.). In addition, a start has been made in the work on adjustment policies and the setting up of the steel committee. That an agreement on industrial policy among the OECD countries alone will not be sufficient should be understood at the outset. Relations between OECD countries (or some of them) and a number of developing countries are involved. How far it might be useful for the OECD countries to go in working out among themselves approaches to developing countries on these matters is a difficult and delicate issue; judgment about it is best left until one has a reasonably concrete idea of the circumstances in which action would be taken.[2]

There should, however, be a clear recognition of North-South issues in what the OECD does. Subject to the caveat just mentioned, this might be provided in several different ways. If the arrangements emphasized consulting about the effects of industrial policies, there should be provision for some consultation with the developing countries most directly involved. To the extent that there are concrete agreements about industrial policy

[2]In this matter I am greatly guided by Miriam Camps's important reassessment of the OECD's best role in North-South and global issues in "*First World*" *Relationships: The Role of the OECD*, Atlantic Institute for International Affairs, Council on Foreign Relations, New York, 1975. She calls for a much subtler handling of such issues as industrial policy than would be suggested by the old view that the industrial countries should use the OECD to arrive at a position for negotiating with others. Here and in the rest of this book, I have refrained from getting into the difficult and complex questions about how to organize international industrial policy cooperation, in part because Mrs. Camps and Catherine Gwin are working on this matter as part of a larger study on international institutions for the 1980s Project of the Council on Foreign Relations. Hence my remarks on procedures should be regarded as first approximations, not final judgments.

arrangements, they should permit developing countries to adhere to them by undertaking specific obligations. In neither case should the question be one of the LDCs joining the OECD, something that is likely to be either too difficult for them or damaging for the organization. In recognition of the strong pressure to make bilateral arrangements about industrial policy (discussed in the next section), there should be acceptance of the principle that OECD countries will not make industrial arrangements with LDCs that damage others. As far as damage to other members of the OECD is concerned, there should be a firm link with arrangements within the group about consultation and avoidance of injury. As far as damage to other LDCs is concerned, the statement is likely to sound somewhat anodyne and pious, but that is probably better than nothing and might someday prove to have been a step forward. In taking these steps two dangers should be avoided. (1) Participation should not be made so open-ended as to lose the advantages of putting the work in the OECD in the first place. (2) The recognition of the North-South dimension should not interfere with dealing as effectively as possible with the major difficulties among the OECD countries that can arise from industrial policy disputes. These are the only ones that could be directly solved through the OECD.

Putting aside the organizational focus and its difficulties, one could think of the most promising like-minded group as making up an *efficiency system*—but with the meaning of *efficiency* modified. The modifications lie first in what was said in Chapter 2 about the breadth with which one must interpret that term. Then there is the common departure from efficiency for a variety of social, political, and security reasons; but, as has been emphasized before, there is a real case for doing noneconomic things as efficiently as possible, and it is not irrelevant that the pursuit of other values is most often seen and measured as a departure from the efficiency norm. Finally, the international play of forces within the system tends to reinforce the idea of efficiency. Practices that work in that direction are: limiting protection for fear of retaliation; taking international competitiveness as the test of success in many activities; the wish to limit subsidies; and fostering competition as a way of avoiding high costs, inefficiency, and monopoly. Even the mutual recognition of the common pressures for protection, everyone's domestic political exigencies, and people's noneconomic aspirations, which together make departures from principle and the infraction of rules inevitable—and tolerable, but only up to a limit—fit the pattern. Such a system depends, however, not only on like-mindedness but on the importance of the members to one another, which is why it is not enough to think in terms of the OECD.

## Intensity of Relations

Part of the case for an OECD agreement is like-mindedness; another part is the intensity of the relation. So much of the world's trade and other exchanges take place among the OECD countries, and so much of the impact of national industrial policies on international economic relations is felt among them, that any substantial progress in dealing with these matters is intrinsically more important than arrangements involving other countries. But the OECD countries are not homogeneous, as even the limited number of examples mentioned throughout this book have shown. Among many other ways of showing differences, an old and familiar one is to stress how much more dependent on international trade the others are than the United States. Real enough, this is not as important a difference as it once was. American foreign trade is now about twice its former share of the GNP and substantially larger still if compared with the production of tradable goods. Some branches of production depend heavily on exports. The funds flowing through investment and service accounts in the balance of payments contribute importantly to the national income. A number of significant firms earn a large part of their money abroad. Much of the pressure for industrial policy measures comes from foreign competition, especially from Japan and some LDCs, while among the issues about which controversy is greatest are foreign investment and the export of technology.

A more significant distinction among OECD countries is the extent to which some have reason to pay special attention to certain others in dealing with industrial policy issues. The European Community is the most important special case, for obvious reasons. How far its members can get in handling industrial policy as a Community issue instead of a national one (as it largely still is) is one of the tests of how much integration will develop in Western Europe. Starting with the occupation and the peace treaty, the postwar relations of the United States and Japan, for all their difficulties, have been closer than ever before and very different from Japan's relations with Europe or any other country. That has had its effect on American policy toward Japan in trade matters, which, though far from consistent or impeccable, has been more accommodating and open than that of European countries. Japan in turn has been sensitive to American views and was a pioneer in restraining exports when threatened with worse consequences. Such trade responses have worn thin and are increasingly seen as needing restatement as industrial policy issues that will require continuing attention in both countries.

Another close relation of a wholly different sort is that between the United States and Canada. Fretful as it makes the Canadians, there is no getting away from the fact that their close involvement with an economy so much larger is bound to do much to shape the economic policy issues facing them and even their economy itself. Canada's importance to the United States is disproportionate to the size of its economy, but, except on a few issues, Canadian interests are not likely to be given as much weight in American policy as Canadians would like. It is unclear what conclusion Canadians should draw. On the one hand, there is the possibility that the United States will not strenuously object to various Canadian practices that it might complain about in other countries. On the other hand, when the United States follows a strongly nationalistic course or pursues particular economic ends of its own, Canada may feel a greater impact than any other country. The first alternative has much history behind it; the second was demonstrated in the early 1970s. A second dilemma that recurs as Canadians discuss their basic economic policy, and especially industrial policies, is whether to accept closer integration with the United States and thus overcome some of the burdens of the small home market or to insist on shaping the national economy in a more separate mode but at what might be a considerable economic cost, particularly if it proves difficult to find willing and helpful partners in the rest of the world.

These examples suggest all kinds of questions about potential international industrial policy arrangements. It would be difficult for a member of the Community to reach an agreement with the United States (or, for that matter, Japan) that put another member of the Community at a serious disadvantage by its temporary restraint of trade, reciprocal concessions to balance costs and benefits of some kind of specialization, or joint financing of some transitional arrangements. It would not be easy for the United States to acquiesce in a European Community arrangement that was especially damaging to Japan (or for Japan to make a European deal that the United States strongly objected to). The relationship between Canada and the United States looks very different if one asks how to make the most of an exceptionally close set of economic connections or sees it as a pure bargaining situation between a middle power and a giant. Only on this hypothetical basis does it carry us into the next sections, where the emphasis is on the effect of bargains on outsiders.[3]

## Bargains

It is the intensity of the issues more than like-mindedness that makes it likely that there will be industrial policy understandings between the principal new exporters of manufactured goods and the old centers where those things are also produced. Enough has been said earlier to show why there are unlikely to be broad, general agreements laying down new trade rules or creating strong multilateral commitments. The principal factor that may

[3] As footnote 1 of this chapter pointed out, a full consideration of the rather special problem of arrangements with the Soviet Union and other centrally planned economies is omitted from this book. It is worth noting, though, that it is not exactly either intensity or bargaining power that forces OECD countries to think about how to absorb the imports from those countries that provide the means of payment for exports to them. It is the wish to have the export business and to get paid and the consequent growth of buy-back arrangements or other forms of barter that make necessary at least rudimentary judgments about what is a satisfactory international division of labor in East-West trade.

keep these from being as restrictive as some people in the OECD world would like is that Korea, Brazil, and other new industrial countries (NICs) have gained bargaining power. They have become major markets for capital goods and will gain even more in future importance if the predictions of slower growth in the industrial world come true. Other developing countries have also gained bargaining power with the industrial world, both as markets and as suppliers of energy and raw materials. Depending on how much those supplies are needed, or how rich their markets prove to be, these countries too will be able to put pressure on the older countries to make room for their exports, even if that requires adjusting their industrial structures.

It is conceivable that the OECD world will meet this situation with a common, across-the-board approach and that means will be found to make orderly changes in structures along the lines suggested by Eugene Staley in the book discussed in Chapter 5. But that is not very likely. The stage seems set for friction and a series of bilateral bargains. Each old industrial country will be anxious to beat the others in the export markets. They will be selling not just machinery but whole factories; they will design them and look for follow-up markets for spares and replacements and for patents, training, and other services that loom ever larger in European, Japanese, and American exports. In the manner suggested in Chapter 5, they will do what they can to assure themselves of a preferred position in each market, if not a monopoly. They will offer access to their markets for the exports of their developing partners; and to make room they will do what they can to keep out competing goods from other developing countries or, if they can manage it without too much retaliation, from other OECD countries.

The prospect is one to be resisted, but that will not be easy. And there will be seductive arguments that in their own way such steps can bring progress. It will be said that since a wide area of agreement on desirable economic patterns and the speed of adjustment is not likely, and if the protectionist pressures in the industrial world can only be overcome by appeals to clear national interests, one should not dismiss the possible value of the narrower arrangements. There is some truth in this. If the agreements were not too narrow and not too discriminatory, if there were some real steps toward adjustment and not just the dumping of burdens on others, would they not represent some progress? One test would be whether the bilateral agreements introduced more new distortions into the international economy than they removed, but it is not easy to pin down such things. And it is very easy to use this kind of argument as a rationalization for purely pragmatic bilateralism of a sort that can be cumulatively very damaging to the world economy.

In pursuing these possibilities one has to think not only of pairs of individual countries but of groups on either or both sides. The main industrial centers all have special relations with certain developing countries; more are likely to be created if the process foreseen here actually occurs. Though regionalism never made the headway in the developing world once expected of it, there are new stirrings and perhaps significant new potentialities connected very directly with the problem of adjustment. There are very real dangers of dividing the world into a series of North-South slices that look like a new form of imperialism. There are questions about what happens to the developing countries that do not fall into one or another of the groups. There are, for that matter, questions about the industrial countries that do not have special affinities with anyone in the developing world. Who, for example, are the natural partners of the United States? The clichés about the unity of the Western Hemisphere are long discarded—or should have been. The special relation with Saudi Arabia, based on oil and security, goes only so far on the most optimistic assumptions. The once comparable case of Iran underlines the point. The relevance of Israel and Egypt are not to industrial policy. Canada and Mexico are very special, and they may be the most important; but the possibilities are limited. The United States may not be the only country in this position. Japan's relation to the countries belonging to the Association of South East Asian Nations (ASEAN) falls well short of meeting its major needs. The ties with China that may develop could be of great significance, but neither partner is likely to see an exclusive bilateralism as its best alternative. As India belatedly shows the industrial strength it was expected to develop much

233

earlier, it does not fit easily into any regional grouping. Nor, for that matter, are many of the new industrial powers likely to be satisfied with such limiting arrangements. So perhaps there will be a new move toward multilateralism, or at least a pressure for it that may work against the clear forces of bilateralism in industrial as well as trade policy.

There is also a cautionary tale of how regionalism in the industrial world may worsen a range of broader problems. The European Community provided an innovative way of dealing with some of the problems of structural change better than its members could have done alone. But when the Community of Nine—still largely northern European and "old industrial" except for half of Italy, parts of a few other countries, and perhaps Ireland (which is northern but not so industrial)—contemplated the addition on some basis of Spain and Portugal and the conclusion of a long tergiversation about Turkey and Greece, the Community faced within itself a number of the problems we have just described in North-South terms. One would like to think that for a result the descendants of the innovators who made the Community would find new ways of dealing with these problems that would point the way to what could be done with the emerging industrial LDCs. Perhaps they will; the process should be closely scrutinized for these lessons. But there is unfortunately another possibility.

To absorb the new countries the Community will work out special measures to deal with agriculture, the processing of raw materials, and cheap-labor industries (not least textiles and clothing). Delicate compromises will have to be negotiated, and the older members of the Community will have to make internal adjustments that are not altogether easy. In the process the Community may "use up" its ability to absorb change for a while and resist any steps to help outside countries in a similar manner. In addition, the enlargement of the sectors within the Community that compete with the exports of the developing countries and probably need protection against them because they are part of an area with higher standards of living and higher prices and costs, will, by the normal laws of politics and economics, harden the resistance of the enlarged Community to further change. This larger Community will still have to import most of its energy and large amounts of raw materials; it will still be anxious to cultivate the growing markets of the developing world and to sell capital goods that are no longer going to be absorbed as quickly as before at home or in the rest of the industrial world. Consequently the pressures for bilateral arrangements described above will continue while the range of adjustment at home is narrowed, with the inevitable result that whenever possible the burdens will be shifted to outsiders, whether they are developed or industrial countries.

So gloomy a prognosis is not a conclusion to this section, only a possibility to be considered. What has been said here about the possible bases for cooperation in industrial policy does not warrant any firm prediction. No single set of affinities or aptitudes dictates an approach to international cooperation on industrial policy that is seen to be satisfactory. Though piecemeal measures are almost certain to be inadequate, they may be all that is possible. Where limited agreements can be realized or pushed further, that should be done, subject to the repeated caveat of concern for outsiders. But there is positive value in a many-faceted approach simply because industrial policy is a complex subject hardly to be encompassed in one set of rules or ideas. Chipping away may be the most promising course even if one does not know what the statue (or statute) will ultimately look like.

## WHO PAYS FOR WHOSE AUTONOMY?

When Korea was a hermit kingdom, or before Lhasa gave way to the troops and bureaucrats from Peking, even when pre-Meiji Japan shut its ports to the world and when Burma as late as the 1970s all but isolated itself from its neighbors, the international system did not greatly feel the effect. Perhaps it simply did not know what it was missing and could not lose what it never had—except in the case of Burma and there smallness and poverty account for enough of the story to ignore the rest. That much is still clear but the connective must be underlined. Neither Swit-

235

zerland or Holland, nor India or China—nor, for that matter, Hong Kong or Singapore—could be omitted from the world without others noticing the difference; so the demarcation line is not obvious (though there must be manufacturers in many countries who wish these and other places off the face of the earth often enough).

Neither disappearance nor isolation is really the issue. The number of countries capable of self-sufficiency at an acceptable level of income is small; those who would put before all else the total preservation of a culture or way of life by insulating it completely from contamination by contact with others are not numerous enough to be taken up in a book on industrial policy. But when it comes to partial isolation, we are dealing with one of the most common phenomena of industrial policy: the closing off of markets, the efforts to be self-sufficient in food or arms or something else, the hope that certain barriers will suffice to permit stability at home no matter how many disturbances take place abroad. To a degree, therefore, it might be redundant to treat the subject once more, but not if we see these efforts less as piecemeal protectionism than as part of an effort to increase national autonomy. This is not only a real phenomenon but something that may increase in importance. It has its advocates, who see a move in that direction not just as something easier to live with than the exigencies of closer cooperation in difficult matters such as industrial policy, but as positive good. There are also pressures in the same direction resulting from very different values, such as greater decentralization of power within the nation or the devolution of decisions to local units.

Finally, there is a case for reading the economic realities of the world rather differently from the way they have been read in most of this book, where the emphasis has been on the value of making the most of global specialization and on the advantages to nations of close economic ties with others. This contrary view is rooted in the belief that the good that governments can do for their own people—however one defines the good—is bound to come largely from how they handle their own affairs, use their resources, and let their people's talents play. What the international system deals with is primarily marginal relations be-

236

tween units; the good to be found in these links cannot possibly be as great as that from the best possible administration of the units themselves. To the objection that a government or society can also do harm, the answer would be that that is a risk one must take and that the disciplinary power of the international system is limited. To the objection that autonomy would amount to anarchy, the advocate's answer is that the law of the jungle can be avoided by recognizing that each can lose freedom if others are free to domineer. Some mutual interference is inescapable, but somewhere in the mutual relation there is a limit to what each can do.

There are at least five separate reasons why many people are led to the conclusion that the primary emphasis should be on permitting each country to do things its own way. The first, which has played a fairly important part in American thinking, is simply that the functioning of the national economy is determined primarily by domestic factors, not by what happens in the rest of the world. This is, of course, not true for many small countries; but for many moderate-sized ones it is at least arguable. As was pointed out earlier, the argument is not as strong as it used to be for the United States, and one can hardly make a case for ignoring the rest of the world. Still, the make-or-break decisions concern the management of the American economy as a whole and not primarily its foreign economic relations.

A second view emphasizing autonomy is, essentially, that the difficulty of trying to achieve great increases in international economic cooperation outweighs the probable gains. Another version amounts to saying, "We have quite enough interdependence, and not everything about it is good." Some argue from the calculation that the marginal gains from further international specialization are fairly small compared to the efforts and costs of achieving them. Others feel that some countries are so well off that the economic cost of a certain number of uneconomic policies is not too burdensome while the political and social costs of adjustment are substantial. Still others stress the fact that efficiency and economic values are the only ones served by increased interdependence, whereas other things may be more important. Many of the arguments appeal primarily to rich coun-

237

tries that are already quite open to one another. There is a tacit assumption about the continued maintenance of a fairly high degree of interdependence, openness of economies, and cooperation. Still, anyone who has taken a hard, honest look at what international cooperation on industrial policy may require has to acknowledge the thought that the results may not be worth the effort or even the possibility that they will be worse than if nothing were tried.

The third line of argument for autonomy stems from fear, or at least dislike, of the consequences of interdependence. It is the view of the weak and has many forms. The most familiar recent one is that of *dependencia*: "There is no way to get the benefits of close participation in the international economic system without exposing ourselves to the great strength of others and losing control of our own affairs." The fear is that interdependence is dependence and that cooperation will always be one-sided. Some who hold this view believe that the economic rewards of participation in the system offset the noneconomic losses but others make the opposite judgment while still others see no economic rewards, only exploitation.

Nationalism, without the fear, provides the fourth persistent set of arguments for autonomy. "What is important to do is what we, the nation, wish to do, in whatever way we wish to do it. We respect the same right in others. We may even join with others on shorter or longer terms to do things, but the starting place is *chez nous*."

The fifth argument is less clear-cut but lurks in some attitudes and is likely to be articulated more often in the future, particularly in response to some of the more elaborate schemes for managing the world of the 1980s. This is the feeling that things have gotten too big for people to handle. "Nations, at least big ones, are bad enough; the world is impossible. The United Nations proves it, maybe even the monetary system, and the hopelessness of resting basic security on anything but the two superpowers." That being so, the advocates of this view—perhaps it would be more accurate to call them merely those who feel this way—think the presumption ought to be that people should run their own nations as well as they can and not venture onto larger international schemes except when tasks are encountered that are plainly beyond the power of the country in question. When the same ideas are applied domestically, they lead to devolution, local option, expanding the powers of states and provinces, and things of that sort—which, we have seen, already considerably limit the ability of some countries to engage in international cooperation about some aspects of industrial policy. If acted on, this would probably be a self-fulfilling prescription, though it remains to be seen what happens when the smaller units feel the need to reach out beyond their jurisdictions to fulfill their own aspirations. Is it inevitable that the partners they will seek will always be others within the same country?

It could be argued that each of the propositions carries the seeds of its own destruction. The argument about managing the domestic economy ignores the fact that what one country does may make it impossible for others to manage their economies; then, unless the United States and some other important countries accept limitations on what they do, the proposition cannot be a general one. The argument about affording bad policies has to cope with the historic question whether one can stand still on a bicycle; if not, the failure to make progress or the acceptance of retrogression would be likely to lead sooner or later to undoing some and perhaps much of the cooperation and interdependence that helps make it possible to afford bad policies in the first place. The *dependencia* view faces the riddle of whether there is greater strength in isolation than in some trade-off between participation and the gains from it. Nationalism is more nearly immune to objections except the classical historical ones: the clash with other nationalisms and the lack of built-in limits. Managing your own affairs may be an illusory ideal if your country is as dependent on the rest of the world as most seem to be.

But it is the last of the propositions that is of most concern to us. It poses a double question: Who can manage units of what size? Who decides who has what degree of autonomy? All the problems of democracy, participation, liberty, and the realization of values that are not held in equal esteem by all members of the unit arise here. It is along these lines that the most radical rethinking of the international order might have to go. It is the line

239

of inquiry that leads through nationalism, separatism, decentralization, ethnicity, pluralism, and all the rest. Summarize them all as autonomy; but recognize that only in a cooperative and pluralistic anarchy, where every individual is free to choose his group and the group its individuals, can the problem be solved. Yet even then failure may once again be imminent if the groups are incapable of performing the functions necessary to realize the values for which they were formed while cooperation and mutual aid among groups runs into the limitations natural to cooperative processes.

If we apply these attractive ideas to industrial policy, the nearest we have come to prescription is a few general propositions: Freedom to do things one's own way is highly valued and should be available to nations; by definition this freedom is limited by that of others; the cost of one country's doing things its own way should be paid by itself, not foisted on others.[4] Just there the questions begin. How do you ensure that a country in fact pays for its choice?

An individual who drops out of the economic system—chooses leisure over work, takes a menial job to devote his creative talents to work done for its own sake and not monetary return, etc.— can pretty well be thought of as paying for his or her choice, even if society has come to think it should provide everyone with some minimum. One could argue that society, too, pays, since it is the poorer for what the dropout has not produced. But the relation is so disproportionate that one can easily dismiss the matter.[5] However, if one took Kant's advice and universalized

[4] In and out of government, Harald Malmgren has been a major advocate of the view that in dealing with the impact of domestic policies on other countries, "the objective of negotiations . . . must be to reduce the scope for passing the costs of national policies to foreign interests and foreign governments, and to prevent conflicts or manage them where they occur." Harald B. Malmgren, *International Economic Peacekeeping in Phase II*, rev. ed., Quadrangle, New York, 1973, p. 203.

[5] There is also the indeterminateness of comparing the uncertainty of what the dropout may someday contribute, which cannot be known in advance, with what he would have contributed if he had stayed at his job, which cannot be known at all. Worse yet, can one assume that if Edison had dropped out no one would have invented the electric light at about the same time?

the maxim, things would be fundamentally different. But then society would not have the wherewithal to support the dropout, and some other process would be set in motion.

Is it the same with nations—that they pay for their own cutting of ties with the rest of the international community, or what we have called the efficiency system?

If a country forgoes certain kinds of production to avoid pollution, the answer seems clear. Nations that make the opposite choice pay for higher production (and maybe more investment and industrialization) by accepting greater pollution. This, too, is autonomy; and it seems to create no burden for other countries so long as the pollution takes forms that do not reach the air, water, and land of others. A country that bans certain products as noxious can hardly be thought to throw a serious burden on the rest of the world because it refuses to import these substances.

Other cases are more complicated. If Americans want to preserve the family farm as a way of life for some of their people and Europeans believe they should approach self-sufficiency in food, do they really pay for their choices? Yes—as taxpayers, for whatever aid is given to farmers, and as consumers, in high prices. But if markets are closed by import barriers and surpluses are dumped on people who would otherwise buy from somewhere else, foreigners are paying too. Direct transfer of resources through services and income with no price supports or import barriers would reduce the impact on foreigners but raise the direct cost to the country helping the farmers. Even then the burden on the rest of the world is not eliminated if the European and American farm policy results in a poorer use of resources than would have been obtained under a different system. The losers then include those producers who have lost a market; the world as a whole, because global production and productivity are reduced; and anyone whose range of choice is narrowed by the whole process as producer or consumer.[6]

[6]The example, incidentally, is a convenient reminder of the inescapability of the problem of units that we have deliberately set aside. The cost of the family farm system has to be shared between the family farmer who needs support, the nonfarmer who is glad to support an institution he idealizes but

When the Soviet Union and other countries establish an economic system that makes the inconvertibility of the ruble and other Eastern European currencies inevitable, that is an inconvenience to the rest of the world; but the worst of the burden clearly falls on the socialist countries who thus pay for the autonomy of their pricing system. But when the dollar was made "inconvertible" in 1971, the impact was not just on the United States. To be sure, the analogy is not exact, since the dollar remained convertible into goods and services in a way that the ruble is not. But the real lessons of the crude comparison (and of the examples that precede it) are that the ability to assign the whole cost of some exercise in autonomy to the exerciser varies greatly and that large changes in the status quo are almost sure to have an impact on others that does not exist, or is discounted, by comparable practices of long standing.

Less clear and more troublesome is the question whether a country whose actions would have an impact on the rest of the world has an obligation either to avoid such action or to do all it can to internalize the cost. Did the United States in some sense have an obligation to other countries, or to the international economic system, to handle the dollar in certain ways because it was not just a national but an international currency? How far could such ideas be carried? If a country possesses scarce raw materials or fuel, does it have an obligation to sell them to the rest of the world (at least if it is not using them itself)? May rich America deny its capital to others, not as gifts, but for the investment vital to expanding production? What if Americans who want to invest their capital abroad are prevented from doing so by a law other Americans have put through? What of the people in a developing country who would welcome employment in a foreign-owned factory instead of a life of poor-but-noble *independencia* but are denied the chance by their compatriots?

does not take part in, and those who do not care whether family farming survives but have to pay anyhow. One must ask, too, whether the same treatment should be meted out to the family farmer who profits and the one who loses, the one who wants to be a family farmer and the one who would quit at the first opportunity. The setting aside of the problem of choice is even more pointed in the next example.

The issues go deeper than simple economics. Suppose a relatively poor country adopts an extraordinarily comprehensive and costly system of education while a richer one spends nothing. It counts on employers to teach what has to be known to do a job (which may be quite a large amount of educating) and for the rest leaves it up to individuals to teach their children and learn what they want to on their own time. Does either of these nations owe something to the other, or to anyone else in the international system? If one nation goes in for a heavy dose of egalitarianism and another for a highly refined system of incentives and differential monetary rewards, there will presumably be some effects on their economic performance. But can one say that either country has attained its autonomy at the expense of others? Should someone be compensated or someone penalized?

Perhaps enough has been said to show that there is no useful way of resolving these issues in general terms. *Autonomy* is too broad and too variegated, ranging from near-withdrawal from the world to selective acts based on the assumption that other relations will remain the same; the protection of a textile industry is a kind of autonomy. The idea that one should pay for one's own choices—take the consequences of one's own actions—is not just a good ethical principle, but something close to an essential of a society of self-respecting and responsible individuals. To apply it to nations or other social units is fraught with difficulty and ambiguity because of the conflicts of individual and group interests and wills that have to be overcome to arrive at the national interest. Even if we put these aside and accept the concept of the nation's choosing, there is no way of being sure that in all cases the nation pays for its choices. Very often it will, especially when the matter involves opting out of the efficiency system. But most of the time there will also be some impact on the rest of the world—some shifting of the burden—either because the country tries to do this or because it is unavoidable. Much of this book is about just that; many of the problems already discussed—industrial adjustment, investment, trade rules—deal with both minimizing and allocating these costs. It is not necessary to restate these matters in any detail to see that the approach via the autonomy issue has been not just a philosophical excursion but a process that has helped formulate some quite practical conclusions.

## TAKING CARE OF THE INTERNATIONAL
## ECONOMIC SYSTEM

Justice aside, the world can tolerate a good bit of opting out by small or weak countries. It is probably also generally the case that these are the countries who pay most of the cost when they choose something other than efficiency. But for big and strong countries matters are completely different. Their impact on the rest of the world is greater and the costs of their choices cannot always be internalized. Often these countries have the ability to dump part of their burdens on the rest of the world, at least initially; but the appearance may be illusory and the cost to them greater than it seems for two interrelated reasons. First, others may retaliate—directly as far as the matter in hand is concerned and by acting in a comparable manner in other cases. Second, cumulative behavior of this sort undermines not only economic cooperation but the international economic system. Therefore unless the country is a net loser from participating in that system, and cannot improve its position in some other way, it may in the end lose more than it gains by imposing involuntary burden sharing on others.

How much a country can do with impunity will vary with the country, the issue, and the time. Disturbances of reasonably well established situations will draw more reaction, and probably heavier penalties, than failures to improve on bad old ways. Among major countries none is so strong that it can always act with impunity or rise above the dangers of the deterioration of the international economic system. Nor does any one of them feel able to absorb the consequences of what others do without reacting, though there are margins of tolerance that differ according to circumstances. The diffusion of economic power is not confined to the great powers but reaches a much larger number of countries than in the past. Although there is a substantial gap in wealth and in economic power between the countries that are old industrial centers and the middle economic powers emerging around the world or rich but underdeveloped countries like some members of OPEC, the gap is not so great that the old industrial countries will treat those on the other side completely differently from the way they treat one another.

These paragraphs have described an international economic system with certain quite familiar characteristics. Autonomy is limited by the tolerance of others, which in turn is a requisite for satisfying the aspirations sought by autonomy. Those who have both a large stake in the system and the ability to do it the most damage, the strongest economies, are the ones whose behavior will largely determine what happens to the system. Hence concern for the kind of autonomy they pursue and how they handle the burden sharing of its costs is crucial. Some aspects of that behavior, making up the main subject of this book, have been shown to present problems that the existing arrangements for cooperation cannot deal with. But when we look at the resulting problems in terms of the measures that might do the job, the basic needs are not very different from those of the earlier system of economic cooperation that mostly concerned the liberalization of trade and payments.

A number of countries have to do a certain amount of "system tending," sometimes at the sacrifice of some immediate interest, as narrowly (or at least conventionally) perceived. As they are thus providing public goods, there will be others who get the benefits of that action without making a comparable effort or paying a fair share of the costs. The free riders will largely be the ones who can also act autonomously with impunity, but they have to pay for most of their nonefficiency choices. Sometimes others, strong powers as well as emerging powers, will have a free ride. The tolerance for free riding on the part of those who, not always willingly, are system tenders is limited and can be strained. There are danger points throughout the system and the process. Existing arrangements are not yet adequate to deal with these matters. Not everyone involved is yet seized with the need. That is what this book is about.

# EIGHT

# Addition and Subtraction

Readers who have come this far know how little has been said about many large issues and also the smaller ones that the study of industrial policy raises in such profusion. They know, too, that the analysis often involves doubtful questions and that the few strong, clear arguments run in opposite directions. As author, I am even more sharply aware of these difficulties, since I know what has been left unsaid. I can only hope that it is not too self-serving to believe that it has been worth the effort to show the nature of this confusion and the reasons for it. But convention calls on an author to draw things together, even at the end of a primer.

Merely to summarize seems unnecessary; the central points have recurred throughout the book. To argue that the thesis set out in the first paragraph has been proved is to claim too much. It has been illustrated and amplified to the extent that it would be surprising to find anyone taking the trouble to read this last chapter who thought that international cooperation was not seriously endangered by conflicts among national industrial policies or that the world economy was not suffering from failures to deal adequately with structural change. The elucidation of these problems in the body of the book should have made clear how very difficult they are and left no room for the belief that the author thinks that he (or anyone else) has a set of prescriptions that would put matters right if only governments would adopt them. However, some ideas have been explored about how the international problems might be approached. The proper function of this last chapter should be to pull these points together to see what they add up to as a possible program for national and international action. And where there is not really a program, one can at least say what ought to be avoided and what is worth aspiring to, even if the chances of achieving it are poor.

To help assess this adding up of possibilities, we begin with a summary look at the situation in which they have to be considered. This involves, first, a restatement of the place of industrial policy in the gamut of national policies and the reasons governments will make more use of it in the future. Concern with the clear evidence of how badly governments generally handle these matters leads to an appraisal of the view that the best course is to keep industrial policy to the inescapable minimum. Because the recession of the mid-1970s was a forcing ground for industrial policy and the unsatisfactory recovery from it continues to present a dangerous passage, the experience has to be looked at once again for what it tells about the future. Running through all this discussion are the indications of the problems to which the rest of the chapter is addressed. What we have in the end is less a set of conclusions about policy than an approach to policy, but in spots it is at least a firm approach.

## THE PLACE OF INDUSTRIAL POLICY

Industrial policy is not a recent invention or some new medicine to cure the ills of the late twentieth century. It is a term for a number of things that most governments already do—good and bad, consistent and inconsistent, thought-out and short-sighted, sustained and sporadic, deliberate and almost accidental. It provides, as the first chapter said, an emphasis more than a sharply defined category. When, in the 1830s, Friedrich List was working out his National System of Political Economy, he was calling for a kind of industrial policy that, warts and all, is not too different from what many countries seem to be pursuing today. It was a developmental policy influenced by American experience, for, List said, "The best work on political economy which one can read in that modern land is actual life."[1] But it was also a theory for developed countries, List would have claimed (if he had used the term), because it was "not founded on bottomless cosmopolitanism, but on the nature of things, on the lessons of history, and on the requirements of the nations." And certainly modern industrialized countries have acted as if their requirements went beyond simply buying and selling in open world markets. As Lionel Stoleru remarked, "to dominate the world market for ravioli is not an objective that mobilizes crowds even though it may well be a more effective way of assuring employment and the increase of incomes than to manufacture a prototype that is unique in the world—and is likely to remain so."[2]

Whether they are wise or foolish, successful or not, governments pursue industrial policies when they prefer one kind of activity over another or want to be sure their economy includes a proper diversity of activities. To get people out of agriculture and into industry where they produce more is an industrial policy, and so is the protection of domestic producers against cheaper foreign food, whether it is done for national security, to preserve farming as a way of life, or not to lose elections. Sometimes industrial policies are aimed at making a national economy stronger by adapting to changes in the world economy, but very often resistance to those changes is the main objective of industrial policy. The common element running through the activities for which *industrial policy* is a shorthand term is their concern with structural change, whether they resist, adapt to, or induce it. Though the question of what is structural is also not crystal clear, it is used here to connote the more or less long-range use of resources and the basic ways economic affairs are conducted.

Industrial policy is not a general substitute for other policies and will not displace them, even if it becomes far more important in the coming decades than it has been. It may replace certain other policies for certain purposes, and a country with a reasoned

---

[1]Friedrich List, *The National System of Political Economy*, trans. Sampson S. Lloyd, Longmans, Green, London, 1904, p. xlii. Both quotations come from the same page.

[2]Stoleru, op. cit., p. 150.

and systematic industrial policy will inevitably tie some scattered measures together and drop others. Basically, though, industrial policy has a place in a gamut that includes the broad measures dealing with the economy as a whole that are usually labeled macroeconomic; the policies (whatever one calls them) that a country has concerning the growth or development of its economy; and the remaining policies dealing with distribution of wealth and income, public welfare, the environment, and the national milieu. Industrial policy involves more than strictly economic factors and is as likely to be affected by foreign as by domestic policy. To speak of it as being in a gamut suggests a place, with boundaries and location, but in fact industrial policy overlaps many of these other activities.

Events have made the need for industrial policy apparent with a persuasiveness that more general arguments lack. The Second World War was a watershed for many things, not least economic policy. The old idea that cycles, including crises, were an essential characteristic of the capitalist system (a necessary cost of its benefits to some, proof of its undesirability to others) was largely displaced by the view that we had learned how to avoid depressions. That view was based more on theory than on the experience of the 1930s. Experience since the 1940s has borne out the new view, though the reasoning is now less sure than it was. Whether economic knowledge could be translated into effective policy was always something one could not be entirely sure of. Now there is the added uncertainty about how Western capitalist economies really work. Even if one accepts the proposition about major depressions, two new facts challenge the basics of the old belief.

Stagflation, already before the oil crisis, went far toward proving that if macroeconomic management was not as effective as it had been, the deficiencies were more than could be explained by mistakes or political choices of the economically wrong trade-off. The persistence of the recession of the mid-1970s, intensified by the oil crisis and both the adjustments to it and the refusals to adjust, underlined this view of stagflation and suggested that structural difficulties were at least partially at fault in making the recession exceptionally troublesome. The evidence on this last point cannot be as conclusive as about stagflation. However, if we accept the hypothesis and combine it with expectations of slower growth (for which the evidence is good and which could be treated as a separate factor), it almost guarantees that macroeconomic measures will not be adequate for the future. They will require the help of structural policies, at a minimum to break bottlenecks and improve the responsiveness of the system to stimuli and restraints, but probably for much more.

The energy crisis of the 1970s also demonstrates the need for industrial policy. Adjustment to higher oil and gas prices, the investment in alternative sources of energy, the determination of how far conservation should be pushed, and the timing of the whole process are all industrial policy problems. The impact of these measures and the changed energy prices on other industries, in reality and in expectation, poses further structural questions. Though the experience in oil is not likely to be repeated in other raw materials, there is good reason to believe that the relative scarcity and cost of some will increase over the next half-century. Even optimistic arguments about the ability of the international economic system to adjust to these circumstances rest on assumptions about structural changes. Any major effort to expand the world's food supplies, especially steps to encourage developing countries to produce more of their own food, calls for structural policies. That is equally true of other efforts to increase the supply and conserve reserves of wood, water, minerals, or any other product. The long time that elapses between exploration for minerals and high levels of production in the mines means that investment requires anticipation of future structural conditions. This is true whether the funds come entirely from private sources or involve some form of government aid or guarantee, as seems increasingly likely in various parts of the world. Changes in population and levels of income mean that some kind of industrial policies will be needed to assure either the growth that is wanted or whatever else is preferred to it.

Another fact that makes industrial policy a greater necessity in the future than in the past is increased concern about the quality of life, particularly in the advanced industrial countries.

The term can be taken to cover a very wide range of things—everything people want that is not directly bought and sold, and some things that are. Whether it is a matter of leisure, purity of the environment, public health, or the realization of social principles—equality, freedom, a floor under poverty—structural measures are involved. The bargaining within a society that determines the trade-off between these values and plain material gain is shaped in part by the wealth and productivity of the economy. Maximizing these is also likely to require measures of industrial policy. The need would be double: to get the most out of new structural changes in the world economy and to reduce the cumulative burden of past resistance to change.

This double need is a factor in all the circumstances calling for industrial policy, but it gains special weight if one accepts the view that the difficulties of the 1970s stem in part from the fact that inefficiencies which were affordable when growth was high became more burdensome in recession. Then the need to undo the effects of much past industrial policy (including measures that have been thought of simply as protectionism) becomes an important reason why industrial policy will be more needed in the future. The more restrictive the measures taken to deal with recession or prop up weak industries to maintain employment, the greater the future burden. If expectations of slower growth in the OECD world prove correct, the need for structural change to gain efficiency increases at a time when most countries will find it hard to satisfy that need.

If a second set of expectations proves correct, those of faster growth in the developing countries, that will also increase the need for structural change in the industrial countries. That is clear if they try to adapt to these changes by importing what they can most advantageously and altering their domestic production accordingly. The easing of such transitions is, as we have seen, a major field for certain kinds of industrial policy. But even if the older industrial centers resist change, they will have to take steps to adapt the structures of their economies.

Quite apart from questions of relative growth rates in different parts of the world, another reason for believing that industrial policy will be important in the future is that the pattern of production in the world appears to change more rapidly than it used to and seems likely to continue to do so. Some of the reasons lie in such familiar factors as the increase in speed and volume of communications, the resulting demonstration effects and their impact on demand, higher levels of learning and skill, rapid growth, increased investment, and the speed with which multinational corporations and others put new technology to use in various parts of the world. Less obvious factors probably play a part—for example, the increased size of the most economical and efficient units of production in many fields. This increase means that each new investment in a new place is likely to increase capacity faster than demand, with a resulting pressure to export, at least for the time being.

Accelerated change almost certainly means that comparative advantage will move about the world more quickly. That means that adaptation to change will be more difficult than in the past, when the pace was slower. Measures of adjustment within industries or through the marketplace that were tolerable when spread over time (and especially when there was also general economic expansion) become unacceptable when telescoped into much shorter periods; so once again governments are called on to take a direct hand in shaping the structure of the national economy, whether to speed or to resist change.

It is probable that governments and their electorates will react differently to all these changes. They may resist increased governmental intervention and favor a freer play of market forces. Something more is said about this possiblilty in the next section; here it is sufficient to note that if this changed attitude developed, it would not only eliminate the need for various specific measures of industrial policy but also create a need for the kinds of measures that make market forces work better and probably also for steps to undo past measures that have inhibited structural change. That would present a very different picture of the world from the one we are used to, in which governments are actively pursuing a series of specific goals concerning the structure of their economy. However, there would still be a need for some measures concerning structural change. And if the change of mood affected some countries but not others and the latter continued to pursue more familiar industrial policy aims, the market-emphasizing ones would find themselves developing criteria of fair trade that were almost bound to include attention to structural issues.

It is implicit in much of what has been said that the need for some kinds of industrial policy measures can be reduced if a good deal of adaptation is allowed to take place or is brought about with the help of other industrial policy measures. The need can also be reduced, or even eliminated, if macroeconomic policy—or luck—leads to satisfactory growth and good flexibility in a national economy or the international economy as a whole. One reason why there was less discussion of industrial policy in many countries in the 1950s and 1960s than there is today was that growth rates, full employment, and affluence made adaptation easier and at the same time made it easier to afford the cost of not adapting where it was politically difficult. However, it appears that part of the price of less attention to industrial policy was the accumulation of resistances that are now showing themselves. That is what is suggested by looking at the textile and steel industries and by the lack of significant progress in trade liberalization after the mid-1960s. The most successful industrial policies, in France and Japan, guided growth rather than creating it.

No amount of industrial policy will serve to assure growth, full employment, stability, a suitable international monetary system, wise national balance-of-payments policies, or many other things that are needed by the international economic system and sought by governments. It makes no sense to think of industrial policy in isolation, nor will it often be an effective substitute for other measures directed to these various purposes. It is essentially a set of policies to be used in conjunction with more general policies and primarily to secure specific objectives: certain kinds of structural change, resistance to market forces for some socially desirable goals, promotion of particular types of development or production. One exception to this almost secondary role for industrial policy occurs when a country goes in for a great deal of planning or shaping of the structure of the economy so that macroeconomic forces operate within a framework set by structural choices. A second exception is the kind of industrial policy that puts primary emphasis on improving the working of the market, assuring the play of competition, or injecting government-stimulated R & D and technology into an otherwise largely unguided economy. Even then one could not usefully put industrial policy at the top of the list of things to do for a government. The burden of the argument of this and earlier sections has been only that the past practice of not putting it on the list at all, or in so limited a sense as to apply only to the odd case, is seriously wrong. That holds true even if a government finally does very few of the specific things that are labeled industrial policy in most discussions.

The increased importance of industrial policy as an international issue follows from its expanded national use. That produces problems that are not yet adequately dealt with and that have played a significant part in slowing down the progress of international economic cooperation. Often national industrial policy measures are aimed at avoiding adjustment to changes in the international economy; sometimes their international impact is secondary to some other aim. In either case they create international problems that are only partially dealt with by existing arrangements for cooperation in general and those pertaining to trade and investment in particular. Measures to deal with industrial policy issues are very likely to fall mainly into those familiar fields, with their very different degrees of international agreement on rules and principles. One major change in the international monetary system seemed to some people likely to reduce the pressures on a number of governments to resort to direct intervention in industry. But floating exchange rates, though making some kinds of adjustment easier than before, have not altogether lived up to expectations in this regard. In any case, issues of industrial policy that affect the differential treatment of an industry within a national economy would not be reached by such across-the-board measures. Efforts to deal with industrial policy by cooperative international action have so far produced only a disappointing series of measures that have for the most part been used to resist change rather than to promote or improve it. Or it has been the kind of international action regarding development that has paid relatively little attention to the global consequences of various elements of structural change that are set in motion. Thus international action as a way of bringing about positive changes, either in anticipation of needs or to facilitate processes already at work, remains largely untried, though potentially very important. The ability of governments to agree on both the diagnosis and the solution of an international industrial policy cannot be taken for granted. Questions about what kinds of agreements, among whom, how negotiated, in which forms, and whether industrial policy as such should be the subject of international action are dealt with later. The need to ask them results from the fact that industrial policy has become a central fact of the international system of economic cooperation.

## THE CASE FOR INACTION

The new interest in industrial policy in the 1970s has stimulated opposition as well as support. Many of the measures advocated in the recession after 1973 were extremely restrictive. Advocates of free markets had long been critical of French *dirigisme*, the symbiosis of Japanese business and government, and the part that nationalized enterprises had played in the difficulties of Italy and the United Kingdom. Believers in the benefits of international trade liberalization found it easy to see how industrial policies were undermining the achievements of 25 years of international economic cooperation. One could have doubts about how far trade liberalization could be pushed without new kinds of supporting measures to deal with adjustment and nevertheless be chary of much of what was being put forward as industrial policy. One could accept the aims and intentions of the advocates of industrial policy and still believe that their efforts would simply play into the hands of industries stronger than they were; protection would be accepted, but not structural change. To see the point, one had only to picture a world in which all activity was governed by policies like those the rich industrial countries applied to their agriculture. The textile example was a warning.

What was done in the case of steel looked dubious. The alleged need for recession cartels, the creation of national champions in computers and other high-science industries that rarely outgrew their bureaucratic tutelage, and the bargaining between multinational companies and national governments about subsidies and tax concessions for investments all looked like an undesirable wave of the future. "Better no industrial policy than this sort of thing" is an understandable point of view and one shared by many people.

Some of the worst dangers might be averted by insisting that industrial policy measures be international. But the requirements for enlightened action along those lines are high: the joining of different national preferences or values, the conscious movement away from a known status quo toward an unknown better state of things, the choice of new activities to replace the old (on which no one has a good record). One calls to mind the hazards: the tendency of the temporary to become permanent, the mixed motives of the parties, the built-in pressures to act in a cartel-like manner, and many others. It is hard to avoid the feeling that the chances of success are poor and those of perversion or deterioration good. A test case could be the worry about excess capacity in some industries. Would not the first step be to prevent their growth in new centers of production? Apart from the unacceptability of rich countries trying to preserve what they already have at the expense of poor countries such a stance would presently burden all the industrial economies as well. The case for not taking steps in industrial policy that would lead to such results is strong.

One of the strongest arguments for inaction is that most of the adjustment to structural change takes place without the "help" of governmental industrial policies.[3] Otherwise the progress of the world economy in the 1950s and 1960s would have been impossible. In many cases these changes took place despite industrial policies that resisted them. The benefits gained by the developing countries as producers, the public of the industrial

[3] A subject that needs more study is just how these unaided adjustments take place. The result might help us to see where a useful push could sometimes be given or a block removed.

countries as consumers, and both business people and workers as suppliers to world markets would all have been less if the forces behind some industrial policies had had their way. No doubt in some hard cases intervention to slow the change was warranted—but why institutionalize the practice and give the already durable "temporary" a legitimate lease on a longer life? No doubt, too, governments are entitled to pursue noneconomic goals, sacrificing the benefits of efficiency; since their choices will usually do some harm to other countries, such problems should be dealt with. But why invite an increase in conflicts, considering the loss through friction and the unsatisfactory nature of the settlement of these disputes? It is not an attractive prospect to set in motion a process in which the squeakiest wheel will get the grease while the strong lay down conditions that the weak have to make the best of.

Still another point in the case for inaction is a new spirit of the times that began to show itself in the late 1970s in several places. In the United States its particular form was deregulation and various kinds of tax revolts. In Europe it was marked by such things as condemnation of nationalization by Italian Communists, the throwing off of old patterns of control by a French government, and the appearance of conservatives in Scandinavian governments that had long been dominated by socialists. The Germans became more articulate than ever about market forces under a socialist government. In Japan the manifestations have been less clear-cut, but they seem to put the stress on the increased ability of some firms to stand on their own feet and so resist guidance by the Ministry of International Trade and Industry; they also show serious doubt whether action according to a collective consensus requires government intervention to succeed. Everywhere there was worry about too much of the GNP's passing through government hands. If inflation was the enemy, was it not the government that did most to fuel inflationary pressures? These attitudes were tied up with widespread disillusionment with macroeconomic measures and some shift of opinion in favor of relying on fixed formulas for government action, such as those called for by the monetarist approach to national economic policy. If movements of this sort were indeed to dominate the next decade, the case for not acting on most industrial policy issues would look strong. But it has yet to be shown that most advocates of these positions would accept the logical consequences of sticking to their view and doing little else.

The case for inaction is not quite the same as the case for not interfering with market forces, but they overlap. And there's the rub. People have in fact *not* been willing to let market forces do their work when the results were not to their liking. That is what trade restrictions, subsidies to investments, steel programs, and cartels mean. Perhaps the world is going to change in this respect, moving toward less market interference, but it is hard to believe so. A more likely result is that the new wave will move it a small distance. It is, after all, a very long step from rebelling against tax increases or irksome regulations to accepting the idea that the government should not protect business against foreign competition, support farm prices, or concern itself about run-down urban areas and public transportation.

Until there is evidence of such change in public attitudes, the valid arguments and fears that have been summed up as the case for inaction become a case for a certain kind of action. It might be of a very limited sort, to make sure that when people did interfere with market forces, they did it in ways that assured that change would take place. Or it might be more general: the anticipation that since there would be more industrial policy intervention in the future, one should work hard to lay down rules and procedures to get better results. Or the emphasis might be on the need to make markets work better. Light-years away from what was done in textiles and agriculture, this kind of industrial policy calls for measures that promote change and make it more acceptable. (Failure to act along these lines may well play into the hands of the advocates of more restrictive industrial policies.) It is but a step to other possibilities: fostering R & D in ways that make for change, a tax policy that favors investment and also risk, an approach to bankruptcy that assures that failures will be permitted to go out of business.

This kind of approach is compatible with the view that industrial policy actions should be minimal, taken only when necessary, and aimed either at permitting market forces to work or at perfecting their operation. It is also compatible with the view that to make the operation of market forces acceptable, politically or morally, their impact on people must be tempered. Indeed, this line of reasoning leads to a position very close to what was considered a call for positive action on structural change, not a case for inaction:

The most feasible and also the most constructive alternative to restrictive intervention by the State is not non-intervention (*laissez-faire*), but intervention of a more constructive kind—namely, a positive programme of industrial adaptation. Such a programme would be designed to assist industry and labour in re-orienting themselves, so that they can take maximum advantage of new opportunities. In this way the enterprise and initiative of citizens will be preserved and will be exerted in the most promising directions. The results of such a programme, assuming that it is successful, might well be in many (but not all) respects similar to that which the automatic market system would accomplish if it were about to function with the theoretical perfection assumed in older textbooks. But the process of adjustment ought to go forward with more attention to the human problems of the individuals directly involved and with less infliction of suffering on particular groups.[4]

Once the argument has been carried this far, there can hardly be any objection to considering what I have called positive industrial policies, national or international. One can believe in putting major reliance on the market and still think that something has to be done to remedy the market's imperfection in forecasting the long future. To overcome the uncertainty that is inhibiting investment there may be a case for some kind of government support or an international understanding that the products of new enterprise will not be excluded from established markets. Another of the 1940s advocates of adaptive policies pointed out that "in adjusting our economic structure, the first step must nearly always be taken by the man who controls capital, and the significance of this truth is not confined to so-called capitalist

[4]Staley, *World Economic Development*, op. cit., p. 177.

economies.''[5] Nor in the modern world is the control entirely private, even in the capitalist economies. Staunch opponents of the restrictive and *dirigiste* kind of industrial policies can equally favor the facilitating kinds of policies, whether they are adopted nationally or internationally. In fact, international action is the more desirable; the need is greater and the market larger.

This line of approach is no longer a case for inaction, but one further step could make it so. Preceding chapters have shown how hard it is to work out altogether satisfactory international measures and how great the pressures are for them to turn bad. A positive effort risks not only waste and damage but a result that may be the opposite of the original purpose. There will be times when it will seem better not to try.

## RECESSION, THE DIFFICULT PASSAGE

The awareness of structural problems was heightened by the recession of the mid-1970s. So was the resistance to change. Those who saw evidence of an increased need for change had to face a diminution of the ability of governments and economies to make changes. Sensitivity to temporary unemployment was one factor, the unwillingness of business to invest another. This unwillingness stemmed partly from the fact that short-term prospects did not justify long-term commitments (though how one could reason from the one to the other was not always apparent); another source was uncertainty about the future of national and world economies, and that was reasonable enough. Still a third factor, contributing to the second, was worry that in their responses to the recession, and afterwards as well, governments would conduct industrial and other policies that penalized business. At the same time, a large number of businessmen resisted such ideas as were abroad about promoting long-term structural change if that seemed likely to diminish their own position or subject them to increased competition. The capitalists and man-

[5] A. G. B. Fisher, *Economic Progress and Social Security*, Macmillan, London, 1945, p. 76.

agers joined with the workers and many of the politicians in a defense of the status quo that, while natural enough, was a threat to the long-run welfare of their countries. It was more than the revival of protectionism that journalists and statesmen saw everywhere. It was a new conservatism that worked against the need for flexibility that seems vital for the future.

The attitudes were matched by the industrial policy record of the recession[6] and the troubled and uneven recovery from it: stopgap arrangements in steel that could turn into almost anything; tightened restrictions on textile trade, especially at the expense of developing countries; national and international cartels or efforts to form cartels; the call for eliminating excess capacity in an inflationary world; uncertainty and squabbling about how to deal with the real issues of energy. The Tokyo Round, the first significant effort to deal with trade barriers in a decade, was almost certainly far less productive than if it had been worked out in better times. There was a smell of the 1930s about and echoes in the language.

If there was some sunlight, it shone through some chinks and one window. The chinks were the piecemeal evidence that the restrictive arrangements did not hold up very well, especially when someone could see a chance to make some money by getting around them, or that governments were not comfortable with unqualified support of business efforts to suppress competition. The Bresciani and others cheated on the European steel arrangements; the trigger-price system in the United States left room for imports; there were bankruptcies in Japan that the government did not stave off; as in the past, textiles moved around the trade barriers; many industries had to adapt, like it or not. The window was the rather widespread recognition of the damage that a nationalistic reaction to the recession could do to each country as well as to the international economic system.

[6] As before, the term *recession* is used somewhat loosely to cover the actual decline of the mid-1970s and the slow and uncertain resumption of growth in Europe and other places, even though a real but also inflationary recovery took place in the United States. The key point is that problems created by the recession and the worry about them (notably unemployment, inadequate investment, and possible excess capacity) were not removed by the unsatisfactory recovery.

The result was a certain prudence in high places, quite a few statements that said the right things, the reasonably successful adherence to the OECD pledge to avoid mutual damage, and the effort to extend it to adjustment measures (described in Chapter 3).

These are legitimate reasons for optimism but one must worry about how far it can be carried. The chinks may be stopped up. If the recession's stumbling recovery gives way to the slow growth so widely expected, governments, business, and the officials of international organizations will work to find ways to penalize the cheating, control trade, enforce the cartel rules, and keep the poachers out of the *chasses gardées* of various industries and trading areas. And the pledge, if it remains a pledge, is hardly likely to be as well honored over time as it was at first. It need not be rescinded or amended to become less effective; a reduced sense of peril will itself weaken the will to adhere to the pledge; slow erosion and pragmatic adaptation to circumstances are easily confounded.

The evidence of this book is that we have not yet found ways to deal adequately with the international problems stemming from national industrial policies. Without better international measures, the chances increase that national measures will become more restrictive. Countries that feel damaged will strike back or seek to compensate themselves in some other field, and the fabric of cooperation will unravel. A deeper reason is that in the absence of adequate international arrangements—or the ability to make them ad hoc—calculations of national choice will have to be narrower and more restrictive. A. G. B. Fisher made that point about the depression. That many bad policies were pursued is clear, and not only with hindsight, he said. But sometimes the reason was that better possibilities were not "within the effective range of choice for national statesmen. . . . In the absence of any efficient framework of international economic institutions they had no alternative but to do what, on a longer view, inevitably proved to be the wrong thing."[7] The point will be as valid for the future if there is no improvement.

In short, one is not entitled to take much satisfaction from the

---

[7]Fisher, op. cit., p. 244.

rays of sunlight as to the way industrial policies were treated in the recession. One may call attention to the danger, hoping that that will do some good, as alarm raising clearly did at the outset. However, substantive progress will be needed. It is not just a matter of new international measures, necessary as they are. It is also the risk that expectations of slow growth will project the troubles of the recession into the indefinite future. If the idea of excess capacity dominates thinking, the results will be to dampen investment, hinder the expansion of production in developing countries, and restrict the markets for its output when it takes place. These tendencies will feed on themselves, and the older industrial nations will become less able to make structural changes just when the need for them increases.[8] It is unacceptable for the rich to say to the poor, "The world has enough, postpone your wants." It is in the direct interest of the inhabitants of the industrial world themselves to make the most efficient possible use of reduced resources, something that requires adaptation.

To escape this heritage of the recession, two lines of action are needed. The first is in macroeconomic policy and measures making for growth; the more they accomplish, the less the strain on industrial policy and pressures on it to move in a restrictive direction. The second line of action is through industrial policy. It points first toward making sure that the restrictive measures taken to meet problems stemming from the recession are kept temporary, if necessary by letting competitive pressures and

[8]Some members of the research staff of GATT have pointed out that the recession measures in several industries provide "higher agreed prices made possible by reductions in output," which not only "run counter to the governments' proclaimed goals" for recovery but "increase excess capacity, the existence of which was one of the motivations for forming the cartel in the first place." Then "the higher prices prevailing in the cartelized market must be protected from lower-cost producers abroad. . . ." If the arrangement also holds down new investment that goes ahead in developing countries, it "tends to widen the productivity gap, with the result that when the cartel arrangement eventually expires their share of the world market is likely to shrink even further." In the long run "the cartel solution" proves costly because it interferes with allocation so that "resources are trapped in less-productive uses." Richard Blackhurst, Nicolas Marian, and Jan Tumlir, *Adjustment, Trade and Growth in Developed and Developing Countries*, GATT Studies in International Trade, no. 6, Geneva, 1978, pp. 59, 60.

cheating undermine them as soon as it is safe to do so. A second step is to use what is not temporary in these measures to bring about adaptation and if possible to turn them into lasting instruments of structural change. The third aim is to provide a better international framework for all these activities. The focus should be on longer-run needs, not on the immediate conditions of the recession and its aftermath. To do these things one must have an idea of where it would be desirable to go. The chapter, and the book, conclude with a sketch of one view of the right direction.

## WHAT THEN MUST WE DO?

My answer is not Tolstoy's, which was long, rambling, and argumentative. Most of what follows has been said before in this book, analytically if not prescriptively. If the statements here are more positive than before, it is only because brevity dictates leaving out the qualifications and caveats needed in real life. A general one is that there are often several ways to achieve a purpose and that though I have preferences, I am not a dogmatist. The following section will be modest about its proposals, cautious about their efficacy, skeptical of the ability of democratic governments to manage microeconomic matters with any nicety, and doubtful that individuals and interest groups will act with the breadth of view that their own long-run interests require. There is an element of idealism in what follows; one ought to aspire. There is no program for immediate action; the focus is the long run.

The underlying conviction of these conclusions is that continuing change is a fundamental fact of the world economy and that adaptation to it is a basic requisite for satisfying the needs of people. Flexibility of national economies should be highly valued. What people want in life is not just economic so economies and societies have to satisfy these other wants as well as those that can be summed up as efficiency. But there are trade-offs, there are limits, and there are mutually exclusive alternatives. People should know what they are doing, what it costs, and who pays. And that raises the question of who is entitled to make these choices on whose behalf. The international arrangements, which are our prime concern, have to allow for considerable differences among national policies, minimize the problems each creates for others, and enhance the ability to meet people's needs and wishes beyond what national governments can do alone.

What can be done internationally depends heavily on national measures, but what is said here about them must remain general and applicable to a number of different economies. The effort to find some common principles that can be applied *mutatis mutandis* is preferable to an emphasis on uniformity of methods. Nationally and internationally the conclusions point a direction in which it would be desirable to move. They do not map a heavenly city where one may some day arrive. That is not for our time.

Structural change is too pervasive; the issues we have designated industrial policy are too complex; and the process of dealing well with them is too difficult, intellectually and politically, to rely on a single effort. Action on trade, investment, and the financing of development all provide points of attack, but what has been in the past is inadequate to future needs. Sectoral measures have a rather poor record, but they cannot be ruled out. Since they are deeply embedded in the ways governments do things, the question is whether they can be used not just as slightly shoddy cover for the protection of such industries but to restore health or even to prevent future trouble by foreseeing it. New kinds of measures should be invented and tested to deal with specific aspects of industrial policy, such as the OECD "orientations." Broad consultation and information measures have a place. Not everything that is needed will be labeled in the first instance "industrial policy" or "structural change." Perhaps someday it will seem wise to draw together many different things in some kind of comprehensive industrial policy agreement or set of principles, but for the time being it will be enough to establish an awareness of structural problems and the need to assess the industrial policy dimension of issues that have usually been thought of in other terms. This is not just a matter of will; it is an intellectual problem as well. We know too little about some of the processes of change or the consequences of various acts. Study is needed to test the impressions and half-formed convictions on which so much of the reasoning about industrial policy is based (including the reasoning in this book). The questions include not only the efficacy of various measures, but how structural change and industrial adaptation to it take place when there is no conscious public effort to that end.

Trade provides the easiest approach, partly because the Tokyo Round itself involved new agreements about industrial policy measures. The new rules about subsidies, government procurement, and other nontariff barriers fall far short of what is needed to deal effectively with the issues raised in this book. Their actual meaning will depend on how governments use the procedures for consultation and the settlement of disputes to broaden the scope of the rules. Even more important is how safeguard provisions are used. When governments are permitted to check imports that upset domestic markets, there should be pressure on them to use the time gained to bring about changes that would eliminate the problem. International surveillance to forward the process and internatonal consultation about the new uses to be made of the shifted resources would be part of a new international industrial policy process.

Even ambitious rules about trade barriers, subsidies, and safe-guards would not dispose of all the trade problems arising from industrial policy. State trading, the conduct of nationalized firms, and the activities of less than national units of government that affect international trade pose further issues. It will not suffice to continue the lame system that has grown up in which rich countries follow one set of rules (more or less) and poor ones are exempted from them and given special treatment. One way of making a change will be to introduce new measures bearing on industrial policies in ways that give emerging developing coun-tries—the Brazils, Koreas, Hong Kongs, Mexicos, and those who follow—an incentive to take part on a more nearly equal basis. A second approach should come through working out new sets of trade policy principles and rules especially applicable to developing countries. They will have to provide greater selec-tivity in the protection of infant industries and more assurance of access for LDC exports to foreign markets, in the developing countries as well as the industrial countries.

This last activity converges with the international attention that needs to be given to questions of investment. The case for a GATT for private investment or a code for investors and governments is a strong one; the difficulty of achieving a meaningful agreement of any breadth is an historic fact that makes it difficult to believe that there will be great steps forward. But whatever the vehicles, there are likely to be some agreements among some countries on a number of investment issues. Pressures for such agreements arise from both restrictions on foreign business and help to investors in the form of subsidies or other measures that affect international trade. If no multilateral rules or standards are developed, the agreements are likely to reflect bilateral bargaining relations and to do some damage to third parties, who may well retaliate in whatever ways they can. As in the case of trade, rules and principles are not likely to suffice without procedures for dealing with cases and perhaps broader consultation. It will not be possible to act as if investment or the behavior of the multinational corporation were something that could be dealt with satisfactorily without regard to what was to be produced and where, which are the underlying issues that affect the economic structure of more than the two countries directly involved.

To see how difficult it will be to deal adequately with investment issues, it is enough to ask whether any government should have the power to prevent or at least penalize investment in fields where there is already excess capacity, by some test. The best placed to do so would usually be the home government of the investing company, but others could have a greater interest. Obviously, such power would be dangerous and almost bound to be abused. On such a matter it would be far better to have an international decision or opinion. But whose? We are immediately in the whole range of issues concerning development financing. Even if there can be safeguards against established producers (or their governments) dominating the process, what else needs to be done? If there is in fact excess capacity in some industry for as far ahead as can be seen, is it not irresponsible to allocate scarce public funds to adding still more instead of using them for something else that is more needed? The rhetorical question is not intended to dictate an affirmative answer. New technology, greater efficiency, or simply lower costs may be sufficient reason for displacing old with new facilities. What is unlikely is that a neat fit can be made, especially when large and lumpy investment requirements for economies of scale mean that the new addition is likely to have a greater capacity than the old, inefficient plant it replaces.

Private funds are another matter, but then the investor should be allowed to fail if he has made a mistake. But governments feel an interest in enterprises not closing down when they provide many jobs and may have other reasons as well—that is what industrial policy is all about. Is it right for governments to defend existing producers against the foolishness of a new venturer who, for whatever reason, feels able to sell (perhaps at a loss) in their markets? Should this be done even if it prevents the creation of jobs in new areas where production might, or might not, be competitive? A panel of international judges is unlikely to escape bias or to have either clear criteria or sufficient wisdom. And yet what can be imagined that would be better? (The Legislator of Chapter 2 is not likely to put in an appearance.) The World Bank and national agencies for development financing have to make judgments that should in some way focus on those issues better than they now do. Even inadequate devices such as the lists mentioned in Chapters 3 and 5 have some value. Then actions that would make trouble can be debated in relevant terms. The MTN codes on subsidies, safeguards, and related matters will be of some help. But it is hard to restrain a combination of public and private people from creating excess capacity, even when they see what they are doing, as is illustrated by the history of chemicals, especially petrochemicals, in recent years.

It is in development that the greatest potential of a positive international industrial policy lies; but it will be immensely difficult to achieve, and one cannot wholeheartedly affirm that it ought to be undertaken. The idea would be that in one form or another—quite a few possibilities can be imagined—the building up of one or more industries in new centers of production in developing countries would be accompanied by the adjustment of the competing industries in the older centers. This might come through complementary specialization in certain products or activities within the same industry. It might be chiefly a matter of

269

contracting the size of the old industry and expanding a different one, perhaps a supplier of machinery to the new activity. The continued existence in the old center of a few producers who are internationally competitive is likely in most industries.

Such efforts would be real international industrial policy, aimed not only at bringing about a smooth transfer but at securing a more efficient use of world resources with benefits for all concerned. The arrangements could deal with matters other than efficiency. For example, they could assure each country that it could retain a certain productive capacity; a government could be left free to subsidize or protect a set of inefficient producers if it did so in an agreed manner and did not increase the burdens of others; a country that held down the speed of its own industrial expansion to make it easier for others to adapt might be compensated. The difficulties of the approach lie only partly in the obvious problem of finding sufficient areas of agreement among governments and among the business groups involved. There is also the doubt one must have whether such large developments can in fact be planned with enough foresight to work out as intended. And finally, one has to ask whether such orderly transfers may in fact prove more modest than what might happen otherwise. Would any planned arrangement have allowed as high a rate of increase of the shipment of LDC manufactured goods to the OECD countries as in fact took place in the 1960s? Still, there is no doubt that if such an arrangement could be made for dealing with some of the hard cases in which the rich countries have insisted on protecting their own least efficient industries, it would be progress.

These positive steps would not have to be confined to North-South relations. They could apply to the reorganization of industry among older countries or the building up of wholly new branches. The problem there is that one doubts the efficacy of such decisions over the working of market forces, at least so long as ideas of fair shares for all countries influence the decisions. However, in industries where scale is important, competition is limited, and the differences in location are secondary in regard to comparative advantage, governmental understandings about the division of labor might not be very different from what would be accomplished by a few large investors or banks and could avoid some international friction as well. Though the principle of the *juste retour* seems to have been responsible for some of the failures in European industrial cooperation, one could imagine a more sensible approach to the division of labor that would increase the benefits as well as spreading them.

Positive policies of this sort make most sense if applied to a number of industries at the same time (expansion in one to offset contraction in another). But they could be confined to a particular sector, which may sometimes be the best course for very practical reasons (there are also some practical difficulties). If one takes the view that governments ought not to get more deeply involved in industrial policy than they really need to, one is almost bound to end up with the sectoral approach. Nothing would be done until a sector really needed attention, and then there would be an attempt to contain the problem by bringing about what change was possible within the industry itself. The sectoral approach could be used to undertake great shifts in production, but it is probably better suited to working out a division of labor in fields no major country is willing to give up entirely. Since the mid-1960s, as pointed out in Chapter 4, there has been discussion of the kinds of agreements about agriculture that would be preferable to the unedifying pulling and hauling that has gone on between the United States and the European Community, as a result of acting as if trade liberalization were the main issue. Japan could be fitted in quite well. Steel may be headed the same way, and a formula that permitted fair and free competition around a hard core of self-sufficiency might have much to recommend it (and improve the productivity of the core as well). The trouble with sectoral approaches is the fairly strong tendency toward cartelization and the equally serious push toward making compromises among the participants at the expense of outside countries. One's evaluation of a sectoral proposal ought to hinge in part on the extent to which safeguards on those points can be devised or forces kept at work that will produce enough competition, either from inside or outside, to put pressure on the participants. Sometimes imperfections in agreements ought to be tolerated because breakdown after a period may be better than tighter restrictions.

All these international devices have to be accompanied by national industrial policies that move in the right direction, or there will be nothing but contradictions and impasses. Enough has been said by now about the virtues of adaptive policies. There is really no doubt that the older industrial countries ought to give much higher priority than they have done to adjusting their economies to structural changes in the world economy. They ought to encourage, not resist, such changes by helping firms to adapt and especially by providing security and assistance to workers. To do this in an orderly manner, they can quite properly set a reasonable pace for the expansion of imports, so long as they do not let temporary trade restraints become an excuse for doing nothing or slow things down to the point at which the loss of competitiveness damages the rest of the economy. Their internal procedures ought to clarify the real conflicts of interest within the society that come from making the change and also from preserving the status quo, as well as showing who pays the costs. It should also be emphasized—as it was in the OECD "orientations" on adjustment policies—that the reason countries should behave this way lies in their own self-interest. It is the effect on their economies rather than on the pattern of international trade that makes this essentially an industrial policy issue rather than simply a trade question.

At the same time governments have to recognize that what they are doing affects others as well as themselves. That is a factor of importance making for adaptive policies; but it applies as well to defensive measures, in which a country forgoes the most efficient use of its resources in order to realize other values (including avoidance of disturbance). In all these cases governments should be prepared to respond to the demands of other countries for adjustments that minimize whatever damage to them is inescapable. Where poorer countries are involved, this compensation may well take the form of actual money payments; generally, however, the emphasis ought to be on providing a pattern of trade, production, and investment that will permit the country to pay its own way in the world. Reciprocity, retaliation, and bargaining power will all affect the balance between the weight given to internal and external factors and probably between adaptive and defensive measures. No government will perfectly satisfy either its domestic constituents or the rest of the world. One can almost think of every country having a sort of ration of noneconomic behavior toward the rest of the world that it is entitled to engage in without much retaliation from abroad. But if it goes too far, the country may not only pay a high price but lose the advantages it was trying to preserve.

These arguments about internal and external pressures and the way national interests are affected both by the domestic content of industrial policy and the reactions of other countries to it apply as well to developing countries. But in the matter of adaptation and initiation, these countries have a somewhat different set of problems. These start with the age-old question of choosing suitable infant industries, knowing how long they require special treatment before they ought to be able to stand on their own feet or be abandoned, and what difference it makes how this tutelage is provided. The record leaves much to be desired. It is also clear that questions about export markets have to be looked at more carefully than before, especially if the OECD countries are likely to experience slower growth. On the one hand, there will probably be more scrutiny of arrangements that amount to export subsidies in some form. On the other, developing countries have a right to expect less restrictive treatment from the richer countries. The past focus on trade policy has not produced adequate solutions, and the problems seem likely to grow. A focus on industrial structures should help put our understanding of the real issues on a clearer basis than when the focus was on preferential tariff treatment, quantitative limits on imports of sensitive items, and so on. It should also test the assumption underlying much of this argument: There are common interests which, if properly pursued, can produce gains for industrialized and developing countries.

Developing countries have more to gain from cooperation and an orderly approach to structural change than from the direction things have been moving in for some time. They cannot expect to be treated as exceptions to all rules and left free of obligations. But they have a right to participate in the making of those rules and the conduct of procedures to apply them. In this activity, as in other matters, their bargaining power will almost certainly grow, especially since the OECD countries count increasingly on selling them capital goods. They will be tempted to agree to privileged bilateral relationships. If they yield too often—and immediate gain will make that seem reasonable—they are likely to do themselves long-run damage. From their point of view, as well as that of analysts, it is not sensible to see everything as a North-South issue. Trade among the developing countries themselves will become more important than in the past, and the emerging industrial countries among the LDCs have some advantages over older industrial centers that they should learn to exploit. There is also some easing of the global adjustment problem when new producers take over old export markets instead of putting all their effort into selling directly into the home markets of the industrial countries. (They will do both.) The emerging middle powers will also face adjustment problems of their own at the same time as they have the opportunity to play a larger part in the international economic system.

Industrialized countries have infant industry problems too, those of the infant prodigies of advanced technology they want to foster. Here too a certain limited protection or special treatment makes sense, but the determination of its limits is just as hard as in developing countries. In all these matters there is a further dilemma. One of the strengths of the industrial countries is that the play of market forces, particularly the power of competition, is a major factor making for efficiency and innovation. But a policy that aims to initiate change by fostering new technologies sometimes has to focus on building up one firm or a few and giving them some kind of monopoly. A highly selective policy can also be cheaper than blanket protection for a whole industry, which helps the strong as well as the weak. It is easy to agree that the target should always be international competitiveness, but not so easy to know either how long to wait before hitting it or how much to pay for near misses.

To be effective in their industrial policies, governments need

274

a good working relationship with business. To provide the combination of the security that labor is entitled to and the mobility that the economy should have will almost certainly require more effective labor policies than all but a few countries have found possible. Not only wise policy calls for this, but also the political acceptability of measures stressing adaptation. On the financial side, industrial policy is likely to work better by providing funds on favorable terms for activities that are being encouraged than by trying to limit the access of enterprises to funds, at least when firms of any size are involved. A government interested in trying to plan much of its economy has a set of problems about fitting various of its industries and sectors into the plan; it will be pushed toward having a fuller industrial policy than a country that does not engage in planning. The energy problem, and probably a number of other factors, will be thought to strengthen the case in many countries for "planning" (written with quotation marks because the word is used in many different ways), but how far governments will get with this is a matter for some doubt. What is clearly useful, however, is the provision of information as to possible future action and its purposes as well as the present situation.

Information is also a key to the international handling of industrial policy. It can take many forms, some of which have been discussed in preceding chapters with regard to both effectiveness and avoidance of the politicization and corruption to which much of it is bound to be exposed. Though data are plentiful, there are deficiencies that ought to be made good. The presentation ought to be not only timely but organized so as to bear on industrial policy issues. Perhaps as much as anything, focus and visibility could help ensure that industrial policy issues are taken into account and fully and fairly appraised. It should not be overlooked that a good deal of what is called consultation is an exchange of information about intention and reaction as well as of "facts." Widely relied on in these prescriptions, consultation should be a very general process, with the flexibility that can come from different groupings of countries at different times and for different purposes.

It would be naive to believe that information alone would bring radical changes in behavior or remove the major international problems concerning industrial policy. But in a field where firm commitments are hard to work out and not always easy to justify, the influence of consultation plus the dissemination of improved and focused data can be significant. It may, for one thing, lay the foundation for concrete action, sometimes to avoid a foreseeable difficulty and sometimes to establish at least some degree of understanding once it was found that certain practices were either particularly offensive or particularly effective (or both). The information could also be a stimulus to governments to facilitate adaptation to structural change and improve the competitiveness of particular industries. For example, if it is true that innovation is sometimes slow because small firms have the ideas but not the access to capital to develop and apply them, the government can help. If there are bottlenecks in the supply of skilled labor while unskilled workers have a high employment rate, there are both immediate and long-run possibilities in training and education. Information may speed up action; a small step taken in advance may be far more useful than two larger, more difficult ones later on. Countries can learn from one another how adaptation or innovation takes place. (French planners tried to create an equivalent of American private venture capital companies by putting state funds at the disposal of a committee of businessmen.)

Like many prescriptions, this one includes a warning. National industrial policies should not let the emphasis on doing certain things create a situation in which other things are prevented from happening. Whatever is done should not suppress the forces that bring about change. These are invention, innovation, entrepreneurship, and competition. Much industrial policy will be dealing with the impact of these activities, but no industrial policy should block them. The government may not finance the mad inventor, but it should not stop a banker from lending to him. Although an adjustment program may be based on the belief that widget making will remain a productive activity in that part of the world for several decades, it would be wrong to suppress an invention that would make widgets obsolete in five years. And if the man who makes a better mousetrap also sells it so effectively that cat breeders lose their market, the state had best help the adjustment, not hinder it.

All this sounds a great deal as if the final case was for relying on the market. There is some truth in this but not the whole truth, for mixed economies require mixed policies. It is an error to reject all measures of industrial policy because complete economic planning seems beyond the power of the government and would be undesirable even if it could be done. Many things will be done that limit the effect of market forces, but the play of these forces should not be totally cut off by government action. It is likely to be sound long-run industrial policy to foster competition, especially if private business tries to suppress it. In spite of all the emphasis on guidance and order, industrial policy in a democracy will do better in the long run if much of the economy is exposed to domestic and international competition; if research, development, and innovation are encouraged and not penalized; and if the financial backing that both competition and R & D require is available, preferably through normal channels but with a governmental supplement should something go wrong. Though directed research and experimentation can achieve important results, it is hard to believe that freedom of investigation in science and technology is not a vital ingredient in assuring maximum creativity and progress. This is more than a matter of setting scientists loose in laboratories and providing mathematicians with enough chalk and computers. It requires opportunities to work in commercial-scale production and to have the feedback and incentives of distribution and use as well.

The opportunities to do things of this sort, the ability to finance them, and the willingness to undertake them are unequally distributed around the globe. Not only do national endowments differ but some social and economic systems will help and others hinder this process. In devising guidelines for industrial policy, whether they are thought of as being globally applied or as coordinating national policies, some attention will have to be paid to this situation. The results may not be unrelated to the way the system accommodates the social unit that wants to do things its own way. The ideal may be that every nation should be organized so as to maximize invention and innovation, but the unattainability of that ideal means that the second-best course must emphasize national autonomy (and its protection against pressures for uniformity or limitation coming from the rest of the system). There might then have to be fewer restraints on national behavior than might be expected in a system that emphasized responsibility (and often compensation) whenever one acted so as to affect others. Uncertainty about what really produces invention and innovation, plus the intrinsic value of the competition of ideas, may give even more weight to the value of having a system that preserves a high degree of autonomy.

For those who have read the foregoing chapters, that last thought should suffice to recall the several different grids, measuring different things and on different scales, that have to be applied to almost all matters affecting industrial policy and structural change. That is in itself the final word of warning: how misleading a simple summary can be. It would also be misleading to read the last few pages without regard to the chapters that came before. The effort to prescribe forces an accentuation of the positive. A little of that goes a long way toward sounding like a preacher—and, when generalities have to take the place of lengthy detail, a fuzzy one at that. But how else do you point a direction if you cannot honestly insist that only one path goes that way?

If the question were "What will happen?" rather than "What ought you try to make happen?" the answer would have to be pessimistic in tone and skeptical about the best end of the range. Therefore, the prescription too must be seen as incorporating more hope than assurance. It would be wrong, though, to say there is no hope. The impact of the mid-1970s recession on international relations was not as bad as it was reasonable to expect. The outcome of the MTN is helpful, if neither stirring in its accomplishment nor likely to be adequate to long-run needs. The OECD "orientations" break new ground, recognize a problem, and set out some desirable guidelines, even if they do not cover all needs, are not binding, and may not be effectively followed up. The handling of the steel problem was better for the limited cooperation and controlled reactions that took the place of the all-out trade war that might have been. Though the willingness to act constructively on restructuring the industry remains doubtful, the idea of equipping the OECD committee with some broad rules and of trying to involve some of the new producers shows a better sense of the real issues than some things that have been done. Though without clear design and with no assurance of continuity, what has been done in the automobile industry has a certain amount of promise.

The list cannot be made much longer. The bad examples are far more numerous. More serious, there is little ground for a favorable prognosis concerning the fragility of these efforts under increased pressure, the conditions that will generate these pressures, or the strength of the widespread simple-minded mercantilism with which national interests in these efforts will be interpreted. What is worse, the strains that national governments are under make it seem natural to seek strength in reducing dependence on others—which is indeed an element of strength—in ways that, thanks to this mercantilism, not only ignore many real national interests but go beyond what all but the strongest countries are capable of. It is here that there may be an educational function for the focus on industrial policy and structural change—to stress one last hopeful note, unless that position is reserved for fear of the alternative.

## THE ALTERNATIVE

This prescription rarely says what the patient *must* do. That is because the author perceived at an early age that writers about international affairs who were free with the imperative were apt to deceive themselves, if not their readers. The "must fallacy" led to the belief that the League of Nations must succeed because it was the only hope of peace. Trade must be freed or we would all get poorer. Fascism must be stopped before it plunged the world into war. And so on. There is no iron law of amelioration in the world. The first 30 years after World War II look quite good by most historical standards, but there is no presumption that the next 30 will be better or even as good. And so it is with the matters dealt with in this book. A situation has been created partly by the success of the past 30 years and partly by the failures and omissions. It is a dynamic situation, but certain lines of development can reasonably be projected as more likely than others. My analysis suggests that there will be a considerable deterioration of international economic relations if things go on as they have.

The analysis may be wrong, and the projection even more so. The discussion has allowed for some factors that could greatly alleviate matters—high growth, a return to full employment, a wave of technological innovation—but they are certainly not to be counted on. What remains need not be a prophecy of doom. That is where the prescription comes in, along with the extensive further analysis needed to test, extend, support, and adopt the prescription. To take the problems of structural change seriously and try to deal with them on a cooperative basis should not be impossible for countries as intimately involved with one another as most of those in the contemporary world. If they showed themselves willing to do this, it would make possible a wholly different projection of events (and it would not take all of them to do that). That neither the will nor the ability to carry it out is easy to come by has been made clear in this book in a hundred ways. But partial progress is not impossible, and it is not fatuously optimistic to see how a great deal might be achieved. The prescription need not be precisely the one given here. But some movement toward the kinds of resolution of the international issues sketched here is a necessary condition of improvement. If it does not come about, then there is something we *must* do: We must face the alternative.

It has been described before and is a familiar pattern—except to those who know nothing but the last 30 years and therefore think it is normal to have a high level of international economic cooperation, great interpenetration of liberal economies, and substantial growth in developing, industrial, and centrally planned economies. A more usual state of affairs, in fact, is a high degree of nationalism pursuing narrow concepts of national interest, slow and uneven growth and sometimes retrogression, less international cooperation, and as a result more opportunities for the strong to use their power against the weak.

Some of the events since 1970 have provided glimpses of such a world not far below the surface of this one. If there is no improvement in the way we handle the conflicts arising from national industrial policies, the world will almost surely move toward greater friction, more fragmentation, and poorer adaptation to structural change. Taken together with the other strains on the international economy, such a development will make for increased efforts to defend the status quo, slower growth, greater difficulties for the poorer countries, more restrictive business practices backed and enforced by governments, and other easily imagined behavior. All this will probably not prevent the emergence of excess capacity in many industries, sharper competition, and more bilateralism as the older industrial countries seek markets for capital goods and offer import privileges to buyers that are denied to others. Divisions will increase among the industrial countries and among the developing countries as well. Cooperation; capital for development; access to markets; and shares in the world's supplies of food, energy, and raw materials will all be bought and sold through a process of haggling that can have only the most accidental relation to the efficient operation of the international economic system, the optimum allocation of world resources, or the freedom of individual nations to pursue their own ways of life.

It is not a very attractive picture, but it is hard to doubt that it is in fact The Alternative.

# Critical Bibliography

Anyone who has read this book knows that a bibliography that listed all its sources would be about as long as the text itself and a full bibliography of industrial policy, as defined here, would fill at least a volume. It might be more honest to present no bibliography at all than to present this truncated one, but other counsels have prevailed. In part this is because if one is treating industrial policy as in some ways a new issue in international relations, it seems desirable to give readers some idea of what has been written by others. Another function of this bibliography is to supplement the *Acknowledgments* in recognizing—though very inadequately—my immense debts. Only in third place, and very weakly, does this bibliography perform the traditional function of telling the reader what sources the author used to write his book.

In a way the narrowness of this bibliography reflects the book's approach to industrial policy, which requires some degree of synthesis of many different kinds of material—national and international, economic, political and social, contemporary and historical. The bibliography could contribute little if it covered each part of the subject: international trade and investment, agriculture—where the past exemplifies so many of the problems that may lie ahead for industrial policy—government-business relations, planning, the multinational corporation, economic development and growth, international economic cooperation, and the record of policy in a series of countries. Moreover, it would be pretentious to put forth lists of source books on these subjects, since in writing this book I reread few such works, relying much more on past acquaintance with them built up by several decades of work in these fields. As I point out in the *Acknowledgments*, talk played a great part in shaping this book, and the reader can provide significant additions to this limited bibliography simply by looking up the books, articles, and reports written by many of the people named there.

There is also the historical dimension. This book talks mostly about the period since the end of the Second World War, but it makes clear in a number of the discussions that some of the most basic issues considered go much further back in history. In addition to works mentioned here and there in the text, the reader could usefully peruse the perceptive analyses and reevaluations of economics books of the 1920s and 1930s by Willard L. Thorp in his contributions to *The Foreign Affairs 50-Year Bibliography, 1920–1970*, edited by Bryon Dexter (New York: Bowker, for the Council on Foreign Relations, 1972). My own appreciation of some current issues increased from rereading Friedrich List's *The National System of Political Economy* while I was writing this book. Then one has to reread Adam Smith, and that was good value too. Alexander Hamilton's *Report on Manufactures* helped, and so did some surprisingly apposite paragraphs from *The Communist Manifesto*.

The rest of this bibliography will, however, concentrate on more recent writings. Some works of general relevance to industrial policy will first be noted and some basic sources of data. Thereafter the comments follow the division of chapters but mention each entry only once, even though some pertain to several chapters. To save space, I have not mentioned here some works cited in footnotes that pertain only to limited topics. The emphasis is on books and reports, because space permits only a few of the many relevant articles to be listed. There seemed little point in listing unpublished papers, though I have used quite a few.

## FUNDAMENTAL ANALYSES

As some passages in Chapter 2 suggest, Lionel Stoleru's *L'Impératif Industriel* (Paris: Editions du Seuil, 1969) and Christian Stoffaes's *La Grande Menace Industrielle* (Paris: Calmann-Levy, 1978), written about a decade apart, are of great value in raising many of the basic issues with which this book is concerned in ways that are both provocative and concrete. Both authors are at once critical and prescriptive; their work is relevant well beyond the borders of France.

Andrew Shonfield, *Modern Capitalism: The Changing Balance of Public and Private Power* (London and New York: Oxford University Press, for the Royal Institute of International Affairs, 1965) is a basic work on the management of mixed economies that provides rich analytical and descriptive material from which I have benefited for many years in thinking about the issues dealt with in this book.

Lincoln Gordon's *Growth Policies and the International Order* (New York: McGraw-Hill, for the 1980s Project of the Council on Foreign Relations, 1979) has much to say on structural change and industrial policy in a different setting from that of this book. Athough we were both writing for the 1980s Project and are old friends, I did not see the Gordon manuscript until this one was in an advanced stage. Then I was happy to find how similar our views proved to be, even though we came at the subject from different directions.

The following books and articles all deal directly with matters of industrial policy and provide a wealth of material, often of a comparative sort:

Raymond Vernon (ed.), *Big Business and the State: Changing Relations in Western Europe* (Cambridge, Mass.: Harvard University Press, 1974).

Steven J. Warnecke and Ezra N. Suleiman (eds.), *Industrial Policies in Western Europe* (New York: Praeger, 1975).

Jean Saint-Geours, *La Politique économique des principaux pays industriels de l'Occident* (Paris: Sirey, 1969).

Joe Staten Bain, *International Differences in Industrial Structure* (New Haven: Yale University Press, 1966).

Helen Hughes (ed.), *Prospects for Partnership: Industrialization and Trade Policies in the 1970s* (Baltimore: Johns Hopkins University Press, for the International Bank for Reconstruction and Development, 1973).

Christopher Layton, *European Advanced Technology: A Programme for Integration* (London: Allen & Unwin, 1969).

Göran Ohlin, "National Industrial Policies and International Trade," in C. Fred Bergsten (ed.), *Toward a New World Trade Policy: The Maidenhead Papers* (Lexington, Mass.: Lexington Books, 1975).

Juergen B. Donges, "A Comparative Survey of Industrialization Policies in Fifteen Semi-Industrial Countries," *Weltwirtschaftliches Archiv*, Vol. 112, Issue 4 (Kiel), 1976.

John Pinder, Takashi Hosomi, and William Diebold, Jr., *Industrial Policy and the International Economy*, A Report of the Trilateral Task Force on Industrial Policy, The Triangle Papers: No. 19 (New York: The Trilateral Commission, 1979).

Since so many of the international issues arising out of industrial policy stem from past cooperation in matters of trade and payments and from the need to reassess those policies, readers might find it useful to examine my book, *The United States and the Industrial World* (New York: Praeger, for the Council on Foreign Relations, 1972). The way in which industrial policy becomes a central element is spelled out on pp. 163–173, but much of the rest of the book analyzes issues that are dealt with rather briefly in this one. There are a number of references to other literature in the earlier book; comments on many related works published since can be found in my quarterly reviews of economics books in *Foreign Affairs*.

Two other works that helped me put industrial policy in a larger setting are:

Andrew Shonfield (ed.), *International Economic Relations of the Western World, 1959–1971*, Vol. 1: *Politics and Trade*, by Shonfield, Curzon, Warley, and Ray; Vol. 2: *International Monetary Relations*, by Susan Strange with an essay by Christopher Prout (London: Oxford University Press, for the Royal Institute of International Affairs, 1976).

Peter J. Katzenstein (ed.), *Between Power and Plenty: Foreign Economic Policies of Advanced Industrial States* (Madison: University of Wisconsin Press, 1978). This was originally an issue of *International Organization*, August 1977.

An article I saw too late to use in writing this book deserves mention for the historical dimension it gives to the politics of structural change. Though it is stimulating and suggestive, I fear it is also a bit too schematic and deterministic: James R. Kurth, "The Political Consequences of the Product Cycle: Industrial History and Political Outcomes," *International Organization*, Vol. 33, No. 1, Winter 1979, pp. 1–34.

## BASIC DATA

The constant flow of current events plays a great part in making a book like this possible, even when only a handful of events are specifically discussed. I have relied heavily on the *New York Times*, the *Financial Times*, the *Financial Post* (Toronto), *Le Monde*, *Neue Zürcher Zeitung*, *Die Zeit*, the *Economist*, *Business Week*, and, more sporadically, a host of other journals that arrive at the library of the Council on Foreign Relations. Summaries of their national press provided by the German, French, Canadian, and British information services in New York have given me material I would not otherwise have seen. A wide variety of reports by corporations, labor unions, and interest groups have helped fill out the picture.

Although relatively few statistics have been used in this book, standard national and international sources have been relied on whenever possible, not only for figures actually cited but to test the accuracy of more general statements. Annual and special reports by the World Bank, the International Monetary Fund, General Agreement on Tariffs and Trade (GATT), and various United Nations agencies have all been drawn on. Among the

287

many publications of the UN Economic Commission for Europe, two of particular value in illuminating the problems of structural change are Ingvar Svennilson's *Growth and Stagnation in the European Economy*, 1954.II.E.3 (Geneva: United Nations, 1954) and a report prepared by the Commission's Secretariat—*Structure and Change in European Industry*, E.77.II.E.3 (New York: United Nations, 1977).

Three members of the Research Division of GATT—Richard Blackhurst, Nicolas Marian, and Jan Tumlir—have made a notable contribution to our understanding of the relations between trade and problems of structural change in two reports published in Geneva by GATT in its series of Studies in International Trade: *Trade Liberalization, Protectionism and Interdependence*, No. 5 (November 1977) and *Adjustment, Trade and Growth in Developed and Developing Countries*, No. 6 (September 1978).

An international organization of particular importance for industrial policy is the Organization for Economic Cooperation and Development (OECD). In addition to doing a good deal of work over the years on various specific industries, it has been the source of a series of reports on national industrial policies. In using these, one must be careful to distinguish the large body of material provided by national delegations from the sections written by the OECD staff. In general, the analysis is not very challenging, but there is much good material. The reports, all published by OECD in Paris, include *United States Industrial Policies* (1970), *The Industrial Policies of 14 Member Countries* (1971), *The Industrial Policy of Austria* (1971), *The Industrial Policy of Japan* (1972), *The Industrial Policy of France* (1974), *The Aims and Instruments of Industrial Policy: A Comparative Study* (1975), and *Selected Industrial Policy Instruments: Objectives and Scope* (1978).

An OECD committee chaired by Jean Rey of Belgium registered early recognition of the relevance of industrial policy to international cooperation in a report by the High Level Group on Trade and Related Problems, *Policy Perspectives for International Trade and Economic Relations* (Paris: OECD, 1972). More recent OECD work on the orientation of industrial policy and on the steel industry is cited in the text. Valuable work has also been done by the Interfutures Project undertaken by the OECD but carried out with a separate staff. A report on the work of Interfutures was in preparation as this book went to press, but unfortunately the detailed studies of several significant industries or sectors are apparently not to be published.

Hearings of several committees of the United States Congress and other publications by some of them, notably the Joint Economic Committee, provide a variety of material that bears on the issues analyzed in this book.

Texts of documents and statements have been taken whenever possible from official sources or *International Legal Materials*, published by the American Society of International Law, Washington, D.C.

## *Chapter 1: The Nature of the Problem*

On the various ways "structural" can be used, see Raymond Williams, *Keywords* (London: Fontana/Croom Helm, 1976), pp. 253–259; Marion J. Levy, Jr., "Structural-Functional Analysis," in *International Encyclopedia of the Social Sciences* (New York: Macmillan, 1968), Vol. 6, pp. 21–28; Judith Maxwell (ed.), *A Time for Realism: Policy Review and Outlook, 1978* (Montreal: C. D. Howe Research Institute, 1978), pp. 1–8 and the material cited there.

The way resistance to structural change may contribute to recession, stagflation, and slow growth and the difficult alternatives facing Western governments are examined more fully than in this book in a paper that I originally prepared for the Bilderberg meetings in the spring of 1978 and that subsequently appeared in *International Affairs*, published by the Royal Institute of International Affairs, London, October 1978, and in German in *Europa-Archiv*, published by Deutsche Gesellschaft für Auswärtige Politik, Bonn, October 10, 1978.

It is impossible to cite all the works that have contributed to what is said here about French planning, other European industrial policy experience, and the highly developed methods used in Japan. There is much material on these subjects in the general works already cited and in others mentioned in footnotes to the chapters. Special mention should be made of an excellent study (of the sort that should be made of other countries and industries): John Zysman, *Political Strategies for Industrial Order: State, Market, and Industry in France* (Berkeley: University of California Press, 1977). One can hardly omit the Colonna Report for the European Community: *Industrial Policy in the Community, Memorandum from the Commission to the Council* (Brussels: Commission of the European Community, 1970). (There are many other Community reports that are relevant, including those on regional policy, subsidies, and scientific cooperation, but the Colonna Report is the most general.)

An excellent survey of the Swedish experience is in Assar Lindbeck's *Swedish Economic Policy* (Berkeley: University of California Press, 1975).

My study of Canadian industrial policy has included many sources used over a period of years, but a few should be singled out. For historical guidance and synthesis I have found invaluable Craufurd D. W. Goodwin, *Canadian Economic Thought: The Political Economy of a Developing Nation 1814–1914* (Durham, N.C. and London: Duke University Press and Cambridge University Press, 1961). The large reexamination of Canadian problems undertaken by the Private Planning Association in the 1960s largely under the guidance of Roy Matthews and published in 13 volumes under the general title of *Canada in the Atlantic Economy* (Toronto: University of Toronto Press, 1968–1972) throws light on problems and potential solutions. Since that time the C. D. Howe Research Institute, the Economic Council of Canada, and the Science Council of Canada have provided a wealth of material.

*Chapter 2: Conflicting Criteria*

It will be apparent from the nature of the issues discussed in most of this chapter that its bibliography could go back to the classics of political theory, social philosophy, and ethics. It could as well include the contemporary treatment of problems of efficiency, equity, distribution, and social justice by Fred Hirsch, Arthur Okun, Charles Schultze, and John Rawls. Bringing more sharply into focus the relevance of efficiency and flexibility to the other goals of society are two works of an earlier period cited elsewhere in the book that are highly relevant today:

Eugene Staley, *World Economic Development: Effects on Advanced Industrial Countries* (Montreal: International Labour Office, 1944).
Allan G. B. Fisher, *Economic Progress and Social Security* (London: Macmillan, 1945).

Much is said in Chapter 5 about the Staley work, but what needs emphasis here is that Staley is not dealing only with the industrialization of new countries; he makes a far more general argument about the need for adaptive policies (and their feasibility), since neither market forces alone nor conventional governmental measures will produce satisfactory results. Fisher's book develops similar ideas more generally and can be usefully supplemented with the same author's application of these ideas (among others) to a more limited set of problems in *International Implications of Full Employment in Great Britain* (London and New York: Oxford University Press, for the Royal Institute of International Affairs, 1946). Somewhat similar ideas, also from the 1930s but concentrated more on how to bring about economic adaptation, can be found in Carl Major Wright, *Adaptation to a Changing World Market* (Copenhagen: Munksgaard, 1939).

Bohuslav Herman's study, *The Optimal International Division of Labor* (Geneva: International Labour Office, 1975), remains the fullest attempt I know of to try to work out an international industrial policy taking several criteria into account.

An enlightening analysis of how measures to improve economic welfare sometimes strengthen productivity and efficiency and sometimes clash with them is Theodore and Frances M. Geiger, *Welfare and Efficiency: Their Interactions in Western Europe and Implications for International Economic Relations* (Washington: National Planning Association, 1978).

An effort to work out a series of criteria for industrial adaptation that stresses economic efficiency but takes account of other considerations is Christian Stoffaes and M. Hors, "Une analyse multicritères des priorités sectorielles du redéploiement industriel,'' in *RCB*, Bulletin interministeriel pour la Rationalisation des Choix Budgetaires (Paris), No. 28, March 1977, pp. 7–48.

On the history of adaptation to change, along with some examples of resistance and initiation, there is much interesting material and stimulating thought in a number of studies by Charles P. Kindleberger usefully brought together (and added to) in his *Economic Response: Comparative Studies in Trade, Finance and Growth* (Cambridge, Mass.: Harvard University Press, 1978).

*Chapter 3: Trade and Investment*

The texts of agreements emerging from the Multilateral Trade Negotiations (MTN) were not public by the time this book went to press, so my discussion is based on official summaries and a constant flow of current statements and reports that seem sufficiently accurate. The underlying approach to the trade and investment issues is largely that of my 1972 book (mentioned earlier), which, naturally, has been supplemented by much other work, too much to be cited here. A few examples of interest appear in the footnotes to the chapter. The subsidy issue is treated very thoroughly in:

Geoffrey Denton, Seamus O'Cleireacain, and Sally Ash, *Trade Effects of Public Subsidies to Private Enterprise* (London: Macmillan, 1975).

Harald B. Malmgren, *International Order for Public Subsidies*, Thames Essay No. 11 (London: Trade Policy Research Centre, 1977).

Steven J. Warnecke (ed.), *International Trade and Industrial Policies* (London: Macmillan, 1978).

A highly relevant article, which appeared too late to be taken fully into account, serves as a note of caution regarding the difficulties of settling disputes about nontariff barriers and applying the balanced judgments required for the approach advocated in this chapter. This is John H. Jackson, ''The Jurisprudence of International Trade: The DISC Case in GATT,'' *American Journal of International Law*, October 1978, Vol. 72,

No. 4, pp. 747–781. Apart from the importance of the case it discusses and its detailed account of how such things are handled, this study can be thought of as a warning about the immense complexity of some of the processes of consultation and agreement referred to in such general language in the text—and at the same time of the importance of making them workable.

### Chapters 4 and 5: Sectors and Innovation

The discussion of textiles is based on a wide variety of materials going back to the beginning of the negotiations for a cotton textile agreement. None of these provides a very full account, and I do not know of any comprehensive analyses. Excellent case studies, of the sort it would be desirable to have for all countries, are Caroline Pestieau's *The Canadian Textile Policy: A Sectoral Trade Adjustment Strategy* (Montreal: Canadian Economic Policy Committee/C. D. Howe Research Institute, 1976), and *The Quebec Textile Industry in Canada*, Accent Quebec, Publication 5 (Montreal: C. D. Howe Research Institute, 1978).

What looks like a valuable study of the negotiation of the multifiber agreement reached me too late to be used in this book: I. M. Destler, Haruhiro Fukui, and Hideo Sato, *The Textile Wrangle: Conflict in Japanese-American Relations, 1969–1971* (Ithaca, N.Y.: Cornell University Press, 1979).

In the case of steel there are many reports and a whole special literature about the European Coal and Steel Community. Among the more recent studies, in addition to the one by Frank Wolter cited in Chapter 4, I used:

Harold R. Williams (ed.), *Free Trade, Fair Trade, and Protection: The Case of Steel* (Kent, Ohio: Kent State University Press, 1978).

United Nations Industrial Development Organization, *The World Iron and Steel Industry* (Second Study), prepared by Sectoral Studies Section, International Centre for Industrial Studies, UNIDO/ICIS.89, November 20, 1978 ([Vienna]: UNIDO, 1978).

United Nations Conference on Trade and Development, *Trade and Structural Adjustment Aspects of the International Iron and Steel Industry: The Role of the Developing Countries*, by Ingo Walter, UNCTAD/ST/MD/16 (Geneva: UNCTAD, 1978).

*Economics of International Steel Trade: Policy Implications for the United States*, An Analysis and Forecast for American Iron and Steel Institute (Newton, Mass.: Putnam, Hayes & Bartlett, Inc., May 1977).

American Iron and Steel Institute, *The Economic Implications of Foreign Steel Pricing Practices in the U.S. Market*, prepared by Putnam, Hayes & Bartlett, Inc. (Washington, D.C.: American Iron and Steel Institute, 1978).

As Chapter 5 explains, my discussion of the automobile industry is not a documented study; nevertheless, it rests on many sources, mostly spotty and scattered. It has proved impracticable to try to list very many. In addition to those cited in the chapter, my thinking about this subject over the years has been influenced by Jack N. Behrman, *The Role of International Companies in Latin American Integration: Autos and Petrochemicals* (Lexington, Mass.: Lexington Books, for the Committee for Economic Development, 1972) and Jack Baranson, *International Transfer of Automotive Technology to Developing Countries* (New York: United Nations Institute for Training and Research, Research Reports No. 8, 1971).

Among other sectors, the only one in which I have relied heavily on a particular piece of work is petrochemicals. During the project mentioned in the text, Louis Turner and James Bedore produced a number of articles, of which two particularly useful ones are "Saudi and Iranian Petrochemicals and Oil Refining: Trade Warfare in the 1980s?" *International Affairs* (London), October 1977, Vol. 53, No. 4; and "The Trade Politics of Middle Eastern Industrialization," *Foreign Affairs*, Winter 1978/79, Vol. 57, No. 2. The complete results of the study will appear as *Middle Eastern Industrialization: The Iranian and Saudi Experience* (New York: Praeger, 1979).

One of the difficulties with international sectoral agreements as means of bringing about orderly adjustment is the pressure to give each participant a "fair share" whether the participant is as efficient as the others or not. An interesting argument to the effect that this is a manageable problem is made by Jack N. Behrman, *Multinational Production Consortia: Lessons from*

*NATO Experience* (Washington, D.C.: GPO, for the Department of State, 1971).

The part of Chapter 5 that deals with the financing of economic development and new ways of organizing North-South relations is, in many ways, a set of variations on some of Eugene Staley's themes; as it draws on everything I know (or think I know) on these subjects, a listing of sources would be so arbitrary as to make no sense.

## Chapters 6, 7, and 8: National Aptitudes, International Combinations, and Directions for the Future

What is said at the beginning of this bibliography about the difficulty of making even a representative list of sources applies with special emphasis to these three chapters, which cut across one huge field of study after another and then try to draw together all the themes of the book. After trying, I have despaired of compiling anything useful. I make only two exceptions.

Chapter 7 could be said to rest on the whole literature of international cooperation and organization, but I suspect it has been especially influenced by the discussions in the 1980s Project that are reflected in a number of the books published so far and others yet to come; a list elsewhere in this volume will be a guide. There is only one reference in the chapter to Miriam Camps's pamphlet on the OECD, but that paper and the earlier one called *The Management of Interdependence* (cited in Chapter 2) contain a number of the basic concepts used here about which groups of countries can work most effectively together and which probably cannot.

The other exception concerns the section on science, technology, and R & D in Chapter 6. This is a field in which I have read much, both as to national policies and the relation of R & D to international trade. I have learned a good deal over the years from conversations with my brother, John. Still, at the time of writing I lacked a sense of how to put everything together. Whether I gained enough of a grasp to write a few sensible pages is a question for the reader. If so, it came from studying the works cited in that section, numerous OECD studies about national science policies, and especially the National Academy of Sciences, *Technology, Trade, and the U.S. Economy* (Washington, D.C.: National Academy of Sciences, 1978) and U.S. House of Representatives, Committee on Science and Technology, *First Annual Report to the Congress Submitted in Accordance with the National Science and Technology Policy, Organization and Priorities Act of 1976*, 95th Cong., 2d Sess. (Washington, D.C.: GPO, 1978).

The Science Council of Canada's report *The Weakest Link: A Technological Perspective on Canadian Industrial Underdevelopment*, by John N. H. Britton and James M. Gilmour (Ottawa: Science Council of Canada, 1978) is of particular interest for the subject of this book, since it so firmly relates R & D questions to the structure of industry both analytically and prescriptively. Lord Rothschild's witty and strong-minded book has particular value because of his experience as a scientist in government, business, and academic life.

# Index

# About the Author

WILLIAM DIEBOLD, JR. is a Senior Research Fellow at the Council on Foreign Relations in New York City. He was educated at Swarthmore College, Yale University, and the London School of Economics, and he thereafter served as a Research Secretary for the Council's War and Peace Studies Project. Before rejoining the Council in 1947, Mr. Diebold served with the Department of State, the United States Army, and the Office of Strategic Services, where he concentrated on economic research and analysis. Mr. Diebold's work has covered a wide range of international economic issues but most recently has focused on the problems of structural change in the world economy and American economic policy toward the communist countries. Among his numerous articles, essays, books, and reviews are *The United States and the Industrial World: American Foreign Economic Policy in the '70s* and *The Schuman Plan: A Study in Economic Cooperation: 1950–1959.*